# A SCIENTIST RESEARCHES
# MARY

## THE ARK OF THE COVENANT

by Prof. Courtenay Bartholomew, M.D.
Foreword by Fr. Slavko Barbaric, O.F.M.

First Printing: 15,000 copies — 1995
Printed in the USA by:
The 101 Foundation
P.O. Box 151
Asbury, NJ 08804-0151

phone: 908-689 8792
fax: 908-689 1957

## ACKNOWLEDGEMENTS

The author is most grateful to Fr. Slavko Barbaric O.F.M. for the many privileges afforded to him in Medjugorje; to Fr. Svetozar Kraljevic O.F.M., Dr. Rosalie A. Turton, John M. Haffert, Sir Ellis Clarke, and Mary Pinder, for reviewing the manuscript; to Basilia Abel-Smith and Kwailan La Borde for their proof-reading. He also wishes to acknowledge the assistance with his research which was given to him by Sr. Marie Therèse Retout O.P.

His sincere thanks are extended to Cherry Araujo, Ed Chong-Ling, Farley Cleghorn, Linda Steele, Susan Isaacs, Valerie Da Silva, Anne Blache-Fraser, Karen Raphael, Roger Moe, Rosemary Dunn, who all assisted over the years in typing the manuscript, and to Patricia Delehaunty Moran who designed the cover of the book. Finally, he expresses his deep appreciation to his wife Mary Martina (Marina) for her tacit support and patience during his daily preoccupation with the writing of this book over the past five years.

**DEDICATION**

This book is dedicated to three sisters
who were three mothers to me:

Marie, Maude and Ethel

— He Loves Much Who Is Forgiven Much —
                                   the author

— He Who Rejects My Mother Rejects Me —
                                        Jesus
                to Gladys Quiroga de Motta,
                     San Nicolás, Argentina

# FOREWORD

Dear Reader,

Peace be with you! "Take this and read it" were decisive words for St. Augustine. He heard them and obeyed. After he read it, and here it concerned Holy Scripture, his conversion began. In your hands you have a book about which I dare say: "Take this and read it. Here you will find a witness to faith yet more than a witness."

This book speaks to you about the Mother of God, who speaks to us in Medjugorje as the Queen of Peace. But this Woman is not foreign to us. From the very beginning she had been announced as the Woman through whom holiness would be brought to the world. She is the Woman who gave God her everlasting "yes," and who is presented to us as the morning glow and the morning star. It is she who, through her descendants, will crush the head of the enemy of human holiness. It is she who is leading her children through this earthly valley and through the darkness of night to God. She is the Mother and teacher of Our Saviour who can, in these times, lead us most directly to Jesus and to God (John-Paul II).

Her life here on earth was for the most part spent in silence. In the background in silence and in complete submission to God, she offered the Son of God and Our Saviour her motherly duties. Shortly before His death on the Cross she was entrusted to us as mother and we to her as children. She accepted her assignment with all seriousness and takes care of us as she did her Son. When He was lost, she sought Him with sadness and found Him with great joy. For nearly twenty centuries she comes to us. She appears and searches for us and wishes to lead us to God. She speaks, she calls out, she prays with us, cries because of us and asks us to assist her in her search for her other children.

If you would like to discover the entire spectrum of her motherly activities then continue reading this book. You will see and it will become clear to you. You will consecrate yourself to her and be ready with her to say your own "yes" to God.

Perhaps when it comes to religious themes you are accustomed to reading the works of theologians and specialists. This is understandable. We in Medjugorje have learned by multiple experiences that the Medjugorje phenomenon is carried by the laity, and most often described by the laity. This confirms the teaching of the second Vatican Council which consigned to the laity an important role. Concerning Medjugorje, one can also say, with nine years of experience, that because the laity responded and gave their witness, the specialists were able to come. God's people are more sensitive to the Word, it seems, than those who hold office within the Church.

This is not a critique toward the hierarchy, but it is entirely normal for the Holy Spirit to penetrate this way into the Church as He recently has. First, the people accepted the Queen of Peace, and only then, the priests. Only when many groups had come without priests did the priests begin to dare to experience Medjugorje. After the priests, then came the bishops, always accompanied by the people of God.

Here I also find the deeper reason why a scientist, as we have here, dares to write a book about God's work in the Blessed Virgin Mary. He speaks here as one of God's people, as a pilgrim of Medjugorje, as a doctor who believes. Take this and read it and many things will become clear to you about God's hand in His humble servant.

I am glad to be reminded of the experience of a world class athlete (a marathon runner), who by coincidence read the messages of the Queen of Peace, and through them came to this deep inner conviction and assurance: "My Mother is speaking to me personally, and if she speaks to me personally, I must obey her!" I wish for you, dear reader, the same experience: that in this book you too will feel in your heart that she is speaking to you personally.

If you are afraid, come to her, she will give you courage.

If you feel lost in this world, come to her, you will find the way because she will show you the way.

If you are sad, she will console you.

If you are without peace, she will lead you to peace.

If you are ill, she will stay by your side in your suffering.

If you feel useless in this world, she will whisper to you; I need you.

If you are destroying yourself with sin, she will pray for you to acquire the strength for change.

If all those around you fail you, she will not.

If all those around you want to cheat you, she stays faithful.

If you want to pray, she wants to teach you.

If you do not know how to love, she will enroll you in her school and you will be able to love.

And if nobody treasures your work, she will say thank you.

And so, dear reader, find the time and read this book and you yourself will see and feel. And, for my part, I bless you and pray for you, that you too will be able to extend your hand to such a Mother and with her, encounter your own peace as well as universal peace. Reach into your heart and you will, despite this torn-apart world, discover joy, hope and strength. To Him who is Almighty, everything is possible. In Mary's life too, this was the beginning.

In deepest gratitude to the author, I extend my best wishes to you.

Father Slavko Barbaric, O.F.M.<br>Medjugorje

### *Faith and Respect for the Ark*

So David gathered all the people together from the Shihor of Egypt to the Pass of Hamath to bring the ark of God from Kiriath-jearim. Then David and all Israel went up to Baalah, to Kiriath-jearim in Judah, to bring up from there the ark of God which bears the name of Yahweh who is seated on the cherubs. At Abinadab's house they placed the ark of God on a new cart. Uzzah and Ahio were leading the cart. David and all Israel danced before God with all their might, singing to the accompaniment of lyres, harps, tambourines, cymbals, trumpets. When they came to the threshing-floor of the Javelin, Uzzah stretched his hand out to hold the ark, as the oxen were making it tilt. Then the anger of Yahweh blazed out against Uzzah and he struck him down because he had laid his hand on the ark, and he died there in the presence of God... David went in fear of God that day (I Chronicles 13:5-12).

# Table Of Contents

Chapter #:                                Page #:

**Revelations and Mysteries:**
1. The Testimony of a Scientist — 1.
2. Science and Religion — 11.
3. On Private Revelations and Apparitions — 20.
4. The Mystery of the Trinity — 24.
5. Mary and the Creation Story — 31.
6. Queen and Co-Redemptrix — 36.

**Covenants:**
7. The Covenants of the Bible — 55.
   — The Old Covenant
8. The Ark of the Covenant — 61.
9. In Search of the Ark — 71.
10. Mount Carmel and the Prophet Elijah — 84.
11. Our Lady of Mt. Carmel — 88.
12. The Covenants of the Bible — 93.
    — The New Covenant

**Mary in Union With Jesus:**
13. The Medical Aspects of the Crucifixion — 99.
14. I am the Immaculate Conception — 106.
15. Mary, The Living Ark — 113.
    of the New Covenant
16. The Ark At Kiriath-Jearim — 120.

**The Eucharist:**
17. The Eucharist — The Sacrament — 126.
    of the New Covenant
18. Eucharistic Miracles — — 131.
    The Confirmation

### Mary, The Visiting Mother:
19. Medjugorje: Mary's School of Prayer — 137.
20. St. James and Mary — El Pilar — 145.
21. The Medjugorje Miracles — 149.
22. "You Are On Mount Tabor" — 157.
23. "Dear Children" — 160.

### The Shekinah:
24. Mary In The Old Testament — 164.
    — The Column of Smoke
25. A Brief History of the Copts — 174.
26. Mary Returns To Egypt — 178.
27. The Ark and the Shekinah in Egypt — 184.

### "Am I Not Your Mother?"
28. Guadalupe: The Year Was 1531 — 191.
29. Betania: The Lourdes of the New World — 199.
30. Mary's Messages in Betania — 213.
31. My Visit To San Nicolás in Argentina — 217.
32. Mary and Noah's Ark — 225.
33. The Messages of Jesus and Mary — 228.
    at San Nicolás
34. Mary And Fatima — 234.
35. Garabandal: The Carmel of Spain — 249.

### Mary's Tears and Mary's Triumph:
36. Why is Mary Crying? — 262.
37. Mary in Akita, Japan — 272.
38. Mother of Mercy — 280.
39. Don Bosco and Mary, Help of Christians — 287.
40. The Messenger of Mary's Royalty — 297.
41. Our Lady of China — 316.
42. The Triumph of the — 326.
    Immaculate Heart of Mary

Bibliography: — 339.

## CHAPTER 1.

## *The Testimony of a Scientist*

**"For I am not ashamed of the gospel."**
**Paul (Romans 1:16)**

The call to research Mary began in Yugoslavia. I could neither pronounce nor spell "Medjugorje" when, in 1983, I first heard about this little-known village. In fact, it almost evoked the response: "Can anything good come from Medjugorje?" Jesus must have smiled when Nathaniel (probably the Bartholomew of the other Gospels) made a similar remark about Him and Nazareth: "Can anything good come from Nazareth?" (John 1:46). But there in that little village where everyone knew everyone's secrets, they did not know the greatest secret of all — that God was also living in Nazareth.

At that time, I could not accept that the Virgin would appear every day for over two years, especially as, to my limited knowledge, there was no precedent for this. And so, I was a little skeptical, albeit not completely unbelieving. If indeed she was really appearing daily, then my logic concluded that there must be a serious reason for this extravagance in apparitions. I then read Fr. René Laurentin's classic book *Is The Virgin Mary Appearing At Medjugorje?*, and became more fascinated with Medjugorje after reading it.

Some time later, when I was invited to a medical conference in Belgrade, Yugoslavia, beginning on October 14, 1986, I saw this as my opportunity to visit Medjugorje en route to the conference. I arrived in Medjugorje on October 13. It was the anniversary of Mary's last apparition at Fatima in 1917. To my surprise, I was invited by Fr. Slavko Barbaric to be present in the Franciscan rectory for the apparition of the Virgin which was expected to take place at 5:40 p.m. Assuming that the apparitions were authentic, my first reaction to this invitation was that I was not worthy to be so close to the Holy Virgin. I articulated this to someone and the reply I received was: "But who is worthy?"

The atmosphere in the room that evening was something which I will never forget. It was a small crowded room charged with vibrations of prayerful supplications as some twenty pilgrim clergy and a few lay people devoutly recited the Rosary while awaiting her arrival. Some seven minutes before the Virgin appeared to the visionaries, I witnessed the strange behaviour of a young Italian girl close to me in the room, suggesting that she was "possessed by an unclean spirit" (Mark 1:23). At the moment when the visionaries knelt in reverent recognition of the arrival of the Madonna, the Gospel according to Mark was re-enacted. The unclean spirit threw her into convulsions and with a loud cry went out of her (Mark 1:26-27). There was obviously a presence in the room who tolerated no evil rival (see p. 8).

This evoked among us a great excitement, a heightened fervour in our prayers, and a wonderful feeling of joy and love. But, for me, it was a most unexpected emotion of love for her *Son* which I experienced at that moment when she appeared in the room, and it left me momentarily bewildered. I seemed to have experienced what Grignon Marie de Montfort had written three centuries ago. It was a conversion *to Jesus through Mary.*" Indeed, it was she who brought Him forth to us in His human form. Obviously, it is not that we can only go to Jesus through His Mother but Mary herself told Fr. Stefano Gobbi, the founder of the Marian Movement of Priests, on July 16, 1980: "I am the way which leads you to Jesus. I am the safest and shortest way."

Of course, many of us give *lip service* to the Lord and praise His name but we can never be sure of our true devotion of the heart unless we are really tested. I sometimes wonder, for example, how many of us Christians of today's world would have chosen to go to the lions in the Colosseum and not renounce Christ? How many of us would pass the test given to our father Abraham? And so, we should always pray: "Do not put us to the test" (Matthew 6:13).

Without going into any detail, something else happened to me in the room that evening and I have believed in Medjugorje ever since. I confess that there is no scientific evidence which I can document to justify my strong belief for it was partly based on *faith*. However, there is scientific evidence to support the visionaries' claim that they do see an apparition.

Never before in the history of the Church has the phenomenon of ecstasy been so subjected to modern scientific tests. In Medjugorje the visionaries have undergone studies with electro-encephalographs, electro-oculographs, eye reflex tests and a study of evoked auditory responses (see p. 8). Professor Henri Joyeux of the University of Montpellier in France and his colleagues performed these sophisticated series of tests with the permission of the visionaries (and *Our Lady of Medjugorje*) during five different periods in 1984, and they concluded that their findings were scientifically inexplicable.

The detailed findings of their investigations are recorded in the book *Scientific and Medical Studies on the Apparitions at Medjugorje* by Professor Joyeux and Fr. René Laurentin, the internationally well-known Mariologist, who, apart from his detailed enquiry and discernment, has recently been using a scientific approach in judging alleged apparitions of the Blessed Virgin Mary.

The medical experts summarized their findings thus: "Clinical observation of the visionaries leads us to affirm, as our Yugoslav colleagues have already affirmed, that these young people are healthy in mind and body. Detailed clinical and para-clinical studies allow us to confirm scientifically that there are no pathological modifications of the parameters studied... There is no question of hallucination in the pathological sense of that word. There is no auditory or visual hallucination... During the ecstasy there is a face to face meeting, as it were, between the visionaries and a person whom we did not see. During the ecstasy they are in a state of prayer and interpersonal communication... The ecstasies are not pathological nor is there any element of deceit. No scientific discipline seems to be able to describe these phenomena. We would be quite willing to define them as a state of active, intense prayer, partially disconnected from the outside world; a state of contemplation with a separate person whom they alone can see, hear and touch."

An Italian team of scientists also ruled out the possibility that any of the visionaries suffered from hallucinations. According to Professor Margnelli, these ecstasies are absolutely authentic. The conclusion of his research team was that the children experienced ecstasies which cannot be explained by contemporary science. Fr. Slavko Barbaric has also given me a copy of a document signed by six prominent Yugoslav neurologists and psychologists who attested in September 1988 that the children were neurologically and psychologically normal.

I have witnessed in Medjugorje many phenomena which science cannot explain to me, and which can, therefore, be classified as supernatural. For example, although there is no electricity on the hill, I have seen the huge Cross on Mount Krizevac light up at 10:30 p.m. on August 15, 1988, the feast of the Assumption of Our Lady. It was at the very moment when the Virgin appeared to the visionaries on the other hill called Podbrdo. There were thousands of pilgrims on Podbrdo that night and many of them witnessed this majestic phenomenon. I have also marvelled at the "miracle of the Sun" for one hour on October 12, 1988, and I have seen several Rosaries, originally silver, which have turned to a golden colour.

In addition, not infrequently, photographs taken by many people in Medjugorje and elsewhere have depicted images of religious significance which were not present at the time of photography. After receiving several of them, especially those depicting the *pillar of cloud*, I slowly and somewhat reluctantly at first, concluded that there must be a purpose for this, namely that they were not meant for my personal library but for a wider audience. I have included in this book many such photographs, most of which were taken by myself, and which have influenced the choice of title of this book. Through them I have learned so much about Mary as the *Ark of the Covenant* and I am most grateful to her for these gifts (see pp. 9 & 10).

My pilgrimages to Medjugorje have had a profound effect on my life and have increased my faith. But when I tell people that I am a "convert," frequently their first response has been: "But I always thought that you were a Catholic!" Yes, I have always been Catholic in *name*, but perhaps the greatest conversions need to take place among Catholics — lukewarm Catholics. We say that we have the true Faith and yet we lack the zeal of some other religions. Revelation 3:15 says it all: *"I know all about you: how you are neither hot nor cold. I wish you were one or the other, but since you are neither, but only lukewarm, I will spit you out of my mouth."* I recognized myself in that passage — about to be spat out!

My dear friend Fr. Svetozar Kraljevic of Yugoslavia, in his book *In the Company of Mary: Thoughts on the apparitions of Our Lady at Medjugorje,* makes this pertinent critique: "I would say that to be indifferent is worse than to be atheistic. Atheists believe there is no God. They cannot prove it, but they believe there is no God. But those who are indifferent, they say: 'There is a God, but I don't need him.' And this is worse than to be an atheist."

But lukewarmness and indifference are not the only problems of many of us Christians, and it was also his awareness of the great threat to the Church *from within* which led Pope Paul VI on June 29, 1973, to warn that "the smoke of Satan has entered the Church."

St. Pius X, one of the greatest Popes of all time and the first Pope to be canonized in 342 years, in his encyclical *Pascendi Dominici Gregis* of 1907, critical of the so-called Modernists, wrote: "The partisans of error are to be sought not only among the Church's open enemies, but, what is to be most dreaded and deplored, in her very bosom ... We allude to many who belong to the Catholic laity, and what is much more sad, to the ranks of the priesthood itself, who, animated by a false zeal for the Church, lacking the solid safeguards of philosophy and theology, nay more, thoroughly imbued with the poisonous doctrines taught by the enemies of the Church, and lost to all sense of modesty, put themselves forward as reformers of the Church... Their method and doctrines are replete with errors... They seize upon professorships in the seminaries and universities and generally make them chairs of pestilence."

Written at the beginning of the twentieth century, this critique is more relevant now at the end of this century when many revolutionary Christians are insisting that God must modernize Himself and conform to society's way of thinking. But as Peter said: "Be not ignorant of this one thing, that one day is with the Lord as a thousand years, and a thousand years as one day" (2 Peter 3:8). In short two "days" after the death of Jesus He is being asked to change His commandments to accommodate the different life styles and philosophies of today's world.

My experiences in Medjugorje, and later in several other Marian shrines, have been associated with an inner call to give testimony to them and to document them in a book. However, it took quite a bit of prodding before I was able to summon the courage to do so, as I was quite aware of the effect it would subsequently bear on my life. And then I read Paul in Romans 1:16, "I am not ashamed of the gospel." Indeed, I have no great virtue except perhaps the courage of my convictions and of not fearing criticism. And so, I began to write.

In the *Mariale*, his monumental work in honour of the Mother of God, St. Albert the Great, one of the greatest scientists of his age, wrote: "It is not my intention to show honour to this glorious Virgin by untruth or to unfold to enlightened minds any new doctrines in pretentious language and thus seek my own praise instead of the glory of the sublime Virgin. It is rather my purpose to speak to humble souls in lowly language, to those who like myself are simple and unlearned. Wherefore, I shall be well content if others more learned than I, who am unworthy and have but little knowledge, shall write something worthier of this Blessed Lady than I can offer here."

On this topic of humility, a devotee once asked a Hindu guru: "Master, what can I do to become humble?" He replied: "Sister, what is there to be proud about?" Indeed! Before Satan fell his pride preceded his disobedience. It is easy, however, to mistake defiance and principled stands in defense of truth for pride. On the other hand, one must also be able to discern the pride that disguises itself as humility.

St. Albert was not seeking his own glory when he wrote on the Mother of God and it is with similar humility that I have eventually responded to the inner call to write this book,especially as I do truly believe that we are living in apocalyptic times. As Lucia, the sole surviving visionary of Fatima, advises about the third unrevealed secret of Fatima: "It is in the Gospel and in the Apocalypse. Read them."

This book is all about the Woman of the Apocalypse whom we greet in the Litany of Loreto as the *Ark of the Covenant*. I believe that it should not be read as a novel but moreso as a text for study and analysis. It is written especially for lukewarm Christians and scientists. It documents a series of experiences I have had on a Marian journey into which I was led, illustrated by many photographs, beginning in Lourdes in 1982, and subsequently to many of her shrines all around the world. The *Ark of the Covenant* was always preceded by the *pillar of cloud* and it was as if the cloud went before me on these trips and was the inspiration to share this journey with you.

Now, I have always been a stickler for the observance of correct protocol, and I thought that it was indeed proper protocol that the first remarkable photograph which I received in Medjugorje seemed to be a symbol of the Trinity since Trinidad, the land of my birth, is named after the Trinity. From the great mystery of the Trinity the journey led to another unusual photograph. This time it actually depicted the *cloud* in front of the living *Ark of the Covenant, Mary*. This was in Cairo, Egypt. Sequentially and otherwise, this too was proper protocol because Mary is so intimately linked to the Holy Trinity. She is the daughter of the Father, the mother of the Son and the bride of the Holy Spirit.

But before you accompany me on this mystical journey by word and picture, a word about that much discussed and often misunderstood topic — Science and Religion.

7.

Above right: Author with Fr. Slavko Barbaric and young Franciscan seminarians in Medjugorje (see p. 1)

Vicka, Ivan and Marija during an apparition

8.

A priest lays his hand on the head of girl possessed (see p. 2).

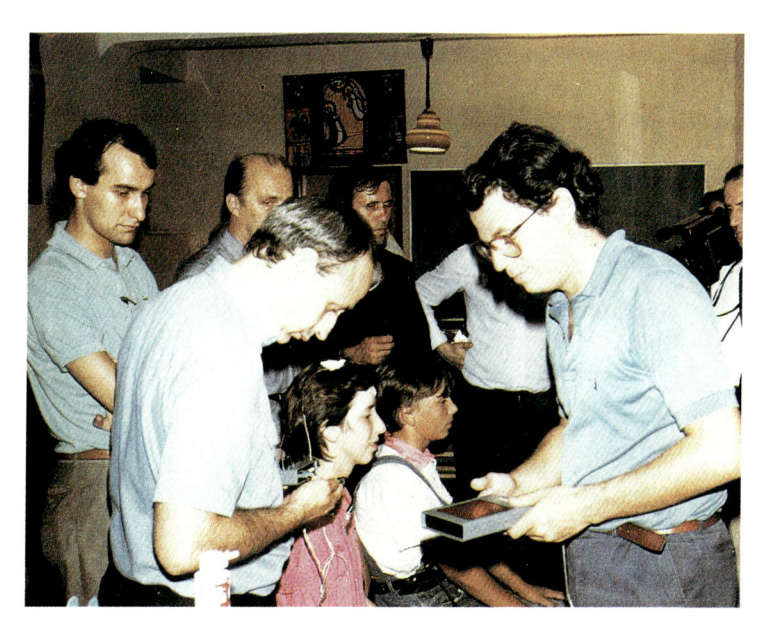

Medical scientist attaching scientific equipment on the visionaries before the apparition of the Virgin (see p. 2).

9.

The Rectory where the Virgin appeared in Medjugorje (see p. 1).

Clouds appear outside the Rectory in a photograph taken during the apparition (see p. 4).

10.

A pillar of cloud appears on a photograph of a painting of Madonna and Child at the author's home (see p. 4).

A procession of Our Lady of Fatima at St. Margaret's Shrine, Bridgeport, Connecticut in 1992 (courtesy of Dr. J. R. Fida).

# CHAPTER 2.

## Science and Religion

> "Science, my son, for all its greatness is nevertheless a small thing; and less than nothing compared to the formidable mystery of the Divinity."
>
> **Padre Pio**

We live in a Universe which is vast both in space and time, the realization of which should truly dwarf our inflated egos. We know that Earth has a diameter of 8,000 miles and the Moon 2160 miles, but I believe that relatively few of us appreciate that the Sun, which is a star, has a diameter of nearly 1 million miles and is about 93 million miles away from Earth. On the other, hand the nearest star (other than the Sun) is 272,000 times further from the Earth than is the Sun.  Scientists have also estimated that the age of the Earth is at least 4.5 billion years (a billion is one thousand million), and throughout this period the Sun must have been shining pretty much as it does now.

This wondrous star, the Sun, is a nuclear reactor and generates its energy by nuclear transmutations.  In fact, it is the conversion of hydrogen to helium which supplies the solar energy generation and the idea of a hydrogen bomb is to produce an extremely rapid conversion of hydrogen into helium, that is, to do what the Sun does, but to do it rapidly.  Indeed, when I consider the Miracle of the Sun which took place at Fatima in 1917, when the Sun was seen spinning and hurling towards Earth, I wonder whether this was not of apocalyptic significance, especially since it was in Japan that the first hydrogen bomb was used, and it was in Akita, Japan, that the Blessed Virgin chose to warn us in 1973 that unless we convert "fire will fall from the sky, and will wipe out a great part of humanity... "

As for time and distance, light travels at about 186,000 miles a second and as the Moon is about 239,000 miles away from Earth, light takes a little more than one second to travel from the Moon to our planet. We speak then of the distance from the Moon as a little more than one light second. The distance from the Sun is about 8 light minutes. We can now appreciate the distance from the stars since light takes about 4.3 *years* to reach us from Proxima Centauri, the nearest star in our solar system. It is about 30 trillion miles away (a trillion is a million million). In short, when we look at that star we are seeing it as it was about 4.3 *years* ago. Therefore, when we look at the distant stars we look back in time. We can never see a star as it is in our 'now' time.

Proxima Centauri can only be seen from the Southern Hemisphere, a faint companion of the bright star Alpha Centauri. They are 2.6 trillion miles apart, and a starship travelling at the pace of today's fastest spacecraft would take millions of years for a return journey to one of the nearby stars. Indeed, all the "twinkling little stars" which we see at night are millions and millions of miles apart.

In Genesis 15:5, God challenged Abraham before He made the Covenant with him: "*Look up at the sky and count the stars, if you can...*" Indeed, with a small telescope we can distinguish only about a million stars, but scientists have estimated that in our Galaxy alone there are about 200 billion stars and there may be as many as 100 billion other galaxies in existence. How many trillions and trillions of stars must there be in God's creation! And yet Psalm 147: 1-4 reads: "Praise the Lord, for He is good... He tells the number of the stars; he calls each by name." We can now more readily appreciate Edward Young's (1683-1754) remark: "An undevout astronomer is mad," and Psalm 14:1 which says: "*The fool says in his heart, 'There is no God.'*"

In spite of this, the question is frequently asked: "Is it possible to be a good scientist and a deeply religious believer at the same time?" Certainly, men like Albert the Great, Newton, Galileo, Mendel and Pasteur, all distinguished scientists and committed Christians, testify to this dual role, but for many, the relationship between science and religion has been one of confrontation.

Religion means a reconnection and it stems from the Latin derivative "*religare*" which means to reconnect. Through religion God desires to reconnect with humanity. He wants to re-establish the same intimate relationship which existed at Creation. Religion, therefore, is the recognition on the part of man of a supreme Power, God, entitled to obedience, honour, reverence and worship in a way *prescribed* by Him, and requiring an act of faith. In fact, it is, above all, an expression of love. It is a love story of obedience to and reverence for God, who *is* Love. It may well be said that it is "for lovers only."

13.

It is true that many religious leaders have actively encouraged scientific research, but as men of science have made new discoveries, each discovery seemed to thrust God further in the background. On the other hand, some religious people have at times felt their faith threatened by science. However, it is important to recognize that ultimately there can be no conflict between science and religion for both deal with truth. If, then, we become apprehensive that scientific research will produce results which are contrary to theological truth, we are forgetting, that God, who is Truth and the Supreme Scientist, cannot contradict Himself.

On September 24, 1989, Pope John Paul II gave a talk on "Science and Faith" to professors and students of the University of Pisa, Italy, where the once controversial, now vindicated, Galileo, the professor of mathematics, taught. He began his address by speaking about the links between the Church and the Chairs of the sciences which make up the University. He said: "People of science are also called upon to practice their own special priesthood. Yes, in a certain sense, every true scientist is a priest... Precisely because they perceive more, and more profoundly, the greater is their duty, on the one hand to recognize, praise, admire and thank God in all the elements of His Creation and, on the other, to make an honest and responsible use of their own ingenuity and the great and small achievements which spring from it."

St. Augustine of Hippo (354-430 AD) was one of the greatest converts in the Catholic Church. He was a Catholic but as I have said before, he was one of many of us who needed conversion within the Faith. His *Confessions* is a classic admission of his sins and his reluctance to convert: "Lord, give me chastity — but not just yet" was one of his slogans. From sinner to saint, he became one of the most brilliant theologians of the Church and soon after his conversion he lamented: "Lord, why did I take so long to know you?"

As early as the fourth century, he had recognized the responsibility of scientists, and in Book Five of his *Confessions* he criticizes them thus: "It seemed to me that the scientists were able to think clearly enough to form a clear judgment of the Universe, even though they could not penetrate through to its sovereign Lord. That is because such men fall into pride. They accurately predict the eclipse of the Sun, then fall into a state of eclipse themselves. They neglect to investigate the source of the intelligence by which they conduct their research. Much of what the natural philosophers and scientists are saying about the Universe is true, but they show no interest in a devout search for the Truth who put the Universe together. So they fail to find Him, or if they do find Him, they do not honour Him as God or give thanks to Him."

Some eight hundred years later, another scholar and saint appeared on the world scene. I have already referred to him. He was Albert the Great. Born in 1206, he was called 'great' because he was a philosopher, a theologian, a renowned scientist, a Doctor of the Church and a saint. He was a man of immense knowledge and erudition, yet he never ceased to project the Scriptures as the fount of man's spirituality or true wisdom. He joined the Dominican Order of Preachers and he taught the sphericity of the earth as Aristotle had taught it. But he went further. He taught that the northern and southern parts of the globe were habitable and uninhabited, and it is said that it is more than possible that it was Albert's teaching that inspired Columbus to set out on his voyage of discovery of the New World.

In the booklet on St. Albert in *The Dominican Saints of the Rosary Series*, it is stated: "Let us remember that Pope Pius XI declared St. Albert the Great to be 'Patron of Science and Peace.' This might seem a strange grouping, but it is true that most of the world's unrest in these days has been caused by the divorce of science from religion and the supernatural. This unrest will continue, and ever increase, unless those who profess to speak in the name of science learn to humble themselves in the presence of Eternal Wisdom and adore Him. True science knows its place, and the true scientist is always humble; we have the example of St. Albert the Great to enforce this lesson. He was truly a scientist because he was humble, and he was humble because he loved the truth. It is for this reason that the Sovereign Pontiff points to him and bids us pray that he will ask God to give peace to a world which knows it not, and wisdom to those whose learning has blinded them to Him."

Now, science is limited by the ordinary laws of nature. It cannot recognize, and so refer to a transnatural or supernatural event which has intervened in the sequence of the natural order, and so, miracles, for example, cannot be fathomed by scientific inquiry. But the God who arbitrarily created all things and who arbitrarily established the ordinary laws of nature is surely not bound to restrict Himself to those ordinary laws. Who would dare argue otherwise? Miracles are then a testimony of the unique personal involvement and interference of God in His Creation.

How can science explain, for example, the numerous bodies of saints which have been found to be incorrupt several decades after death without any preservative being used, except through divine intervention? I personally have seen three of these favoured bodies (see pp. 18 & 19 ). How else can one account for the hundreds of holy people of the Church who have inexplicably received the stigmata of the crucified Jesus in their hands and sometimes their feet, as were seen in the case of the first stigmatist, St. Francis of Assisi?

However, once the scientist believes in God, he must then appreciate that with God all things are possible. Indeed, it was Luke, the physician and saint, who recorded that the angel Gabriel said to Mary: "Nothing is impossible to God" (Luke 1:37). Therefore, when a supernatural phenomenon occurs, scientists can only testify to the historical occurrence of the event and then declare that the nature of the event is outside the boundaries of ordinary scientific knowledge. And there science stops!

That there is a supernatural force which is responsible for Creation is relatively easy to accept. In fact, can there possibly be any alternative belief? But the ultimate humbling of the creature becomes manifest when he asks himself: "Who created this Force whom we call God?" He then discovers the limit of his human intelligence. Psalm 8:4-5, speaking of the Majesty of God and the dignity of man, queries: "When I behold your heavens, the work of your fingers, the moon and the stars which you set in place — what is man that you should be mindful of him...?" Indeed, Psalm 14:1 says it all: "The fool says in his heart 'There is no God!'" In fact, when disbelief becomes a faith it is much less rational than a belief in religion.

That God always was and that He had no beginning humiliates scientific logic and human understanding, and so, true science often needs to bow to religion, for as Bishop Renfrew from Scotland once said: "These (supernatural) mysteries level us all, the brainy and the brainless, for they save us from self-esteem and pride." It brings to mind God's taunting question to Job: *"Where were you when I laid the earth's foundation? Tell me, since you are so well informed!"* (Job 38:4). True science therefore walks hand in hand with religion, and anyone who thinks otherwise knows too little science and, above all, too little religion.

In the 19th century it was widely assumed that religion and the religious were on the wane and an age of materialism, liberalism and scientific revolution began to replace earlier ages dominated by religion. Indeed, by the end of the 19th century, Friedrich Nietzsche felt justified to exclaim that "God is dead!" and in the middle of the 20th century this same cry was repeated by many. However, in the last decades of this century, Marx's threat of a totally secular world, cleansed of the "opium" of religious superstition, has become an illusory fantasy as religion has been revived in many countries, particularly in Eastern Europe, clearly filling some deep-felt need, unsatisfied by scientific and technological developments. In fact, this technological age appears to have generated precisely such a religious revival. Nietzsche is now dead but God is very much alive today! It is the realization of the familiar maxim that "a little science takes one away from God but a great deal of science brings one back to Him."

Indeed, the story of the Virgin birth is a particularly striking example of faith. C. S. Lewis in his book *Miracles* writes: "When Joseph discovered that his fiancée was going to have a baby, he not unnaturally decided to repudiate her. Why? Because he knew just as well as any modern gynecologist that in the ordinary course of nature women who 'know not a man' do not have babies. No doubt, the modern gynecologist knows several things about birth and begetting which Joseph did not know. But those things do not concern the main point that a virgin birth is contrary to the course of nature. And Joseph obviously knew that. When he finally accepted the view that his fiancée's pregnancy was due, not to unchastity, but to a miracle, he accepted the miracle as something contrary to the known order of nature. If Joseph had lacked faith to trust God or humility to perceive the holiness of his spouse, he could have disbelieved in the miraculous origin of her Son as easily as any other man; likewise any modern man who believes in God can accept the miracle as easily as Joseph did."

In December 1968, three astronauts set off on a mission to orbit the Moon. In a historic broadcast to Earth on Christmas Eve, Major William Anders was heard reading from the Book of Genesis the passage describing the creation of the world: *"In the beginning, God created the heavens and the earth..."* Then from a quarter of a million miles out in space Captain James Lovel continued: *"And God called the light day and the darkness he called night..."* Colonel Frank Borman completed the reading with the verse: *"And God said, let the waters under the heavens be gathered together unto one place, and let the dry land appear also."* It was a new dawn for them as they looked down at God's creation.

In July 1969, countless millions all over the world watched Apollo 11 lift off on schedule on a two-and-a-half days quarter million miles journey on a mission to land on the Moon. It was a "giant leap for mankind" in his quest for knowledge of the Universe. It was July 16, the feast of *Our Lady of Mount Carmel*, a very special feast day of the *Ark of the Covenant* and *Queen of Peace*, and on Sunday, July 20,

Neil Armstrong and Edwin Aldrin landed on the Sea of Peace (Sea of Tranquility). It was man's first step on the Moon.

The fourth manned lunar landing by Apollo 15 was in July 1971. Astronaut James Irwin returned from the Moon and in an emotional speech he testified that he had felt the presence of God there. He then devoted the last two decades of his life to sharing his lunar experience and conversion: "God had a plan for me," he said to a journalist, "to leave Earth and to share the adventure with others, so that they too can be lifted up."

The Russians were no less impressed. The book *The Home Planet* records the remark of Aleksei Leonov, the first man to "walk" in space in 1965: "We have come to consider the planet a holy relic." In like manner, Russian cosmonaut Boris Volynov, one of the cosmonauts of the world's first Space Station in 1969, returned to Earth saying: "Having seen the Sun, the Moon, the stars and our planet... you begin to look at things differently and with greater trepidation."

And so, as the anxieties and dilemmas of this advanced technological and scientific age heighten, as the menace of materialism, greed and human discord become more onerous, a sense of tragedy arising from the threat to human existence has set the stage for the resurgence of religious fervour, not *despite* science and technology but precisely *because* of them. The irony is that while part of one of the most sophisticated scientific and technical enterprises yet devised by man, these explorers gazed back from where they had come and rediscovered the sacred. In so doing, as Edwin Bobb put it, they did a favour for mankind, especially that segment which has never appreciated the practical value of the aesthetic and religious perspective. Perhaps they found the missing link between science and religion — FAITH!

This book researches the most controversial Woman in the history of the world, that great Woman of *faith*, who once said: "Behold the handmaid of the Lord, be it be done unto me according to thy word" (Luke 1:38). Her Hebrew name was Miryam. We call her Mary.

**18.**

Above and Below: Incorrupt body of St. Bernadette behind the altar rail in Nevers, France (see p. 15 & p. 110)

19.

The incorrupt body of St. Margaret Mary Alacoque in Paray le Monial, France (see p. 15).

The incorrupt body of St. Catherine Labouré in Paris (see p. 15)

## CHAPTER 3.

## *On Private Revelations and Apparitions*

**"There were many other things that Jesus did; if all were written down, the world itself, I suppose, would not hold all the books that would have to be written."**

**John 21:25**

God speaks to us first and foremost through the Holy Scriptures, then through the teachings of the Church and also through private revelations. However, no Catholic is obligated by the Church to believe in any private revelation, the reason being that private revelations do not constitute part of the original Deposit of Faith, the official public revelation given to the Church which was closed with the death of the last of the apostles, John the Evangelist.

This is the standard statement that is recited repeatedly in theological and scriptural arguments. Indeed, many Bible "scholars" are often quick to retort that such and such is not in the Bible. They conveniently forget that John ended his witness with these words: "There were many other things that Jesus did, if all were written down, the world itself, I suppose, would not hold all the books that would have to be written" (John 21:25).

God, in His Wisdom, has frequently used private revelations in the past and continues to do so today. The Church, however, when it approves private revelations, does not make an infallible pronouncement. She merely declares that the private revelation contains nothing contrary to Sacred Scripture and to Catholic teaching. Apparitions do not provide new revelation; what they do is corroborate the Scriptures or Church doctrine. Nevertheless, a Catholic could certainly and legitimately refuse to believe them. However, Pope Benedict XIV's caution is most commendable, namely, "provided this is done with suitable modesty, for good reasons and without contempt."

21.

Father Albert Hebert, S.M., a Marist priest, in his book *The Tears of Mary and Fatima*, recognizes the difficulties that are sometimes associated with private revelations, both inside and outside the Church. He remarks: "Not all private revelations achieve their stated purpose. It would seem that some suffer so much harassment, interference and opposition from various sources, including, if not especially the clergy, that it is reasonable to believe that Christ or Mary would have to withdraw their activity and influence at the site and terminate the mission." This, he observes, is not novel. It is what Christ Himself had expected when He instructed the apostles, when a city or a town would not receive them, to shake the dust off their feet and to go elsewhere (Matthew 10:14).

According to Father Hebert, it is also well known that there have been persons, even ecclesiastics, who in all sincerity meant well, but lacking full knowledge, practical investigating abilities and/or courage, or all of these qualities, have caused loss of graces and other supernatural favours through not believing. Judicious authorities will know how to make contingent statements until the matter of a private revelation is finally and definitively settled, and sometimes the best action is to let it run its course without interference.

God has often chosen simple, sometimes unlearned, and ordinary members of the laity to be messengers of His private revelations and this has sometimes created disbelief in several people, particularly among those who consider themselves more worthy. If only Bernadette Soubirous of Lourdes were alive to tell us all about that. Some of the present day visionaries certainly can.

As Bill Reck, the publisher, says in the book *Our Lord and Our Lady In Scottsdale*: "Our Lord and Our Lady have not always manifested themselves to those we mortals might consider most worthy or even most receptive... Our own inability to comprehend the ways of the Lord, in and of itself, gives glory to Him."

This is nothing new. In his first letter to the Church at Corinth, Paul criticized the dissentions among the faithful: "As scripture says, I shall destroy the wisdom of the wise and bring to nothing all the teaching of the learned. Where are the philosophers now? Where are the scribes? Where are any of our thinkers today? Do you see now how God has shown up the foolishness of human wisdom?... For God's foolishness is wiser than human wisdom, and God's weakness is stronger than human strength. Take yourselves, for instance, brothers, at the time you were called how many of you were wise in the ordinary sense of the word, how many were influential people, or came from noble families? No, it was to shame the wise that God chose what is foolish by human reckoning, and to shame what is strong that he chose what is weak by human reckoning; those whom the world thinks common and contemptible are the ones God has chosen — those who are nothing at all to show up those who are everything" (1 Cor. 1:19-28).

Yet, as one of a cadre of professionals who are trained to analyze the facts in an unprejudiced way and to arrive at a logical and unbiased conclusion, I find it difficult to understand how, apart from blind prejudice and ignorance of the evidence, anyone could dare question the authenticity, say, of Fatima and the miracle of the Sun which was witnessed by over 70,000 people there. I find it equally difficult to understand how any critic, non-Catholic or Catholic, could deny the reality of the miraculous painting of Our Lady on the tilma of Juan Diego, which is there for anyone to see in Guadalupe, and I invite the skeptics and unbelievers to investigate the evidence or remain silent.

I find it hard to fathom how anyone who has researched the evidence of the miraculous spring and healings in Lourdes could do anything other than believe, and I have no ear for those who babble without researching the evidence. However, as Franz Werfel, a Jewish convert to Catholicism, on whose book was based the film *The Song of Bernadette*, said about Mary's apparition at Lourdes: "For those who believe, no explanation is necessary. For those who do not believe, no explanation is possible." If, then, these apparitions of the Mother of Jesus are truly authentic, why is it that the rest of the Christian world with its many divisions pay little heed to her messages? Will they be apologizing profusely to her in the heaven they hope to see?

I have leaned heavily in this book on several carefully selected private revelations, including those of the Venerable Mary of Agreda (Maria de Jesus de Agreda), as recorded in her four-volume book, *The Mystical City of God*. In 1667, when the precious remains of this Spanish Franciscan nun were exhumed two years after her death, they were found to be incorrupt and permeating the surrounding air with a most sweet fragrance.

Three hundred and twenty-one years later, on November 18, 1988, I visited the Convent of the Immaculate Conception in the small village of Agreda in the Province of Soria in Spain, and I saw the still incorrupt body of the Venerable Mary and the original manuscript of *The Mystical City of God*, begun in 1655 and finished in 1665.

I have also quoted from the private revelations of Sr. Faustina Kowalska of Poland, "the apostle of the Divine Mercy," who was beatified on Sunday, April 18, 1993. Indeed, the private revelations of Sr. Faustina were kept under wraps for years and her Divine Mercy messages were only recently approved (as she had foretold that they would be) by a decree of April 15, 1978, influenced by Pope John Paul II, then a Cardinal in Poland. Now her life, private revelations and the devotional literature on the Divine Mercy are being spread all over the world.

There are chapters dealing with the apparitions in Saragossa, Guadalupe, Lourdes, Fatima, Medjugorje, Garabandal, Akita, Amsterdam, Betania, and Argentina. I have visited all these shrines and after in-depth analyses, I believe what I have seen and heard. It was the result of historical research, scientific analysis and *faith*, and as far as I am concerned, any critic will have to fulfill at least the first two of these.

Sir William Osler (1849-1919), one of the most revered physicians in the world of medicine, once warned that "the greater the ignorance the greater the dogmatism," and at a farewell dinner in his honour in 1905 he praised the humility associated with faith: "Nothing in life," he said, "is more wonderful than *faith*. It is the one great moving force which we can neither weigh in the balance nor test in the crucible."

## CHAPTER 4.

## *The Mystery of the Trinity*

**God said: "Let us make man in our image, after our likeness."**

**Genesis 1:26**

When, in 1498, Christopher Columbus discovered an island in the West Indies with three tall mountain peaks, seen from afar before landing, he called the island *La Trinidad*, the Spanish word for The Trinity. Since then, Trinidad has been called the "Land of the Trinity," and Trinity Sunday is celebrated with great solemnity by the Catholic community of the island. It is the only occasion when the National Anthem is sung during the Mass.

Coincidentally, the very first "mystical" photograph taken with my camera was a depiction of what has been interpreted by many as the Trinity. I was on the hill of Podbrdo in Medjugorje on October 11, 1987. It was about midday and by the time I reached the top of the hill where the Virgin Mary first appeared to the visionaries, rain began to fall. Consequently, I spent a very short time on the hill. There were no other people on Podbrdo at that time.

I hurriedly took a photograph of the Cross which was planted on the spot where the Virgin appeared on June 24, 1981, and as I was about to take a second snapshot, I distinctly heard a voice within me say: "Take a shot of the hill." I looked around and could see nothing about the hill to my right which could be considered camera-worthy. Nonetheless, I felt with unruffled certainty that I should obey the request and take a photo of the hill nearby.

When I developed the film a few days later in London, to my surprise, a series of images appeared on the photographs. The first photograph showed the Cross, but in front and to the left of it, three figures appeared on the print. I said: *"appeared on the print,"* because I am certain that there were no other people on the hill with me that afternoon.

One was the figure of a person covered from head to foot with *a bright red cloak*, and very close to him, apparently embracing him gently, was another person who was partially seen. The third figure was that of a man whose back was turned toward the person covered in red, and he appeared to be walking away from him. At the bottom left hand corner of the photograph there was the distinct side-view of the head, neck and shoulder of a woman, covered with a blue mantilla. Her face was dark and as unrecognizable as the faces of the three figures just described.

My immediate interpretation of the prints was confirmed by a Jesuit priest in London and by many other people as being symbolic of the Trinity. The person who was covered from head to foot with the bright red cloak was said to be a symbolic interpretation of the second Person of the Blessed Trinity, Jesus, covered with a "cloak of blood," as indeed he was, when he was nailed to the Cross. The person *walking away* from him was considered to be symbolic of the first Person of the Trinity, God the Father, and a depiction of Mark 15:34 — "My God, my God, why have you forsaken me?" The third figure who was embracing him was interpreted as a representation of the third Person of the Trinity, the Holy Spirit, that expression of eternal love between the Father and Son. Finally, the image of the head and neck in blue at the left bottom corner of the picture was seen as symbolic of Mary at the foot of the Cross.

The second photograph ("Take a shot of the hill") which was taken within twenty seconds of the first was equally remarkable. This time the positions of the three figures were rearranged. The first and third figures could now be seen seemingly congratulating each other. However, the figure who previously was most prominent and covered from head to foot with a red cloak, was now barely seen to the right and behind them. The cloak which was now removed from his head, rested on his shoulders, and his head was bowed in an expression of deep humility. It was symbolic of the second Person of the Trinity, who had humbled Himself through His Passion and death on the Cross and who had successfully "consummated" His mission. It was the triumph of failure.

Emanating from the top right-hand corner of the first print was a luminous shaft of cloud, obliquely zooming down from the heavens onto the three figures. It was the first of a series of pictorial symbols of the *Shekinah* which I was to receive. I have included in this book these two photographs and many others which subsequently also depicted the *Shekinah* (see p. 30).

But, who can understand the Trinity? It is the supreme mystery of the Christian faith. Surely, the finite mind can never fully comprehend the infinite Being, and if it did, then, God would not be God. It is a revealed mystery to be accepted as true because God Himself taught it. Indeed, if the doctrine of the Trinity is false, that would be the end of the Christian religion, for the very essence of that religion is that the eternal Son of God became man for our salvation.

It is a religion which teaches that before the second Person appeared on earth in human form, He existed as the eternal Son of God, equal with the Father in all things. This eternal Son of God, in becoming man, took His human nature from the Virgin Mary. And so, the Son, who is born of the Father without a mother, was born of a woman as man without a father. Thus was born a Being who was both God and man. In His divinity He is one with the Father and in His humanity He is one with us. But this human nature, which began in *time*, was due to the operation of the Holy Spirit. Frank Sheed's *Theology for Beginners* was a great help in my attempt to try to understand the basics of this mystery, limited as I am by my finite mind.

This doctrine of the Holy Trinity contains four tenets. In the one divine nature there are three Persons: the Father, the Son, and the Holy Spirit. No one of these Persons is either of the others and each is wholly Himself. The Father is God, the Son is God, the Holy Spirit is God. Yet, they are not three Gods, but one God.

"Hear, O Israel, the Lord thy God is one God." This is the *Shema*. It is the cry of Judaism. Obviously, by not accepting Christ as the Messiah and the Son of God, Judaism does not accept the doctrine of the Trinity. Islam, likewise, rejects that Jesus was the only begotten Son of God and that God is a triune God: "Those who say: 'The Lord of Mercy has begotten a Son,' preach a monstrous falsehood, at which the very heavens might crack, the earth break asunder, and the mountains crumble to dust. That they should ascribe a son to the Merciful, when it does not become the Lord of Mercy to beget one" (Koran 19:88).

Koran 4:171 also reads: "People of the Book, do not transgress the bounds of your religion. Speak nothing but the truth of God. The Messiah, Jesus the Son of Mary, was no more than God's apostle and His Word which He cast to Mary: a spirit from Him. So believe in God and His apostles and do not say: 'Three.' Forbear, and it shall be better for you. God is but one God. God forbid that He should have a Son! Allah is the all-sufficient Protector."

As far as the Holy Spirit or the Paraclete is concerned, Ahmed Deedat, in his booklet *What the Bible says about Muhammad*, states: "It was prophet Muhammad (peace be upon him) who was the Paraclete, Comforter, helper, admonisher sent by God after Jesus. He testified of Jesus, taught new things which could not be borne at Jesus' time..."

It is true that the term "Trinity" is not found in the Bible, but the essence of it most certainly is. Indeed, the trinity of Persons in God was taught as a fact by Christ Himself. Thus, He said: *"The Father and I are One"* (John 10:30). And in Matthew 11:27, He says: *"No one knows the Son but the Father, and no one knows the Father but the Son and anyone to whom the Son wishes to reveal Him."* And so, there are two Persons, yet one. Then, at the very end of St. Matthew's Gospel, after Jesus rose from the dead, He introduces a third Person, still within the oneness: *"Go, therefore, and make disciples of all the nations. Baptize them in the name of the Father, and of the Son, and of the Holy Spirit."*

Of course, it may seem quite inconceivable and a contradiction in terms that one nature should be possessed by three Persons. Moreover, as Frank Sheed says, immediate difficulty presents itself in that we can hardly help thinking of sons younger than their fathers. Therefore, the question arises as to whether the second Person is younger than the first? If not, how can He be His Son?

Now, fathers are always older than sons, simply because a human being cannot start generating the moment he exists at conception; he must wait until he develops at a point where he can generate. But God lives in *eternity*, not in *time*. He does not have to wait for a certain amount of eternity to pass by before He can generate. Eternity does not pass by and there is no yesterday nor tomorrow in eternity. God lives in the eternal present where there is neither past nor future. It is an abiding *now*. There is no succession of time in eternity. What we call "now" in time is only the indivisible instant, which is the last moment of the past and the first moment of the future simultaneously. As someone once said: "Time is nature's way of keeping everything from happening all at once."

But, as stated in Professor Stephen Hawking's, *A Brief History Of Time*: "the Universe does have a preferred direction of time... animals get older and people remember the past rather than the future... There is a universal arrow of time... What would happen if and when the Universe stopped expanding and began to contract? Would the thermodynamic arrow reverse? Would we see broken cups gather themselves together off the floor and jump back onto the table?"

We reverse time, as it were, when we use the reverse mode on our videos and recorders, and in like manner, the God who has determined the direction of time can certainly reverse it at His will. In my view, the resurrection of our bodies can well be explained in this context and can be compared to the broken cups cited by Hawking.

Someone very special to me has requested that I should not be too scientific in this book, but I hope she will permit me this indulgence. One of the most interesting discourses on the doctrine of the Trinity was given by Dr. D. James Kennedy, a Presbyterian minister and television evangelist in Florida, whose sermons I have always enjoyed. He started by saying what the Trinity is *not*, and cited someone who, in an attempt to explain the Trinity, compared it to a pie divided into three pieces. However, as Dr. Kennedy remarked: "That may work well with cherry pies, but it does not work well with the living God, because God is not like a pie. You see, the Bible does not teach that the Father is a third of God, and the Son is a third of God and the Holy Spirit is a third of God. The Bible teaches that God the Father is God, that the Son is God and the Holy Spirit is God. So that just won't work."

He then went on to quote Dr. Nathan Wood, formerly the President of Gordon College, who wrote an interesting book, now out of print, in which he makes a scientific analogy to the Trinity: "Anyone who manufactures anything will no doubt leave his fingerprints on the article which he has made. In like manner, the Universe also contains upon itself the impress or fingerprints of its Maker. And so, impressed upon this Universe are the fingerprints of the triune God... who has revealed Himself in nature.

"Now, we will find, if we examine this Universe, that it consists, as any scientist will tell you, of *space, time,* and *matter*. These three, no more. Furthermore, it is not possible in this Universe which we know, to have any two of those without the other. This Universe always existed of space, time and matter, and cannot exist, as we know it, in any other way but with all three of these. Take away any one of them and you have no Universe... And now, let us look at each of these and, in turn, we will discover that each one of these elements of this triniverse is itself triune.

"For example, take the first one, *space*. Space is made up of longitude, latitude and altitude, that is, of length, breadth and height. These three, no more. Furthermore, it is not possible in the physical Universe to have anything that does not contain all three. Everything that we know of in the physical Universe always, under all circumstances, contains length, breadth and height, and if you take away any one of these it ceases to exist. You cannot have one without having all. Furthermore, may I point out to you that length is not a third of space, neither is width a third of space nor height a third of space.

"Now, let us move on from space to *time*. Time, as every school boy knows, is composed of the *past*, the *present* and the *future*. These three, no more. And in this world, as we know it, you cannot have time without having all three...

"Now, what is *matter?* Scientists will tell you that matter consists of energy in motion, producing phenomena. That pew upon which you are sitting is not solid. It is made up of tiny minute particles of electricity, of tiny *electrons, protons* and *neutrons*, and these are whirling at tremendous speeds, so fast that it boggles the mind... These particles, moving at tremendous speed, are producing all manner of phenomena, whether it be hardness or solidity, heat or cold, or softness... All matter is thus composed of energy in motion, and the same sort of procession and relationship that exists with time and space exists here also.

"And so, we see that the single Universe in which we live is made up of a *triniverse* of space, time and matter, and each of these, in its turn, is also triune. So, we also see in this Universe the very fingerprints of the triune God who made it - the Father, Son and Holy Spirit."

However, it appears that God had no intention of revealing the doctrine of the Trinity in its fullness to the Jews prior to the coming of Christ. It was eventually given to man explicitly when He sent His eternal and only begotten Son in human form as the Christ, and it was left to Him to reveal it to us. But, was it not hinted in the very first pages of the Bible? The Book of Genesis, Chapter 1:26 reads: *"Then God said: 'Let us make man in our own image, after our likeness.'"* By *"us"* and *"our"* He must have been referring to the triune God. He could not be referring to the angels. They do not create.

Yet, if after all this we still do not understand the Trinity, that, too, is understandable. It is meant to be a mystery!

Three figures appear next to the Cross in a photograph of Podbrdo Hill (see p. 25)

The appearance of the pillar of cloud on the photograph. The three figures have changed position (see p. 25)

## CHAPTER 5.

## *Mary and the Creation Story*

"**And now war broke out in heaven, when Michael with his angels attacked the dragon.**"
**Revelation 12:7**

Any history of Mary must begin, not merely with her birth, but with Creation and God's eternal plan. Now, as the Apostle Paul wrote, Jesus was "the first born of every creature. For in him were all things created in heaven and on earth, visible and invisible, whether thrones or dominations, principalities or powers. All things were created by him and in him. And he is before all, and by him all things hold together" (Col. 1:15-17).

Indeed, Jesus Himself made this awe-inspiring statement: *"Before Abraham ever was, I **Am**"* (John 8:58). What a magnificent play with the tenses! It carries the stamp of divine authority — a God with neither beginning nor end. But around 1290 BC the Father also identified Himself thus to Moses from the burning bush: "I **Am** who **Am**." And so, Jesus confirms in John 10:30, "The Father and I are one."

There was a great love of the Father for the Son and of the Son for the Father and from this love, the third Person of the Holy Trinity, the Holy Spirit, was begotten. Francis de Sales calls Him the eternal "Sigh" of that great love. But science could never conceptualize its reality. It is beyond scientific understanding.

The second Person of the Trinity was predestined to be incarnated as He was to be the link between the Godhead and the whole of Creation. The question, of course, has been raised, namely: "Would God have become incarnate if man had not sinned?" The twelfth century Benedictine monk, Rupert of Deitz, was one of many theologians who considered the Incarnation too magnificent a work on God's part to have been conditional on sin and, indeed, several decades later the Dominican friar and scientist, Albert the Great, agreed with him.

Fr. Martindale, S.J. has also expressed this viewpoint in his writings: "I hold (and though this is not a Catholic dogma, yet it is in harmony with it and is held by many) that, even had sin not been sinned, the Incarnation would have taken place, so that in every possible way communion between man and God might be established. Imagine saying that because there had been no sin, therefore there would be no Jesus, no Mary!"

When God determined to take upon Himself a human nature it immediately implied His predetermination of a human Mother. It is as though God saw His need for a Mother and this was also the only way to achieve this. As Cardinal Suenens rationalizes: "If the Incarnation lies at the heart of God's creative action, it is Mary who makes the Incarnation possible and therein lies her incomparable greatness. Her pedestination to be the Mother of Jesus is therefore absolutely fundamental and she was so predestined from the beginning of Creation." St. Peter Damian also voiced his opinion: "This most Blessed Virgin had been already elected and predestined in the decree of the eternal Wisdom before the world was made."

The story of the Creation is recorded in the Book of Genesis and brief mention is made of the fall of the angels in several passages in the Old and New Testaments. Great theologians such as Scotus, John of St. Thomas and the Dominican Suarez, among others, maintained that the object of Satan's envy was the hypostatic union of God with man in Jesus, and that he considered himself more worthy than any human creature to be one with God and to sit at His right hand. Above all, he refused to recognize the Son of God as made of a mortal woman. It is believed that Satan was the greatest angel in the choir of the cherubim, with an exalted beauty and wisdom before his fall. In the New Testament Christ Himself testifies to his fall: *"I watched Satan fall like lightning from heaven"* (Luke 10:18).

The Sacred Scriptures also relate the fall of Satan in the fourteenth chapter of Isaiah: *"How did you come to fall from the heavens, Daystar, son of Dawn? How did you come to be thrown to the ground, you who enslaved the nations? You who used to think to yourself, 'I will climb up to the heavens; and higher than the stars of God I will set my throne. I will sit on the Mount of Assembly in the recesses of the north. I will climb to the top of thunderclouds, I will rival the Most High.' What! Now you have fallen to Sheol, to the very bottom of the abyss!"* (Isaiah 14:12-15).

*The Mystical City of God* by the Venerable Mary of Jesus of Agreda (1602 - 1665) is a monumental four-volume history of the life of the Blessed Virgin, as privately revealed by Mary herself to this seventeenth century Spanish Franciscan nun. It is said that this holy nun saw in ecstasy all the events recorded in her book. The Blessed Virgin told her to write them down and the book *The Mystical City of God,* acclaimed by popes, cardinals and theologians, has inspired the laity and the clergy for over three hundred years. The mystic relates in greater detail the account of the creation of the Universe and the role of Mary as predestined by God.

She says in Book 1, Chapter 1, that in the beginning God created heaven and earth. He created heaven for angels and men, and the earth as a place of pilgrimage for mortals. The angels were created in the empyrean heavens and in a state of grace by which they might be first to merit the reward of glory. At first, they received a more explicit intelligence of the Being of God, one in substance, three in person, and they were commanded to adore and reverence Him as their Creator.

Heaven and earth were scarcely created when God dared to reveal His divine plan for the first time, proposing it as a test for the angelic creatures. The angels were then informed that God was to create a human nature and reasoning creatures lower than themselves, in order that they too should love and reverence Him as their Author.

They were informed that these were to stand in high favour, and that the second Person of the Blessed Trinity was to become incarnate and assume their nature, raising it to the hypostatic union, and that they were to acknowledge Him as their head, not only as God, but as God and man, the God-Man, adoring Him and reverencing Him.

To this command, using their *free will,* all the obedient and holy angels submitted themselves and they gave their full assent and acknowledgment with a humble and loving subjection of the will. But Lucifer, full of envy and pride, resisted and induced his followers to resist likewise, as they in reality did, preferring to follow him and disobey divine command.

When it was revealed to the angels that they would have to obey the Incarnate Word, a third precept was given to them, namely, that they were to admit as a superior conjointly with Him, a Woman in whose womb the Only Begotten of the Father was to assume flesh, and that this Woman was to be their Queen and the Queen of all creatures.

He then presented her to them not in reality, since she did not exist as yet, but in a sign or image. It was a Woman, adorned with the sun, standing on the moon, and with twelve stars on her head for a crown. St. John describes this image in the Book of Revelation (Rev. 12:1-2). This Woman was shown in her condition of motherhood, that is, in a state of maternity. The angelic spirits understood at once the role of this Woman.

And so, it seems to me that in one masterly stroke God "equalized" His Creation. Not only did He announce that the second Person of the Blessed Trinity would incarnate into the human family, He also made a mortal being, one of us, Queen of the angels. It was another test of humility for the angelic corps.

The mystic went on to relate that the good angels obeyed this command of the Lord with still increasing humility, praising the powers and the mysteries of the Most High, accepting also the Woman of the sign as their Queen. Lucifer and his confederates, however, rose to a higher pitch of pride and boastful insolence. In disorderly fury, he aspired to be himself the head of all the human race and of the angelic orders, and if there was to be a hypostatic union, he demanded that it be consummated in him: "It is only I who will be like the Most High. All will render me honour."

Above all, the decree constituting him inferior to the Mother of the Incarnate Word, he opposed with horrible blasphemies. Turning against God in unbridled indignation and calling upon the other angels, he exhorted them saying: "Unjust are these commands and injury is done to my greatness. This human nature which You, Lord, look upon with so much love and which You favour so highly, I will persecute and destroy. To this end I will direct all my power and all my aspirations. And this Woman, Mother of the Word, I will hurl from the position in which you have proposed to place her and at my hands, the plan which You set up shall come to nought."

This proud boast aroused the indignation of the Lord and to humiliate and punish him, He spoke thus to Lucifer: "This Woman whom you refuse to honour, shall crush your head and by her shall you be vanquished and annihilated. And if through your pride, death enters into the world, life and salvation of mortals shall enter through the humility of this Woman. Those that are of the nature and likeness of this Man and Woman shall enjoy the gifts and the crowns which you and your followers have lost."

Then happened that great battle in heaven which St. John describes in Apocalypse 12. The good angels, led in battle by Michael the Archangel, cast one third of the angelic host down to earth. It was the first warfare in eternity, a war beyond human imagination. It was a disaster unparalleled in eternity and in time. It stemmed from the *free will* which God in His Wisdom had to give His creatures, both angelic and mortal. He had no choice!

After the fall of the angels, in the fullness of time God created man. Adam and Eve who were to be the first parents of humanity prefigured the Redeemer and His Mother, the second Adam and the second Eve. However, as related by the Venerable Mary of Jesus of Agreda, knowing the precepts given to him by the Creator and believing that they were the God-Man and His Mother, Lucifer resolved to tempt them. He began with Eve in the hope of attaining his end more surely, and great was his joy when he succeeded in leading her to be disobedient to God. He gloried in his triumph, thinking that he had thwarted for all time the divine plan. Sin had entered the world.

But grief would soon be his when once more he heard this rebuke from the mouth of God Himself: *"I will put enmity between you and the woman, and between your seed and her seed; (s)he will crush your head..."* (Genesis 3:15). According to the Jerusalem Bible, the Latin version has a feminine pronoun ('she' will crush your head...) and since, in the messianic interpretation of the text, the Messiah and His Mother appear together, the pronoun has been taken to refer to Mary.

Following the fall of our first parents, thousands of years would elapse before the Redeemer and the Co-Redemptrix appeared in the world to redeem us from sin. Of course, it is theoretically, but perhaps not theologically possible, that the Creator could have been evil, but the God of heaven and earth is Goodness and Love. He hates sin. As Henry Edward Manning, Cardinal Archbishop of Westminster, said over one hundred years ago: "God wrote upon the conscience of man the nature of sin. He made man to know right from wrong, and in the conscience of man the obligations of this law are written. Every man born into the world has this outline of God's law written upon him, and sin is the transgression of that law. Venial sin is the disease of the soul; mortal sin is the death of a soul."

## CHAPTER 6.

## *Queen and Co-Redemptrix*

**"Near the cross of Jesus stood his mother."**
                                                                    **John 19:25**

"From the beginning and before all ages God elected and predestined for His Son a Mother from whom He was to take flesh and be born in the fullness of time, and loved her so much above all creatures that in her alone was He perfectly pleased" (Pope Pius IX *In Ineffabilis Deus*).

When, in this fullness of time, the Ambassador Gabriel relayed God's invitation to Mary to be the Mother of the second Person of the Holy Trinity, she bowed her head and replied: "I am the handmaid of the Lord. Be it done unto me according to thy will" (Luke 1:38). It was the voice of *humility* replying to God. A virgin, barely in her teens, thanked God for looking "with favour on the lowliness of his servant" (Luke 1:46).

There were many ways in which God could have made His appearance on earth. He could have come into the world at the age of a perfect man, independent of others, but He chose to come as a poor little babe dependent on the care and support of Mary. In His wisdom He found no more perfect means, no shorter way to do it than to submit Himself for thirty years to the most "blessed" of all women. It is this divine *humility* which the proud cannot understand, and so, in their eyes, Jesus could never be God.

According to Cyril Papali, O.D.: "Mary is the most perfect creature possible, for she has attained the peak of perfection that God has decreed as realizable by creatures, and has given God the maximum glory He wishes to derive from creation... It is philosophical, of course, but idle all the same, to argue that no creature is the best possible, because God can always make a better one. However, it is one thing for God to have the power to create, but another to have the will... To express it in our own imperfect terms, God has exhausted His omnipotence in creating her. That was what St. Bonaventure meant when he wrote: 'Mary is that being which God cannot make greater. He can make a greater earth and a greater heaven but not a greater Mother.'"

Indeed, she was God's greatest creation. As William Wordsworth put it — she is "our tainted nature's solitary boast." She is God's masterpiece. God asked for her consent and this she freely gave. The Word was made flesh and for this, in a sense, God is forever indebted to Mary. She was the sole human parent. No human father was involved and she alone furnished the sacred body of her Son. And just as the Son came *eternally* from the substance of the Father alone, so too, in *time*, He came from the flesh and blood of Mary alone.

As Fr. Michael O'Carroll, the Irish theologian of Blackrock College, Dublin, so scientifically put it: "In a sense they were the same flesh. He took His body from her. He took it from no one else. His entire genetic substance and constitution is Marian. His DNA is Marian. He is the first Marian in all history, and His Sacred Heart and her Immaculate Heart are *one* Heart."

And so, the God who always was, created His own Mother and became man. The Regulator allowed Himself to be directed; the omniscient God had to experience being man, and therefore the omnipotent God became impotent and vulnerable, dependent on a woman for His survival; the Bread of life, who satisfies every hunger, had need of nourishment and from her breasts she gave milk to this Bread. Only Son of God, as Man, He is the only Son of Mary. But the title of Mother does not change and in eternity God still calls her *"Mother!"*

But the maternal rights exercised by Mary over her Son are much more of privileges than rights, and the authority which she has over Jesus is only an authority conceded out of His goodness, kindness and love for mankind. As Son of God, begotten from all eternity, Jesus does not and cannot depend on any creature, not even His Mother. But in His human nature He is a servant of His Father and subject to the authority of His Mother. The 19th century Bishop of Bourges in France, Monseigneur de la Auvergne, had this to say: "By the fact that Mary at the Incarnation became the Mother of God, she acquired over Him a real and legitimate authority, a natural jurisdiction, a sacred and incontestable right, a maternal right which Our Lord Himself has recognized and to which He has voluntarily submitted, not by necessity of nature, but out of humility and love..."

### Veneration Not Worship

It is often said that Catholics worship the Virgin Mary, and in spite of the consistent denials of the Church over the centuries, the unread and the ill-informed continue to give lip to this erroneous criticism with boring regularity.

Timothy Ware, an Orthodox priest, speaks of the similarities of the Roman Catholic Church and the Orthodox Church with respect to this aspect of Mary when he said in his book *The Orthodox Church*: "Among the saints a special position belongs to the Blessed Virgin Mary whom Orthodox reverence as the most exalted amongst God's creatures, more honourable than the cherubim and incomparably more glorious than the seraphim. Note that we have termed her 'most exalted among God's creatures'; Orthodox, like Roman Catholics, *venerate* the Mother of God but in no sense do the members of either Church regard her as a fourth person of the Trinity, nor do they assign to her the *worship* due to God alone... The appellation *Theotokos* is of particular importance for it provides the key to the Orthodox cult of the Virgin. We honour Mary because she is the Mother of God. We do not venerate her in isolation, but because of her relation to Christ. Thus, the reverence shown to Mary, far from eclipsing the worship of God, has exactly the opposite effect. The more we esteem Mary, the more vivid is our awareness of the majesty of her Son, for it is precisely on account of the Son that we venerate the Mother."

Fr. Tadros Y. Malaty, a Coptic Orthodox priest, in his book *St. Mary in the Orthodox Concept* also makes this distinction: "In all our genuine Marian books and hymns, the Church makes a clear distinction between Jesus Christ to whom worshipping is due and to St. Mary to whom veneration is due." But as far back as the fourth century St. Epiphanius of Salamis (315-403 AD) in Cyprus also said: "Let Mary be honoured, but let the Lord be worshipped," and St. Ambrose added: "Mary is the Temple of God, not the God of the Temple. And, therefore, He alone is to be adored."

But who knows and insists on this more than the holy Virgin herself? She is not very prominent in the Bible for it is the Word of God and the Good News of her Son Jesus Christ, not the Gospel of Mary. She therefore remains hidden in the Old Testament as the humble handmaid of God would wish, but she is contained mystically, directly or indirectly, in all the Sacred Books. She is the Woman promised in the beginning who will crush the serpent's head (Genesis 3:15). She is the Virgin foretold by Isaiah, who shall conceive and bring forth Emmanuel (Isaiah 7:14). She is the rod shooting up from the root of Jesse that shall bear the divine flower (Isaiah 11:1) and she is the *Ark of the Covenant* (Rev. 11:19).

Certain aspects of all the great women of the Old Testament also foreshadow Mary, who is the greatest of all women.

Indeed, she is the First Lady of the world. She is like Sarah, whose life was one continuous trial of her faith in God's promise, as she was to be the mother of nations and she was the woman whose faith helped to achieve one of the miraculous births of the Bible, Isaac. She is like Esther, that great Queen who had the courage to intercede for her people at the risk of her life. She is Rachel, weeping for her children: "A voice was heard in Rama, weeping and loud lamentations; Rachel weeping for her children, and she will not be comforted because there are no more" (Jeremiah 31:15). She is Deborah who successfully led the Israelites against the Canaanites (Judges 4-5) and rallied her troops by predicting that they would be victorious. In like manner, in these apocalyptic times, Mary is rallying her troops, having already predicted in Fatima in 1917 that she will be victorious in her battle with Satan: "In the end my Immaculate Heart will triumph," she said.

In the New Testament Mary's role is more evident. The story of the conception, birth and infancy of Jesus is in fact the story of His Mother and, in a sense, He was almost lost in her shadow. When at last He did manifest Himself to the world it was her maternal authority that brought about His first miracle even though He had said: *"My time has not yet come,"* (John 2:5). Then Mary retreated into the background as John the Baptist eventually did: "He must increase, but I must decrease" (John 3:30). In this and in several other ways she is a prototype of John. John came to announce His First Coming and she is appearing now all over the world, preparing us for His Second Coming.

*True Devotion to Mary* by Louis Marie Grignon de Montfort (1673-1716) is considered to be the greatest single book on the Blessed Virgin Mary ever written. He talked about the providential function of Mary in the latter times: "It was through Mary that the salvation of the world was begun, and it is through Mary that it must be consummated. Mary hardly appeared at all in the first Coming of Jesus Christ, in order that men, as yet but little instructed and enlightened on the Person of her Son, should not remove themselves from Him and attach themselves too strongly and too closely to her... but in the Second Coming of Jesus Christ, Mary has to be made known and revealed by the Holy Ghost in order that, through her, Jesus Christ may be known, loved and served. God, then, wishes to reveal and make known Mary, the masterpiece of His hands, in these latter times... Being the way in which Jesus came to us the first time, she will also be the way by which He will come the second time, though not in the same manner." Spoken nearly three centuries ago, undoubtedly, the world is now in de Montfort's "latter times."

## The Co-Redemptrix

"When the fullness of time had come God sent his son, born of a woman... to redeem those who were under the law so that we might receive adoption as sons" (Paul in Gal 4:4-5). And so, it was the will of the Father that this Woman be intimately involved in His wondrous plan of human redemption. According to Mark Miravelle in his book *Mary Co-Redemptrix Mediatrix Advocate:* "Mary's intimate cooperation with the Redeemer began at the Annunciation, where she freely participated in the work of man's salvation through faith and obedience (Luke 1:28). The cooperation of the Mother of the Redeemer in the work of redemption started with her *fiat* to the angel."

On the morning when the Prince of Peace was born, a multitude of angels began to sing: "Peace on earth to men of goodwill." Mary then became the *Queen of Peace*. Thirty-three years later, in the closing phase of His life, and on the occasion of that most perfect sacrifice offered at that "Holy Mass" on a mountain called Calvary, there were no pews. *Stabat Mater*. The Woman stood at the foot of the Cross. Before He died, the Prince of Peace made His last will and testament and gave us all the Queen as our Mother. It was on that Friday that some men call "Good."

But do we really understand and appreciate what it means to be "at the foot of the Cross" for three hours? Hers was the most spiritual, the most intense and incomparable suffering ever known, and if there were one thousand mothers standing beneath the crosses of their thousand crucified sons, the sum total of their anguish could not describe the pain and suffering of that Mother *whose heart was pierced with a sword*; one solitary creature suffering *with* God, who in turn was suffering *for* all mankind and *from* them. She was a martyr whom God preserved from dying! That was the meaning of being the second Eve. That was the price of being *Co-Redemptrix*, for from the very beginning of Creation she was thus chosen.

It is in light of Mary's unique and intimate cooperation with the Redeemer, beginning at the Incarnation and ending at the work of redemption at Calvary, that the Church has evoked Mary under the title *"Co-Redemptrix."* I said *"Co,"* and by *"Co"* I do not mean *"Co-equal."* As Mark Miravelle wrote: "The title of *Co-Redemptrix* applied to the Mother of Jesus never places Mary *on a level of equality* with Jesus Christ, the divine Lord of all, in the saving process of humanity's redemption. Rather, it denotes Mary's singular *sharing with her Son* in the saving work of redemption for the human family... Mary, who is *completely dependent and subordinate* to her redeeming Son even for her own human redemption, participates in the redemptive act of her Son as His exalted human Mother."

Mary Co-Redemptrix gave to the Saviour the very instrument of redemption — His human body. Eve, on the other hand, was the Co-peccatrix (co-sinner) with the Peccator (the sinner) Adam, whose sin, as father of the human race, led to loss of grace for us, for it was through the instrumentality of the Co-peccatrix that the Peccator effected the death of the human race. The situation had to be reversed. While the first Eve received her bodily substance and being from Adam, it is the second Eve who gives the second Adam His body. Eve and Adam were the destroyers of the human race; Jesus and Mary were the restorers.

## Mediatrix

As Paul says: "There is one God, and there is one mediator between God and man, the man Christ Jesus, who gave Himself as a ransom for all" (1 Timothy 2:5-6). And so, Jesus Christ, true God and true man, is the one mediator between God and the human family.

At the wedding in Cana Jesus performed the first of His signs, which manifested His glory and thereby commenced the public ministry of the one Mediator. But this first public manifestation of the glory of the Mediator was, in turn, mediated by His Mother. We all know the event.

When the wine ran out, the Mother of Jesus said to Him: "They have no wine." And Jesus said to her: *"Woman, what have you to do with me? My hour has not yet come."* His Mother, quietly disregarding him, exercised her motherly authority and then said to the servants: "Do whatever he tells you." Jesus immediately responds to this intercessory request of His Mother by miraculously changing the water, not only to wine, but into the *best* wine. And so, at Cana, thanks to Mary, Jesus begins His hour, but it was Mary's day. On that day the Woman of Cana also began the public revelation of her own role as Mediatrix with the Mediator.

## Mediatrix of All Graces

St. Pius X, however, adds: "It cannot be denied that the dispensing of graces belong by strict and proper right to Christ, for they are the exclusive fruits of His death, who by His nature is Mediator between God and man. Nevertheless, by this union in sorrow and suffering which existed between the Son and the Mother, who, at the foot of the Cross of Redemption, died a martyr's death without dying, it has been allowed to the august Virgin to be the most powerful mediatrix between Jesus and man." It was an act of appreciation from the Godliness of the God-Man and the gentlemanliness of the Man-God. He also, I dare say, in His wisdom, decreed that Mary, as Mother and as daughter of Adam, had a legitimate right to intercede for mankind. It is God's logic!

On July 16, 1980, Fr. Stefano Gobbi claims to have received this message from Mary, and in all my research on the topic of grace I could find no better teaching, no more lucid explanation than these words of the Mediatrix herself:

"Grace springs from the bosom of the Father and is merited for you by the Word who, in my virginal womb, became man to share with you that same divine life, and for this He offered Himself as a ransom, becoming thus the one and only Mediator between God and all humanity.

"From the bosom of the Father, grace, in order to reach you, must therefore pass through the divine Heart of the Son, who communicates it to you in His spirit of love. This life of grace also has a relationship with your heavenly Mother. I am truly the Mother of Jesus and your Mother and my mediation is exercised between you and my Son Jesus. This is the natural consequence of my divine motherhood. In my virginal womb this first act of my mediation was carried out. As your Mother I was the means chosen by Jesus, and through me, all of you may reach Him. My task is that of distributing grace to all of my children, according to the particular needs of each one, which the Mother is very good at knowing.

"I am ever carrying out this duty of mine. However, I can carry it out fully, only in the case of those children who entrust themselves to me with perfect abandonment. I am the way which leads you to Jesus. *I am the safest and shortest way*, the necessary way for each of you, and if you refuse to go along this way, you run the danger of being lost in the course of your journey. This is my great work which I am still carrying out in silence and in the desert, and under my powerful action as Mediatrix of graces, you are evermore transformed into Christ.

"I am the Mother of intercession and of reparation and my maternal task is that of interceding each day for you before my Son Jesus. For my sinful children. I have obtained the grace of repentance, of a change of heart, of return to the Lord. For my sick children, I grant the grace of understanding the meaning of every suffering, of accepting it with docility, of offering it with love, of carrying one's own cross with trust and with filial obedience to the will of God, and for my good children, I obtain the gift of perseverance in good."

Let us recall the event of November 27 in the year 1830, 150 years earlier. It was the Saturday before the first Sunday of Advent at half past five in the evening. That event took place in the chapel of the Rue du Bac in Paris, a shrine which I have visited on three occasions.

St. Catherine Labouré was in the chapel praying when she saw the Blessed Virgin. She was standing, dressed in a robe of white silk, her feet resting on a globe. In her hands, held at the level of her breast, she held a small globe. The rings on her fingers were covered with jewels, some large and some small, from which came beautiful rays. The Virgin spoke to her: "This is a symbol of the graces which I share on those who ask me." It was reminiscent of her Son who said: *"Ask and you shall receive."*

At that moment an oval shaped frame formed around the Blessed Virgin, and on it were written in letters of gold: "O Mary conceived without sin pray for us who have recourse to thee." Then a voice was heard to say: "Have a medal struck after this model. Those who wear it will receive great graces; abundant graces will be given to those who have confidence." However, some of the precious stones gave forth no rays of light: "Those jewels which are in shadow represent the graces which people forget to ask me for," she explained.

"Suddenly the oval seemed to turn," said Catherine Labouré. "I saw the reverse of the medal: the letter M surmounted by a cross, and below it, two hearts, one crowned with a crown of thorns, and the other pierced by a sword. I seemed to hear a voice which said to me: 'The M and the two hearts say enough.'"

### Advocate

The Blessed Virgin is also invoked in the Church under the title of "Advocate." Mary not only mediates the graces of God to humanity as Mediatrix, but she also meditates the petitions of the human family back *to* God. She intercedes *to* God the Father, *through* the Son and *by* the Holy Spirit on behalf of humanity as our Advocate, especially in times of dangers and difficulties.

The Old is revealed in the New and, as Dr. Mark Miravalle points out in his book, we can see an authentic foreshadowing of the role of the Mother of Jesus as *Advocate* for the people of

God in the Old Testament role of the *queen mother*, the role and office held by the mothers of the great kings of Israel.

In the kingdom of Israel, the mother of the king held the exalted office of the queen mother, and because the kings of Israel normally had numerous wives, the mother of the king was chosen to be the queen of the kingdom, due to her singular familial relationship with the king. The office and authority of the queen mother in her close relationship to the king thus made her the strongest advocate to the king for the people of the kingdom.

It recalls the response of King Solomon to his mother Bathsheba in this queen mother's petition for a member of the kingdom as recorded in 1 Kings 2:19-20: "And the king rose to meet her, and bowed down to her: then he sat on his throne, and had a seat brought for the king's mother: and she sat on his right": 'I have only one small request to make of you; do not refuse me.' And the king said to her: 'Make your request, my mother, for I will not refuse you.'" In like manner, it is the teaching of the Church that Christ will never refuse His Mother's requests.

### Lady of All Nations/ Mother of All Nations

The title Co-Redemptrix was the main theme of one of the most interesting and important series of apparitions (1945-1959) which took place in Holland. On March 25, 1945, the feast of the Annunciation, the Virgin clad in a white robe, appeared to Ida Peerdeman, a visionary in Amsterdam. On February 11, 1951, the anniversary of her first apparition to Bernadette Soubirous in Lourdes, she appeared to Ida preceded by a dazzling light: "I am the Lady, Mary, *Mother of All Nations*. You can say the *Lady of All Nations* or the *Mother of All Nations* — who in the beginning was Mary. I come today, on this very day, to tell you that this is who I want to be. After all, the children of men of all nations one day will be one... Everyone will return to the Cross; then and only then, will peace reign."

Then she said: "Repeat after me this prayer in front of the Cross: 'Lord, Jesus Christ, Son of the Father, send me your Spirit over the earth. Let the Holy Spirit live in the hearts of all nations that they may be preserved from corruption, disaster and war. May the *Lady of All Nations*, who was once Mary, be our *Advocate*.'"

She spoke of many spiritual topics and then enlarged upon them over the years. She explained how her role should be summed up in a doctrine to be proclaimed as **"The final**

**Marian dogma."** On April 29, 1951, she said to Ida: "I stand here as the *Co-Redemptrix, Mediatrix and Advocate*. Everything should be concentrated on that. The new dogma will be '*the dogma of the Co-Redemptrix.*' Notice I place special emphasis on 'Co.' I have said that it will arouse much controversy. However, I tell you that the Church, Rome, will carry it through and silence all objections..."

The dogma of the Assumption of the Blessed Virgin Mary was proclaimed in 1950 and on May 31, 1951, Mary explained to Ida: "The dogma of the Assumption had to precede it. The last and greatest dogma will follow." On another occasion she said: "The nations must know that the *Lady of all Nations* has come as *Co-Redemptrix, Mediatrix and Advocate*. So be it!"

She then prophesied that this final dogma will be proclaimed in some future year on the 31st of May. May 31 is the last day of the month dedicated to Mary by the Church. It ushers in the month of June, dedicated to the Sacred Heart of her Son, the Redeemer, Christ the King. It makes much sense. Proper protocol! Significantly so, at that time May 31 was the feast of *Mary, Queen of the World*.

On April 4, 1954, she said to Ida: "Satan is still the prince of this world. That is why the *Lady of all Nations* had to come *now*, into *these* times, for she is *the Immaculate Conception* and therefore also the *Co-Redemptrix, Mediatrix and Advocate*. These three are but one. *Is that clearly understood, theologians?*"

Note the authority with which she spoke and the implication that certain theologians would attempt to deny her this title! This announcement ("These three are but one") also interested me in that it identified a trinity of concepts and titles of the Bride of the three-in-one God.

"Satan is still the prince of this world," she said. And on another occasion she added: "Only God knows how powerful is the kingdom of Satan!" Indeed, Pope Paul VI went further and warned us that "the smoke of Satan has even entered the Church." And so, the Virgin frequently asks for prayers for the clergy as they are under constant and intense attack by her enemy.

Three years earlier, on December 31, 1951, the thirty-eighth apparition, she revealed to Ida: "In Russia a great change will come about." Then she paused before she said: *"after much conflict."* Then she added: "China will turn to the Mother Church." Again she paused before repeating very slowly: *"after much conflict."*

Upon reading this latter prophecy in Ida's book the *Lady of All Nations*, I recalled an interesting experience in November 1974. China had just opened its "bamboo curtain," as it were, and had already invited President Nixon to visit China two years previously.  Dr. Eric Williams, Prime Minister of Trinidad and Tobago, and at that time the senior politician of the Commonwealth Caribbean, was then invited to make a State visit to China, representing the Third World, and I was included as a member of his small entourage.  On November 6 at 11 p.m. we met Chairman Mao Tse-tung.  He was obviously suffering from Parkinson's disease and died three years later.

Six years later in 1981, I met a lovely sixteen year old Chinese girl who was allowed to emigrate to America via Ireland, following interventions made by an influential relative who was residing in Dublin.  At that time she was the house-help of relatives of mine there and was learning to speak English.  One evening as I was talking about some aspects of religion, she was obviously surprised that I could be so misinformed and in a most gentle voice she asked: "But how could you believe that there is a God?  Chairman Mao has always said that there is no God!"

Over the next week I spent several hours explaining simple theology to her.  Later that year I received a letter from her, dated October 30, 1981.  She had left Dublin and was then studying in New York.  The letter read in part: "Dear Courtenay, It has been over three months since I met you in Ireland, but everything is so clear in my memory... It is you who enlightened me to believe in God.  I treasure the books you gave me very much.  I specially like that book *Letters to God From Teenagers*.  When I feel lonely or meet difficulties I often think that God is with me, which always gives me confidence, courage and great relief...  With love — Wei-Hong."

This was but one Chinese convert who "turned to the Mother Church."  By coincidence, October 30, the day she wrote the letter, is the feast of St. Marcellus the Centurion, a martyr for the faith, who converted from Roman paganism to Christianity in 298 AD.  "China will turn to the Mother Church," said Mary in Amsterdam in 1951.  Is this single conversion a herald of things to come?

### The Eucharist And Amsterdam

The apparitions of the *Lady of All Nations* to Ida Peerdeman have not been denounced by the Church, and so, on Friday, July 17, 1992, when I was in Amsterdam for a meeting of the Scientific Committee of the World AIDS Foundation, I visited the home and private chapel of Ida, then in her late eighties.  As I entered the hallway she told me that the day of my visit was the anniversary of her "Eucharistic experience," which occurred in 1958 when, before the celebration of the Mass began, she suddenly saw a huge and almost blindingly-white Host in front of the altar: "It was white fire — magnificent." The vision slowly faded away and the altar was then bathed in a beautiful light. It all lasted for a moment.

I spent an hour in front of the oil painting of the *Lady of All Nations* beside the altar in Ida's private chapel. The painting was a reproduction of a vision which she saw when Mary appeared to her standing in front of the Cross of the Redeemer. It was obviously the appropriate place for the Co-Redemptrix. The Virgin stood on a globe around which were hundreds of sheep, both black and white, representing the peoples of the world.

She stood in front of the Cross, dressed in white and her long black hair fell loosely on her shoulders (see p. 54). To me, it was as though she had "let her hair down," as she said what she had to say with great authority in Amsterdam. "So be it!" she exclaimed many times. *"Is that clearly understood, theologians?"* she also said decisively.

In time it was this painting of the *Lady of All Nations* in Amsterdam which a Japanese sculptor used as the basis for his carving of the famous weeping statue of *Our Lady of Akita,* where again in 1973 Mary "let her hair down," as she had also done in 1961 in Garabandal, Spain, and gave the world stern warnings of a terrible chastisement to come if we did not convert.

It was on the following day as I was being taken around Amsterdam by a Dutch friend that I learnt about the "miracle of the Host" in Amsterdam on March 15, 1345, when a consecrated Communion wafer remained intact and rose spontaneously into the air after accidentally falling into the flames of a fireplace in the home of a sick man. Two years later a chapel was built there, and from far and wide believers from all ranks of society made pilgrimages to this shrine. Nowadays, the Begijnhof Chapel in Amsterdam is the starting and finishing point of a silent procession which takes place every year on a night in March.

The Eucharist also held a prominent place in the messages of the *Lady of All Nations* and as Raoul Auclair wrote in the Introduction to his book on the Amsterdam apparitions: "It is through the Eucharist that the world, in the peril which threatens it, can be saved. Moreover, the Lady tells us that this is why she has chosen Amsterdam, the city of the miracle, which took place in 1345, exactly 600 hundred years before."

Indeed, it is not without significance that at the end of Mary's last apparition on May 31, 1959, before she said her parting word to Ida: *"Adieu,"* a voice was heard to say: *"Who eats*

*Me and drinks Me takes eternal life and receives the true Spirit."* It was Jesus in the Eucharist speaking.

**World Affairs and Marian Feasts**

Twenty-eight years before her prophecy in Amsterdam she had also promised in 1917 at Fatima that Russia will be converted. Who would have thought that 1989 would have seen such sweeping and sudden upheavals in the Soviet system? Once unified by Moscow's iron grip, the countries of Eastern Europe broke free. Poland and Hungary led the way, then East Germany, Czechoslovakia, Romania and Lithuania. A colossal statue of Lenin was torn down in Romania and the new state seal of St. George replaced the bolshevik hammer and sickle on the door of the Republic's legislature in Lithuania.

But the influence of this great Woman on world affairs is neither fully recognized nor appreciated, and the recent events in Europe tend to be seen in political terms only. However, the Fatima message has had such an influence on many of us that the *Wall Street Journal* chose, after the fall of the Iron Curtain, to make the revelations of Fatima the subject of a feature article.

On March 5, 1990, the *London Daily Telegraph* also published an article by Anthony O'Hear, Professor of Philosophy at Bradford University in England, under the caption *The Lesson The East Can Now Teach The West*. To my surprise, the article in this secular press began with this quotation in italics from *Our Lady of Fatima*: *"If you heed my requests the world will be saved, Russia will be converted and there will be peace. If not, Russia will scatter her errors through the world, provoking wars and persecution against the Church, the good will be martyred, the Holy Father will have much to suffer and several nations will be wiped out."*

Professor O'Hear then continued his article: "It is not surprising that many people in Poland see events in East Europe over the past 70 years in terms of these words of *Our Lady of Fatima*, revealed in 1917. They believe that it is through God's grace and the power of faith that the godless regime in their country has crumbled..."

He went on to add: "Neither Marxism nor liberalism can give expression to what has come to be central to the East European experience: the living recognition that evil exists, that we have all sinned and are as individuals answerable to a higher order, that human life is sacred and that individuals may not be manipulated beyond a certain point, and that political Utopia is an illusion based on the denial of evil and an arrogant over-estimate of human powers.

The Church — the traditional Church, not the Marxising Church of "liberation" and social concern — stands for these truths, and so for the dignity of man. Even if we cannot bring ourselves to bend the knee before the Virgin, we in the West should surely attend to the testimony of those in the East who have lived through the totalitarian experience, and are finding something of irreplaceable value in religious faith." Professor O'Hear is not a Catholic.

But the Virgin's footprint was not only seen in these recent events in Europe. Italy, so devoted to the Blessed Virgin, surrendered to the Allies on September 8, 1943, the feast of the *Nativity of the Blessed Virgin Mary*. She is the *Queen of Peace* and it is no coincidence that the signing of the Peace Treaty in Japan at the end of World War II took place on August 15, 1945. It was the feast of the *Assumption of Mary*. Six years later on September 8, 1951, Japan also signed a formal pact in San Francisco pertaining to their surrender. It was called the Second World War peace treaty. It was again on the feast of the *Nativity of the Blessed Virgin Mary*.

The signing in Washington of the intermediate range nuclear forces treaty (INF) by Mikhail Gorbachev and Ronald Reagan, abolishing medium range missiles in Europe, took place on December 8, 1987, the feast of *the Immaculate Conception*. The Berlin Wall fell on January 1, 1990, on the feast of the *Mother of God*. It is also no coincidence that the Communist party died in Russia on August 22, 1991, when Mikhail Gorbachev survived the aborted coup by the diehard communists. It was the feast of the *Queenship of Mary*.

It did not stop there. The leaders of Russia, the Ukraine and Byelorussia announced the dissolution of the Soviet Union and said that they had agreed to establish a "Commonwealth of Independent States" — in effect, a new nation. It was Sunday, December 8, 1991, the feast of *the Immaculate Conception!*

Meanwhile, in the Europe which gave this planet two World Wars, the churches are opening again in the East, and it is of momentous significance that the flag of the twelve member community of Western Europe, adopted officially by the countries of the European Economic Commission (EEC), is a blue flag with twelve stars. Blue is the colour which the Church identifies with the Virgin, and the Woman of the Apocalypse was seen wearing a crown with twelve stars! (Rev 12: 1-2).

Is it another coincidence that the date on which the flag of Europe was accepted was December 8, 1955, the feast of *the Immaculate Conception?*

## The Marian Movement of Priests

Fr. Stefano Gobbi, the founder of the Marian Movement of Priests, is said to have received this inner locution from Our Lady in 1988: "Walk in my light and become the apostles of your heavenly Mother in these last times. Spread everywhere the perfume of my presence and of my Motherly tenderness... The period of time granted by the Lord to humanity for its conversion is about to come to its end... My times have come, and now I about to leave the desert where I am to accomplish my greatest prodigies and to obtain my foretold victory... These are my times. These are the times of the great mercy. These are the times of the triumph of my Immaculate Heart. These are the times of my strong admonition: "Come back, come back, O humanity!

"You are being called to be my apostles in these last times. These are ten very important years. These are ten decisive years. I am asking you to spend them with me because you are entering into the final period of the second Advent, which would lead you to the triumph of my Immaculate Heart. In this period of ten years there will come to completion the time of the great tribulation, which has been foretold to you in Holy Scripture before the Second Coming of Jesus. In this period of ten years all the secrets that I have revealed to some of my children will come to pass and all the events which I have foretold to you will take place...

"Do not allow yourselves to be seized with fear... Beloved children, the Lord who has come in His first birth is about to return to you in His glory. His Second and Glorious Coming is close at hand, and it is my maternal duty to prepare you to receive Him, as I received Him in His First Coming... And so, enrapped in the light of my Immaculate Heart, you too should prepare a precious crib for His glorious return."

## Beauty and Love of Mary

It is a message of urgency from the Mother of mothers. In emergency rooms of hospitals **CPR** is the acronym for an emergency procedure in near-death situations. It means **C**ardio-**P**ulmonary-**R**esuscitation, and it sometimes restores the apparently dead to life. Mary is appearing all over the world in this century with an emergency call to all her children, Christian and non-Christian alike. Her **CPR** means *Conversion, Penance* and *Reparation*. It is also a call for a return to the *Covenant, Prayer* and *Reconciliation*, and it is meant to restore souls to life and save us from eternal death.

## 51.

There is a cry of distress and a warning of impending disaster coming from the motherly Heart of the one Woman who loves with a greater love than any other woman is *capable* of loving. It is Rachel crying for her children. It is a cry from the Queen of Hearts and the Mother of Love. The visionaries in Medjugorje once asked her: "Gospa, how is it that you are so beautiful?" She smiled and in a soft musical voice she replied: "I am beautiful because I love much. Love, and you too will be beautiful."

Albertus Magnus once said: "As our Lord Jesus Christ was the most beautiful among the sons of men, so was the Blessed Virgin beautiful and fair above all the daughters of Adam. Mary, whose beauty surpassed that of all women who ever lived, now glorified and made immortal in heaven, is a paradise of incomparable pulchritude." Indeed, Wordsworth called her "our tainted nature's solitary boast." This beauty is indescribable by all the visionaries to whom I have spoken and who have had the privilege of seeing her. Indeed, it is written that St. Bridget once heard Our Lord address His Mother: "Your beauty surpasses the beauty of the angels and of all created things" (*Lib Revelate.* C. 16).

Alphonsus Marie Liguori (1696-1787), Doctor of the Church and founder of the Redemptorists, in his classic writing *The Glories of Mary*, relates the romantic story of the brother of a king of Hungary who used to recite the Office of Our Lady daily. He fell seriously ill, and then made a vow of chastity to Mary if she would restore him to health, and he immediately recovered. His brother, the king, however, died soon afterwards and a bride was chosen for him. But sometime before the nuptial ceremony he retired to his room to say his accustomed Office. When he came to the verse in the *Song of Songs*: "How beautiful you are, how charming, my love, my delight! (Song 7:7), the Virgin appeared to him and said: "If I am as beautiful as you say, why do you now leave me for another? Know that if you leave her, you shall have me for a spouse, and the kingdom of heaven instead of that of Hungary." The prince then fled to a desert near Aquileia in Italy where he lived a holy and chaste life. He kept his vow to the fairest of them all.

Beauty, as we all know, is frequently accompanied by great pride and vanity. In fact, it was the cause of Lucifer's fall. Mary, on the other hand, was most pure and humble in her great and unique beauty, and the saints and mystics have often said that her beauty was such that it extinguished all passion in the beholder and created an intense love of chastity.

As for love, in Book Three of his *Confessions*, St. Augustine confessed: "I was in love with love... To love and be loved was sweet to me." Of this human love, Fr. J. Boudreau, S.J. wrote in 1872: "Think of this, you mortals, who crave after human love. You desire to love and to be loved. Love is the sunshine of your lives. But do what you will, it can never give you perfect happiness here below; for when you have at last succeeded in possessing the object after which you so ardently sighed, you discover its imperfections which you had not suspected before, and these lessen your happiness. But suppose even that you are of the few who are happy as they expected to be — how long will your blessedness last? A few years at most. Then death with a merciless hand tears away from you the object of your love, Is not this the end of all earthly happiness?"

D. Roberto, a hermit of Monte Corona, has written most eloquently on this topic. His book *The Love of Mary* was first published in 1856. He talks of the love of creatures thus: "Behold how inconstant, how changeable is earthly love. A slight suspicion, an incautious word, a negligent act, is enough to cool or extinguish it... And if this love is based on the purely natural qualities of beauty, vanity or ambition, as years increase, as the face becomes wrinkled and the hair turns gray, and as interest subsides, love becomes lukewarm, then cools, and at last entirely disappears." He went on to add that "the foolish lovers of the world even try to conceal their defects, both natural and moral, which might diminish them in the eyes of those they love."

"But," he continues, "it is not so with the true love of Mary in whom there is no change, nor shadow of vicissitude. Neither our low and vile condition, nor our misery and poverty, neither disgraces nor sufferings, infamy nor dishonour, natural defects nor failings, neither age nor youth, infirmity nor death itself, can cool in the least the ardour of her love. She loves us although we are ungrateful, faithless and sinful. She loves us with an insuperable love, more than all the mothers, sisters and lovers in the world." Hers is the *Love* of God.

Indeed, she is one of us and only her love for God surpasses her love for us. "Am I not of your kind?" she once said to Juan Diego in Guadalupe, Mexico. She is the *Queen of Love* and those who have experienced her love can readily understand why St. Bernard of Clairvaux called her *"Ravisher of Hearts."*

In her call for the renewal of the *Covenant of Love* there is no room for *compromise*, no room for sitting on the fence. We are being called to *take a side* in this *final hour* of the battle between the serpent and his seed and the Woman and her seed

(Genesis 3:15). It is the Woman who, according to the inspired writings of several saints, Satan fears and hates even more than God Himself ever since he was made aware of her before the battle in heaven.

As Louis Grignon de Montfort wrote: "The most terrible of all the enemies which God has set up against the devil is His Holy Mother Mary... Satan, being proud, suffers infinitely more from being beaten and punished by a little and humble handmaid of God, and her humility humbles him more than the divine power." And so, those who tend to deride and even hate the name of this great Woman unwittingly have one thing in common with Satan!

54.

Painting of Lady of All
Nations in Amsterdam

Pillar of fire in front of
Ida and the painting

Below: The private chapel of Ida in Amsterdam (see p. 47)

**CHAPTER 7.**

## *The Covenants of the Bible —*
## *The Old Covenant*

**"We will observe all the commands that
Yahweh has decreed."**

**Exodus 24:3**

In order to appreciate fully the significance of Mary's title, the *Ark of the Covenant*, it is appropriate that we recall and study the biblical history of the Covenants. Indeed, the Covenant is the basic theme of the Bible. It is the heart of the Old and New Testaments in which God made Covenants with some of his favourite sons with whom He had very personal and intimate relationships.

A covenant is an agreement or bond between two parties. The first Covenant between Yahweh and man is found in the Book of Genesis, chapters 6 9: "When Yahweh saw that the wickedness of man was growing on earth and that the thoughts in his heart fashioned nothing but wickedness all day, he regretted that he had made man on earth and his heart grieved, but Noah had found favour with Him. And so God said to Noah: *"The end has come for all things of flesh. I have decided this because the earth is full of violence of man's making and I will blot out all mankind from the face of the earth. Make yourself an Ark out of resinous wood... For my part, I mean to bring a flood and send the waters over the earth to destroy all flesh on it; every living creature under heaven, every living thing on earth shall perish but I will establish my Covenant with you. You must go on board the Ark, yourself, your sons, your wife and your sons' wives along with you."*

The flood lasted forty days on the earth. Noah then sent out the dove from the Ark and in the evening the dove came back to him and there it was with a new olive branch in its beak. So Noah realized that the waters were receding from the earth. Then God said to Noah: *"Come out of the Ark, you yourself, your wife, your sons and your sons' wives with you... Never again* will I strike down every living thing as I have done... Here is a sign of the Covenant I make between Myself and you and every living creature with you for all generations. I will set My bow (rainbow) in the clouds and this shall be a sign of the Covenant between Me and the earth, but when I gather the clouds of the earth and the bow appears in the clouds I will recall the Covenant between Myself and you and every living creature of every kind, and so the waters shall never again become a flood to destroy all things of flesh..."

And so, the sign of the first Covenant was a "rainbow in the clouds" (see p. 60). It bespeaks the significance and importance of water in God's creation. Indeed, water covers three fourths of the earth's surface and the human body is about seventy percent water by weight. Life on earth cannot be sustained without it. The Moon, for example, lacks air and water, and life as we know it is not likely to exist there.

Water from the oceans, lakes and rivers is evaporated by the Sun's heat to form water vapour, and clouds form when moist air rises and cools. A rainbow, on the other hand, is formed when the Sun's rays pass through tiny droplets of water which linger in the air after rain. The raindrops act like tiny mirrors or glass prisms. We see a rainbow when the Sun is behind us and the rain is in front of us. It is a band of colour which starts with red (the least bent part of the light), then orange, yellow, green, blue, indigo and finally violet (the most bent part of the light).

The Covenant with Noah cannot be related to any historical time as the Bible offers no real clue as to when Noah lived, and it is only with the story of Abraham that we begin to get details which enable historians to guess the approximate dates of biblical history. However, modern historians now believe that the flood took place about 5000 years ago and archaeologists have recently provided overwhelming evidence that segments of the broken Ark have been found on Mount Ararat in Turkey at about 15,000 feet in the ice-packed mountain. However, the Turkish authorities have since prohibited further explorations.

The second Covenant of the Bible was made between God and Abraham. Abraham is the biblical patriarch from whom the Jews and the Arabs trace their ancestry. It is said that the people of Abraham were originally idol worshippers who emigrated about 2000 BC from the ancient city of Ur, near the Persian Gulf, to the city of Haran in what is now Turkey. It was there that Abraham rejected his father's gods, and set off with his own flock to lead an independent life, spurred by the heavenly command to found a nation of people who would serve a single God.

57.

The great cities and civilizations of Egypt and Mesopotamia were already old, but the Hebrews, like many of the wandering people, lived on the fringes. It was during this time that the Lord first promised the itinerant Hebrews a land of their own and numerous descendants in return for obedience and exclusive loyalty: *"Have no fear, Abram, I am your shield; your reward will be great... Look up to heaven and count the stars, if you can. Such will be your descendants..."*

That day Yahweh made a Covenant with Abram in these terms: *"To your descendants I give this land from the border of Egypt to the great river, the river Euphrates"* (Genesis 15:5-18). God was speaking of Canaan (Palestine), which in our own contemporary history is now the source of religious and political conflict in the Middle East.

The second part of this Covenant was made when Abraham was 99 years old: *"I am El Shaddai,"* said Yahweh to him, *"Bear yourself blameless in my presence and I will make a Covenant between myself and you and increase your numbers greatly ... You shall no longer be called Abram; your name shall be called Abraham ... I will give you, and your descendants after you the land you are living in, the whole land of Canaan, to own in perpetuity, and I will be your God. You on your part shall maintain my Covenant, yourself and your descendants after you, generation after generation. Now this is my Covenant which you are to maintain between myself and you, and your descendants after you... When they are eight days old all your male children must be circumcised, generation after generation of them..."* (Genesis 17:1-22).

Thus, circumcision became the sign of the Covenant and a requirement for the people of the Covenant, the Israelites. Yahweh then promised Abraham a son whom he was to name Isaac. According to Hebrew and Catholic teaching, He then told Abraham: *"With him I will establish my Covenant, a Covenant in perpetuity, to be his God and the God of his descendants after him"* (Genesis 17:19-20). God later renewed the Covenant with Abraham's descendants by a personal manifestation to Isaac (Genesis 26: 1-5) and then Jacob (Genesis 28: 10-22).

Prior to this, God had put Abraham to the test: *"Take your son Isaac, your only one whom you love and go to the land of Moriah. There you shall offer him up as a holocaust on a height that I will point out to you."* Broken-hearted, he obeyed God and "tied up his son Isaac, and put him on top of the wood on the altar. Then he reached out and took the knife to slaughter his son. But the Lord's messenger called to him from heaven, *"Abraham, Abraham! Do not lay your hand on the boy. Do not do the least thing to him. I know now how devoted you are to God. Since you did not withhold from me your own beloved son."*

As Abraham looked about, he spied a ram caught by its horns in the thicket. So he went and took the ram and offered it up as a holocaust in place of his son. Again the Lord's messenger called Abraham from heaven and said: *"I swear by myself,"* declares the Lord, *"that because you acted as you did in not withholding from me your beloved son, I will bless you abundantly and make your descendants as countless as the stars of the sky and the sands of the sea shore... all this because you obeyed my command"* (Genesis 22:1-18).

However, the Islamic version states that the Covenant was between God and Abraham's first son Ishmael, who was conceived by Hagar, the Eqyptian maid-servant of his wife Sarah. Islam teaches that it was Ishmael and not Isaac who was supposed to be sacrificed. According to H. M. Baagil, M.D., in his booklet *Christian Muslim Dialogue*: "Because of (Jewish) chauvinism the name Ishmael was changed to Isaac in all of Genesis 22." According to the Koran, Ishmael goes to Mecca and his descendants growing up in Arabia are Moslems, whereas those of Isaac, who remained in Palestine, are Jews.

With the passage of time, about 430 years (Exodus 12:40; Gal.3:17), and the continual breaking of the Covenant, the tribes of Israel eventually became slaves of the Egyptians, and the story of the Sinai Covenant begins as the Covenant people suffer oppression in Egypt later in the thirteenth century BC. God eventually hears their cry and moves to deliver them through His chosen prophet Moses, as he remembers His Covenant with Abraham, Isaac and Jacob (Exodus 2:24-25).

The Covenant with Moses was made in the midst of the theophany (the visible manifestation of God in a cloud to man) on Mount Sinai and with the Ten Commandments. Moses then went down from the mountain and told the people all the commands of Yahweh and all the ordinances. In answer, they all said with one voice: "We will observe all the commands that Yahweh has decreed" (Exodus 24:3). Early next morning Moses built an altar at the foot of the mountain with twelve standing stones for the twelve tribes of Israel.

Now, flesh was offered to Yahweh as burnt offerings. Blood was a particularly powerful sacrificial symbol. Indeed, it is stated in the Bible that blood that is spilled, especially innocent blood, "cries out" to God (Gen. 4:10), and blood that is shed serves to "cleanse and save" (Heb. 9:22). And so, like Noah who sacrificed burnt offerings, Moses directed certain young Israelites to offer holocausts and to immolate bullocks to Yahweh as communion sacrifices.

Half of the blood Moses took up and put into basins, the other half he cast on the altar... then he took the blood and cast it towards the people: "This," he said, "is the blood of the Covenant that Yahweh has made for you, containing all these rules." The sprinkling of the blood on the altar signified Yahweh, and on the people, it signified that Yahweh and the people had become blood relatives, next of kin (Exodus 24:1-8). God and Israel were therefore bonded together as Covenant partners in a blood-rite at Sinai.

However, the Sinai Covenant was broken even before the people left the mountain (Exodus 32:1-29) as the fashioning of the golden calf was an attempt to create a god whose presence the Israelites could control and see. When, after forty days, he came down from the mountain and saw the golden calf, the angry Moses broke the tablets of the Law, symbolic of the broken Covenant. The Covenant with Abraham still stood, however, and after Moses "reminded" God of this, the Sinai Covenant was renewed. Moses then cut two tablets of stone like the first and, with the two tablets in his hands, once more he went up the mountain of Sinai in the early morning as Yahweh had commanded him. Another Covenant was made.

The breaking of the Covenants, however, continued throughout the history of the twelfth to the sixth century BC, and the prophets warned that the result of breakage of the Covenants would be loss of Covenant privileges, loss of land and descendants and the return to slavery in foreign lands.

There was, however, yet another Covenant to shape Old Testament theology, the Covenant of David. In the year 1004 BC, a millennium after Abraham's time, David was king in Jerusalem. He began to plan a Temple, a magnificent house for the *Ark of the Covenant*, but that same night the word of the Lord came to him through the Prophet Nathan (2 Samuel 7:4-17). Instead of David building a house for the Lord, the Lord will build a house for David, that is, a dynasty. His house and his sovereignty will remain forever. A descendant of his will forever reign. Psalm 89 speaks almost entirely of this agreement between God and David: *"I have made a Covenant with my chosen. I have given my servant David my sworn word. I have founded your dynasty to last forever. I have built you a throne to outlast all time."*

With David, therefore, God's plan of salvation takes another significant step forward. While Abraham was the father of all Israelites and the one person with whom God initiated the first Covenant with the chosen people, and while Moses was the mediator when God bound His people to Himself in the true Covenant-religion, David was the king whom God chose to found the kingdom which one day would be both eternal and universal and from which salvation would finally spring through the Mediator of the new and everlasting Covenant, Jesus. This Covenant was signed and sealed with the blood, not of bullocks, but with the Precious Blood of the true Lamb of God on Calvary.

With this brief summary of the Covenants of the Old Testament, let us now look at the history of the *Ark of the (Old) Covenant* and its relationship to the Virgin Mary.

The rainbow — the sign of God's first Covenant.
Photo taken in Tobago (see p. 56)

## CHAPTER 8.

## *The Ark of the Covenant*

> "You shall put into the ark the covenant that I shall give you."
>
> **Exodus 10:16**

In the Old Testament there was no object so sacred and holy as the *Ark of the Covenant*. After the terms of the Covenant were given by Yahweh to Moses on Mount Sinai, He also described to Moses how the Ark or chest for the tablets of the Covenant, the Ten Commandments, written in the hand of God, was to be built. Yahweh Himself chose two master craftsmen, Bezalech and Aholiab, to oversee the construction. He also gave the details for the sanctuary which was to enclose the Ark: *"And let them make me a sanctuary that I may dwell among them"* (Exodus 25:1-9).

The sanctuary or tabernacle for the Ark itself was a colourful tent embroidered with cherubim. It was called the Tent of Meeting. It was the place where God and man met, and they met there because of the Covenant which He had made with the Hebrews. It was pitched in a courtyard, a rectangular area cordoned off from the outside by four walls of curtains, and was divided into two rooms by a veil of fine linen.

In the outer room stood a gold lampstand and an altar for incense. In the inner room, the *Holy of Holies*, stood the beautiful *Ark of the Covenant*. The Ark was in the shape of a chest, some three feet long and two feet in breadth and height, and was made of sweetly smelling setim wood, an "incorruptible" acacia. It was covered with gold inside and outside and at the four corners there were four golden rings through which passed two bars of setim wood covered with gold to carry the Ark. Only the priestly tribe of Levites was allowed to carry the Ark.

On the level top of the Ark was a flat slab made of pure gold of the same length and breadth of the Ark itself. This was adorned at the ends with a pair of carved cherubim facing each other. The slab was called in Hebrew the *kapporet*, variously translated as the *mercy seat* or *propitiatory*, on which God was enthroned and dispensed mercy to His people. In etymological fact, *kapporet* is derived from the verb *kippur* which has to do, not with "covering over," as has often been claimed, but with "wiping away," and in the cultic context, with wiping away sin from the sinner.

### The Pillar of Cloud and of Fire — the Shekinah

The two cherubim extended over the propitiatory, spreading their wings and covering the slab (see p. 68). There, between the golden wings of the cherubim and above the Ark, rested the *cloud*, the visible presence of Yahweh. It was a *cloud by day* and a *fire by night*, who spoke to the prophets from the propitiatory or throne of mercy. Once a year the High Priest, and only the High Priest, would enter the *Holy of Holies* where the Ark was kept. It was on the feast of Yom Kippur (the Day of Atonement). The High Priest would then sprinkle the blood of animals on the kapporet of the Ark so as to cleanse Israel from all its sins before the Lord. A cloud of incense always covered the Ark (Lev. 16: 1-13).

We recall that the sign of the first Covenant was the rainbow in the clouds and in the Old Testament clouds cover Yahweh when He reveals Himself, especially on Mount Sinai when God gave Moses the Ten Commandments — the Sinai Covenant (Exodus 19:16; 24:15, etc.). In the New Testament when Jesus manifested His divine glory, clouds overshadowed Him at His Transfiguration on Mt. Tabor (Matt. 17:5; Mark 9:7; Luke 9:34; Acts 1:9). The day of His Ascension the cloud also surrounded the ascending Christ — "and a cloud took Him from their sight" (Acts 1:9). On the day of Pentecost, the fiery cloud, the Holy Spirit, filled the Cenacle and rained down tongues of fire on the apostles (Acts 2:3), and when the Son of Man reappears, He will also be on a cloud (Matt. 24:30; Rev. 1:7).

When the Israelites left Egypt at night, "the Lord went in front of them in a *pillar of cloud* by day, to lead them along the way, and a *pillar of fire* by night, to give them light, so that they might travel by day and by night. Neither the *pillar of cloud* by day nor the *pillar of fire* by night left its place in front of the people" (Exodus 13:21-22). However, when the Pharoah, all his army and his chariots pursued them, the *pillar of cloud* moved from in front of them and took its place behind them. It came between the army of Egypt and the Israelites and protected them (Exodus 14:19-20).

During the Sinai trek the cloud in the shape of a *pillar* occasionally descended to stand at the door of the Tabernacle or Tent of Meeting when there was conversation between Yahweh and Moses. This visible appearance of God in the form of a cloud the Jewish writers called the *Shekinah*. This word is not found in the Bible and most of the references to the *Shekinah* are found in the Haggadah, the non-legal portion of the Rabbinical literature. It is from the Hebrew word "to appear," "to dwell." It was Yahweh Himself dwelling among His chosen people.

Now, the *Ark of the Covenant* was intended to contain only the tablets on which the Law was written, namely, the Ten Commandments. However, upon subsequent command, a golden vessel containing some of the miraculous manna which fell from heaven during the wanderings of the Hebrews across the Sinai desert (Exodus 16:34) and the miraculous rod of Aaron were also enclosed in the Ark (Hebrews 9:4).

When the Israelites had renewed their Covenant with their Lord (*"We will observe all that Yahweh has decreed: we will obey."*) and had built a sanctuary for Him (Exodus 24:7), it was time to leave the sacred mountain and head northwards towards Canaan (present day Israel). They then carefully dismantled and packed the sanctuary and placed the sacred *Ark of the Covenant* which the priests always carried at the head of the caravan. The Ark in turn was always preceded by the *pillar of cloud* by day and the *pillar of fire* by night to give them light.

We are told in Numbers 10:33-36 that the Ark, in preceding the Israelites when they left Sinai, indicated where they were to stop and pitch camp. It is also recorded in Numbers 14 that when some of the Israelites first attacked the Canaanites and the Amalekites, in defiance of Moses' orders, the Ark remained in the camp, and the Israelites were defeated and harried all the way to Hormah as the Ark was not with them. Indeed, following this defeat, it would be many years before the morale of the Israelites grew strong enough to invade Canaan successfully.

Many years later, after the death of Moses and in the time of his successor Joshua, such was its powers that as soon as the bearers of the Ark reached the Promised Land, and the feet of the priests bearing the *Ark of the Covenant* touched the edge of the Jordan River, the waters of the Jordan parted, and "the priests who carried the Ark stood on dry ground." All the Israelites crossed the ground dry-shod just as occurred in the miracle of the parting of the Red Sea (Joshua 3:14-17).

Later on, before attacking Jericho, the Israelites performed a strange rite. The Ark was carried around the strongly fortified city daily for seven days. Seven priests walked before the Ark of Yahweh sounding their trumpets as they went. On the seventh day they marched around seven times and at the seventh time the trumpets sounded, after which the city walls miraculously fell down (Joshua 6:6-21). The Israelites then took the city. It was the first Israelite victory in Canaan under the leadership of Joshua.

Eventually their claim to the heartland of Canaan was threatened by new and powerful intruders. These were the Philistines who migrated from the Aegean region in the 13th century BC. Eventually, at the battle of Ebenezer in Shiloh in 1050 BC, the Philistines launched a ferocious attack on the Israelites. Suffering defeat, the Israelites called for the sacred Ark, hoping that it would reverse their ill luck. However, the Ark fell into Philistine hands and was carried off in triumph by them (1 Samuel 4:11). This disaster was interpreted as God's departure from their midst because of their infidelity (1 Sam. 4:22). It was a time of unspeakable sadness and shock for the Israelites: "The glory is departed from Israel, because the Ark of God was taken ..." (1 Samuel 4:21).

When the Ark was captured, the Philistines had it for seven months and carried it to Ashdod and elsewhere. It was put into the temple of the great (so they thought) fishtail god of the Philistines, Dagon. However, the Ark wreaked havoc among the pagan Philistines while they had it in their territory and they were punished severely for keeping it. The statue of Dagon immediately crashed down on its face and after the idol was righted, it fell on its face again and this time the head of Dagon and both the palms of his hands were cut off (l Samuel 5:1-5).

In addition, the Ark instilled terror into them in Ashdod itself and in Gad and Ekron, afflicting them with tumours, suspected to be bubonic plague. It was then that the Philistines eventually decided that the Ark had brought them such misfortune that it should be returned to the Israelites immediately (1 Samuel 5:6-12).

The Philistines then put it on a cart and gave the oxen their heads, and they carried it back to the Israelites at Beth-shemesh. But disaster also befell the people of Beth-shemesh because "the sons of Jeconiah had not rejoiced when they saw the ark of Yahweh, and He struck down seventy of them. The people mourned because Yahweh had struck them so fiercely. The men of Beth-shemesh then said: 'Who is able to stand before the Lord, this holy God, and to whom shall he go up away from us?' So they sent messages to the inhabitants of Kiriath-Jearim saying: 'The Philistines have returned the Ark of the Lord. Come down and take it back. And the men of Kiriath-Jearim came and took up the Ark of the

Lord, and brought it to the house of Abinadab on the hill'" (1 Samuel 6:19-21).

However, by that time the Israelites seemed to have lost faith in the Ark and the Ark remained in Kiriath-Jearim all through the reign of Samuel and Saul (Israel's first king) for about 80 years. Because of their apostasy, the recovery of the Ark failed to improve the fortunes of the Israelites, and for twenty years the Philistines continued their aggression. Eventually, it was David who would rid Israel of the Philistine menace and establish a powerful united kingdom over his people.

In the year 1004 BC when he was king over Israel, he brought the *Ark of the Covenant* from the house of Abinadab in Kiriath-Jearim. Uzzah and Ahio, the sons of Abinadab, then led the cart. Uzzah walked alongside the Ark and Ahio went in front. However, when they arrived at a certain spot, as the oxen were making the cart tilt, Uzzah stretched his hand out to the Ark and steadied it. Then the anger of God blazed out against Uzzah and for this crime (touching the Ark), even though innocently, God struck him down on the spot and he died there beside the Ark.

Quite naturally, David went in fear of the Lord that day. It was at that time that he uttered the words: "How can the Ark of the Lord come to me?" So David decided not to take the Ark into Jerusalem and he then carried it into the house of Obededom, the Gittite. The Ark of the Lord stayed in the house of Obededom for three months (2 Samuel 6:3-11).

David eventually brought the Ark from Obededom's house to Jerusalem, the citadel of David, the city which he had just made the capital of his kingdom. This time he appointed Levites to carry the Ark as was ordained by Yahweh ever since the Ark was built (Numbers 1:48-50). He danced, whirling round the Ark with all his might, wearing only a linen loincloth round him (see p. 68).

After they had placed the Ark in a tent and as David was retiring to his house, Michal, the daughter of Saul, went out to meet him: "What a fine reputation the king of Israel has won for himself today, displaying himself under the eyes of his servant maids as any buffoon might display himself," she said. David answered: "I was dancing for Yahweh not for them. As Yahweh lives who chose me in preference to your father to make me leader of Israel, Yahweh's people, I shall dance before Yahweh and demean myself even more. In your eyes I may be base, but by my maids you speak of I shall be held in honour" (2 Samuel 6:20-23).

However, although David himself planned to build a permanent Temple for the Ark, Yahweh decreed otherwise. It was to be built by his son, Solomon. David died around 965 BC, shortly after he had appointed Solomon as his successor, and from about 960-953 BC Solomon began to build a house for the Lord on Mount Moriah, the site chosen by his father. The best possible materials were obtained as Solomon's majestic Temple was intended to be the permanent home of the *Ark of the Covenant*. With the Ark within the city, Jerusalem then became the religious centre of the whole of Israel (see p. 69).

The Ark itself stood majestically in the *Holy of Holies* in the Temple, its walls covered with gold plates. This *Holy of Holies* was enclosed by a great veil, 60 by 30 feet, so thick and heavy that it took three hundred priests to hang it. It was woven with coloured strands — white, violet, red and green. Significantly, these colours are now the liturgical colours of the Church. However, this Temple was not to last until the time of Christ. It was burnt to the ground by the Babylonian commander Nebuchadnezzar in 587 BC, for under Solomon Israel once more broke the Covenant which their fathers had made with God, agreeing to adore Him alone. Instead, they worshipped the idols of Solomon's wives on the Mount of Offense where he built temples for them.

After this we hear no more about the Ark in the Bible. According to one tradition, the Ark was saved by Jeremiah on the eve of the destruction of the city, and he hid it with other precious things on Mt. Nebo where it was to remain undiscovered "until Yahweh gathers his people together again and shows them His mercy" (2 Maccabees 2: 6-7).

Now, a second Temple which was more modest than Solomon's, was built on the same site between 520-550 BC, and is associated with Zerubbabel, a descendant of David. This too was plundered in subsequent wars until in 20 BC, Herod the Great began its restoration on a grander scale. This magnificent Temple which Herod spent 46 years in building was not entirely finished when Jesus entered His "Father's House."

However, at the time of Jesus its *Holy of Holies*, although veiled, was empty. The nation had fallen from the state of grace of the days of Moses and the prophets. The Ark was not there. The *Shekinah* did not dwell in it. The *Glory* had left Israel. Nonetheless, as prophesied by Jesus, this Temple was also totally destroyed in 70 AD by the Romans: *"You see these great buildings? Not one stone will be left upon another — all will be torn down"* (Mark 13:2)

After it was razed to the ground, the main archaeological remnant was a retaining wall of the Temple. It is believed that some of the foundations of that wall go back to the first Temple of Solomon, and for centuries, especially on the 9th of

Av, the anniversary of the destruction of the Temple, hundreds of Jews still flock to the wall to pray, to weep and bemoan their bitter fate. This is why it is called the "Wailing Wall." It is one of the most historic sites in Jerusalem and in several pilgrimages to the Holy Land I, too, prayed with the Jews at the Wall. I do not know, however, if our prayer was the same (see p. 70).

In the 7th century AD the conquering Moslems ravaged Jerusalem again, especially the area where the Rock of Moriah is situated. This rock was in the middle of the Priests' Court in the Temple and was the great altar of sacrifice. Most significantly, it is said that the Temple and its altar stood on the summit of Mount Moriah, the very site where Abraham, dutifully obeying God's command and test, was on the verge of sacrificing his son Isaac when God held back his hand (Genesis 22:1-12). He had passed the test of fidelity to Yahweh.

At the present time, in place of the Jewish Temple which was built to house the Ark and where Jesus prayed and taught, the great Moslem Mosque of Omar, called the "Dome of the Rock," covers the Temple area and the rock. This rock rises several feet above the floor of the eight-sided mosque ornamented with passages from the Koran. With its golden dome, the Mosque of Omar is the most outstanding edifice in the old city of Jerusalem (see pp. 69 & 70).

68.

Above: The Ark of the Covenant (see p. 62)
Below: David dances before the Ark of the Covenant (see p. 65)

69.

A depiction of the magnificent Temple of Solomon (see p. 66)

Mosque of Omar replaces the Temple on Mt. Moriah (see p. 67)

The Wailing Wall - the only remnant of the Old Temple

The author praying at the Wailing Wall (see p. 67)

## CHAPTER 9.

## *In Search Of The Ark*

**"The place is to remain unknown until God gathers his people together again and shows them his mercy."**
**2 Maccabees 2:9**

There is much controversy about the fate of the ancient *Ark of the Covenant*. Now, the *Kibre Negest* (the Glory of Kings) was written by Nebure Id Yishaq, the administrator of Axum in Ethiopia, in the 14th century AD. It is the royal chronicle which records the glory of the sovereigns of Ethiopia. It also tells the story of Solomon and the Queen of Sheba, and how Ethiopia came to make the audacious claim that the *Ark of the Covenant* is in its possession.

From it we are told that the first people to settle in Ethiopia were the descendants of Noah. Noah's son, Ham, begat Cush who in turn sired Ethiopic, from whom the name of the country was derived. Ethiopic's son was Aksumai, and he is said to have founded the holy city of Axum about 1000 BC.

Apart from texts such as the *Kibre Negest*, we are also told in the Bible that the river Gihon encompassed the whole land of Ethiopia (Genesis 2:13), and that Moses had married an Ethiopian woman (Numbers 12:1). Her name was Zipporah (Exodus 2:22).

The river Gihon, which is known as the Blue Nile, flows over Lake Tana, then to the Sudan and Egypt before it finally enters the Mediterranean sea. In gratitude, the ancient Egyptians called Ethiopia "the land of God," as their livelihood depended on the annual flooding of the Nile and the fertile soil which the river carried from the fertile land of Ethiopia. Truly, Egypt is the gift of the Nile, because without the Nile Egypt would not have existed as a center of ancient civilization and almost all of the country would have been a desert.

In early times the Empire of Ethiopia stretched in the north as far as the Sudan, in the east up to Yemen, in the west to the white Nile and in the southeast to the Indian Ocean. It was a highly developed civilization with impressive palaces and beautiful works of art and literature, some of which still exist today. In the *Kibre Negest* it is stated that the Queen of Sheba brought Judaism to Ethiopia after her visit to King Solomon (970-971 BC) in Jerusalem (1 Kings 10:1-13). From that time on it became the official religion of the country until Christianity took its place in 320 AD. According to tradition, Axum was the capital city of the Queen of Sheba. Her name was Makeda.

Present day Axum has a population of about thirty thousand and in its ruins there is still evidence of the glory that was ancient Axum. It is the site of some of the most outstanding and mysterious objects of antiquity in the world, including giant obelisks made of single blocks of granite larger than the Egyptian obelisks. As Belai Giday said in his book *Ethiopian Civilization*: "The engineering skill involved in erecting these single blocks of granite baffles the imagination, the more so when one realizes that they were built over 2000 years ago." The second tallest obelisk of Axum, twenty-six meters, was looted and taken to Rome in 1937 by the Italian Fascists on Mussolini's personal orders. It now stands in the Piazza di Capena near the Arch of Constantine.

I visited Axum on January 17-19, 1994, after reading Graham Hancock's book *The Sign and the Seal*. This British researcher had spent five years tracing the path of the *Ark of the Covenant* from Jerusalem through Egypt, the Sudan and into Ethiopia. I was impressed with the thoroughness of Hancock's research and flew to Addis Ababa, and then after a two hour flight on a turbo-jet from Addis, I arrived in Axum around 4:00 p.m. on Monday, January 17.

What was once the pride of Ethiopia is now a poor town, but whereas its wealth is a thing of the past, the religious fervour of its impoverished inhabitants apparently has not diminished over the centuries. I was fortunate to have a knowledgeable guide from whom I learnt much about the history of Axum and the object which was the reason for my visit there — the *Ark of the Covenant*.

Now, there is an old Ethiopian tradition which claims that the Queen of Sheba had a son fathered by King Solomon, and whose name was Menelik. It is said that Menelik is a corruption of the Hebrew "Ben melek" ("Son of the king"). According to the *Kibre Negest*, Menelik was twenty years old when he went to visit King Solomon in Jerusalem and was well received by his father. He stayed in Jerusalem for three years, after which he decided to return to Ethiopia. As he was his first-born son, Solomon tried to persuade him to remain. Menelik, however, kindly refused the offer, and when Solomon saw that Menelik was set upon leaving, he summoned the high officials of his realm and commanded them to send their first-born sons to Ethiopia as he was sending his.

Among the people chosen to leave for Ethiopia was Azariah, the son of Zadok, the High Priest of Israel. It is the legend that Azariah was told by the Archangel Michael in a dream that he should take the holy Ark to Ethiopia, in anticipation of the future destruction of the Temple by Nebuchadnezzar. Menelik and the sons of Israel's princes and high priests, along with more than twelve thousand people, then set forth to Ethiopia. On the way they told Menelik how they had brought the true Ark with them. Menelik was filled with joy and he reasoned that they could not have succeeded in so bold a venture unless God had willed it. They then proceeded to Ethiopia.

However, to many scholars this legend does not appear to satisfy chronological history since King Solomon's reign was from 961-922 BC. There is reference to the Ark during the time of Jeremiah (628-583 BC) and during the reign of the Judean King Hezekiah (728-693 BC), when the latter made an emotional plea to God "enthroned upon the cherubim" to save Jerusalem from Sennacherib's army (2 Kings 7: 14-20).

At the death of Hezekiah his son Manasseh succeeded him and became king in Judea around 687 AD. From this time on there is no reference to the Ark in the Bible. This holiest of holy objects in Israel disappears without any explanation in the pages of the Holy Scriptures.

However, the second Book of Maccabees quotes a tradition that the prophet Jeremiah saved it from the Babylonian siege and hid it in Mount Nebo. It is said that the prophet, warned by an oracle, gave orders for the Ark to go with him to Mount Nebo, which Moses had climbed to survey the Promised Land, and that on his arrival, he found a cave into which he placed the Ark and afterwards blocked the entrance. Some of his companions came with him to mark the spot but they were subsequently unable to find it. Jeremiah then prophesized: "The place is to remain unknown until God gathers his people together again and shows them his mercy. Then the Lord will bring these things once more to light, and the glory of the Lord will be seen, and so will the *cloud*, as it was revealed in the time of Moses and when Solomon prayed that the Holy Place might be gloriously hallowed" (2 Maccabees: 2-9).

According to the Jerusalem Bible, the two Books of Maccabees were not in the Jewish Canon of scripture, but their inspiration has been recognised by the Church. The second Book of Maccabees was originally written in Greek and is said to be the work of one Jason of Cyrene. The author wrote for the Jews of Egypt and the work was completed sometime after 124 BC. He used for his purpose, documents and narratives, the veracity of which he did not necessarily guarantee. However, the book is important for its affirmation of certain teachings of the Church which other Old Testament writings had left vague.

On the other hand, Maimonides (1135-1204 AD), philosopher, physician and codifier of Jewish law, theorizes that when Solomon built the Temple, he foresaw its destruction and constructed a secret cave below, in which King Josiah (640-609 BC) hid the Ark before Nebuchadnezzar destroyed the Temple. However, Hebrew University professor Menachem Haran, a leading expert on first Temple times, is certain that the Ark disappeared during the reign of King Manasseh, who ruled the kingdom of Judea from 687-642 BC.

Manasseh, the son of King Hezekiah, ruined his father's reforms and restored idol worship and Baal worship in Israel: "He did evil in the sight of the Lord, following the abominable practices of the nations whom the Lord had cleared out of the way of the Israelites... He erected altars to Baal and also set up a sacred pole, as Ahab, king of Israel, had done... The Asherah idol he had made, he set up in the Temple" (2 Kings 21:1-7).

Graham Hancock also speculates that King Manasseh had introduced an idol into the *Holy of Holies* of the Temple, and in taking this monumental step backwards towards paganism, it was inconceivable that he could have allowed the *Ark of the Covenant* to remain in its place — since the Ark was *the sign and the seal* of Yahweh's presence on earth, and the ultimate symbol of the fiercely monotheistic Judaic faith.

He suggests that the most likely scenario was that Manasseh would have ordered the Levites to remove the Ark from the Temple before he installed his Asherah in the inner sanctum, and that they must have carried the Ark to a place of safety far away. But what was the Ark's fate after its removal from the Temple?

Hancock's research traced the Ark's journey southwest down through Egypt and along the Nile to Elephantine Island at Aswan. Indeed, on this island archaeologists have found ruins of a substantial Jewish settlement and papyrus correspondence in which repeated mention is made of a Temple of the Lord that stood there from 650 to 410 BC.

It is believed that the Ark remained in Elephantine Island for about two hundred years and that a Temple was erected there, specifically to house the Ark. It is also said that the ancestors of Ethiopia's black Jews, the Falashas, might have been migrants from Elephantine.

Egypt was eventually invaded around 525 BC and many churches were destroyed. Then, towards the end of the fifth century, the Jewish Temple on Elephantine was also destroyed, but not before the holy Ark was taken safely to the island of Tana Kirkos in Ethiopia. There it rested for eight hundred years until the time when Ethiopia was converted to Christianity in the fourth century AD. It was then removed to its present resting place at Axum by Emperor Azana (300-350 AD), who furthered the spread of Christianity.

When the Christians took it to Axum, they placed it in the great church they had built there and which was dedicated to Mary. It was the first Christian church of Ethiopia and was built in 321 AD. It was called St. Mary of Zion. What an appropriate name for the church which was to house the Ark! It rested for many hundreds of years in this church, and some twelve hundred years later in 1535, it was razed to the ground by the Moslem invader, Ahmed Gragn. However, the sacred relic had already been removed to some other place for safe keeping.

One hundred years later, with peace restored throughout the Empire, it is believed that the Ark was installed in the second St. Mary's, built on the razed remains of the first. There it stood until 1965, when it was moved to a new and more secure chapel put up at the same time as a large cathedral, which was built next to the old 17th century Church of St. Mary of Zion.

When Christianity became the official religion of Ethiopia in the fourth century AD, Alexandria, as the Holy See of St. Mark, was at that time the centre for the spread of Christianity. For many centuries the bishop of Ethiopia was always an Egyptian Copt, under the authority of the Patriarch of Alexandria. However, the Ethiopian Church preserved a distinct Judaic culture. The Church continued to be under the authority and the administration of the Egyptian Coptic Church until 1958, when a native Patriarch was named as the head of the Ethiopian Orthodox Church. So came an end of one thousand six hundred years of dependency, and since 1959 the Ethiopian Church has been completely independent of Egyptian control.

Fifty-two percent of the population of Ethiopia are Orthodox Christians, thirty-one percent are Moslems and Roman Catholics are a relatively small minority. Today the Ethiopian Church claims about thirty million members, twenty-four archbishops and about two hundred and fifty thousand clergy, which makes it the largest Eastern Orthodox Church after the Russian Orthodox Church. In fact, the number of Orthodox churches in Ethiopia is now over twenty-two thousand with each administrative region having its own bishop under the overall leadership of the Ethiopian Patriarch. However, St. Mary of Zion Cathedral is considered the mother church of the Ethiopian churches.

All twenty thousand churches have a central *Holy of Holies*, containing *tabots*. These are replicas of the Ark and once a year, on the feast of *Timkat*, the feast of the Epiphany, which in the Ethiopian Orthodox Church commemorates the baptism of Christ by John the Baptist, the Ark is publicly paraded from the *Holy of Holies* to a tent as in Old Testament times. There it stays overnight, accompanied by the prayers and chanting of the priests and the people. However, whereas replicas of the Ark or tabots are paraded from all the churches, the true Ark is said to reside in the Church of St. Mary of Zion in Axum. Indeed, there is a great devotion to Mary in the Ethiopian Church with thirty-three festivals in her honour.

On the morning of January 18, 1994, through arrangements made by my Ethiopian guide, I was allowed into the chapel built for the Ark, but not into the *Holy of Holies* as only the custodian of the Ark can enter the inner sanctum, not even the Patriarch (see p. 80). For generations a priest has been charged with the life-long responsibility of guarding the Ark and of handing it on to a worthy successor at his death bed. This privileged and holy guardian spends all his life in the chapel and at appointed times during the day and night he appears before the holy Ark to burn incense and to pray.

I had the good fortune of being allowed to meet the present custodian Abba Tesfa Maryam, who succeeded Abba Gebra Mikail in 1991. He is a man in his early fifties, very serene and soft spoken. He showed me a papyrus at least one thousand years old, and chose to highlight a magnificent and colourful Ethiopian painting of the Annunciation. I consider it to be a significant coincidence for it was at the Annunciation that Mary became the *Ark of the Covenant*. I took a photograph of it and I have included it in this book. Through my interpreter he related the emotion he feels in the presence of the Ark. It was one of love and privilege, but also of filial awe (see p. 81).

At the end of our discourse I asked him: "Do you think that one day Ethiopia will return the Ark to Jerusalem?" After a short pause, he slowly and calmly replied with a smile: "*We* did not bring it here, you know." It reminded me of a statement that Rabbi David Rosen of Jerusalem once made, referring to the Ark, as quoted in *The Jerusalem Report* of May 21, 1992:

"And if it is meant to come back, it will come back. The Almighty will see to it."

That afternoon, January 18, I witnessed the annual ceremony of the parading of the Ark from the *Holy of Holies* to the tent pitched for it some two miles away. It was an experience which I will never forget.

It was a clear sunny day and at about 5 p.m., at the repeated sound of a horn, dozens of priests and deacons with brightly coloured ceremonial umbrellas, fringed at the edges and decorated with crosses, stars, suns and moons, accompanied the guardian who carried the Ark on his head. It was covered with a thick blue and red brocade, embroidered with a large white dove (see pp. 81 & 82).

As in Old Testament times, the Ark was carried in procession against the background sound of horns, tambourines, trumpets, drums, cymbals and the ancient music of the sistra. I was part of ancient history as I recalled how David danced before the Ark when he led it to Jerusalem. Escorting the precious sacred relic were armed soldiers on both sides of the procession. I joined the crowd of Ethiopian worshippers and was grateful for the privilege of being there to witness this great enactment of Hebrew history.

As the Sun began to disappear beneath the horizon, the thousands of Ethiopians, all dressed in white, made a beautiful contrast against the dry brown earth and the blue and almost cloudless sky above. It was as though we were wedged between the canopy of Mary's colours — blue, the colour of the sky, and brown which is the colour of the earth and the colour she chose for her Scapular. They are the colours of the Queen of heaven and earth.

After about half an hour's journey to the tent, the Ark was then paraded once around the tent and then placed inside, where it was separated by a veil from the chanting priests who spent the whole night inside the tent in prayer. Outside were the thousands of Ethiopian worshippers, singing and praising God. I spent a long time in the tent with the priests and deacons, and I have never witnessed such soulful chanting, with a fervour and devotion which bespoke their conviction that the object of their celebration was truly the *Ark of the Covenant*.

However, my own stamina did not allow me to stay all night with them as I had just arrived from a long journey from Trinidad. I took dozens of photographs that day and when I developed the slides several days later, in one photograph of the chapel containing the *Holy of Holies*, which housed the alleged *Ark of the Covenant*, a cloudy shaft of light was seen beaming down from the sky onto the building. Then, in a photograph of the huge crowd of Ethiopians following the Ark as it entered the tent, a bright *pillar of cloud* appeared in front of the tent! These photographs are also included in this book (see pp. 80 & 83).

On the following day, January 19, I was in Addis Abba en route to Trinidad and I was able to speak to the Patriarch of the Ethiopian Orthodox Church, His Excellency Abuna Paulos, and his assistant, a deacon, Tewolde Yohannes. During the conversation I asked the deacon: "Is it true that the *Ark of the Covenant* is in Axum?" There was a pause and a tone in his gentle response, which expressed surprise at the question: "Of course, it is in Axum!"

The Book of Maccabees testifies that the Ark was hidden in Mount Nebo and it is possible that this was indeed so at some stage. Nonetheless, several expeditions to Mount Nebo in recent years have failed to find the Ark. There are also those who believe that the Ark is somewhere under the Temple Mount. However, attempts to explore the tunnel under the Temple Mount, which is now covered by the great Mosque of Omar, have been prohibited by the Moslems.

Be that as it may, the claim that the Ark is indeed in Axum must be considered to be true. It was Moses who was God's instrument in providing the holy Ark to the Israelites, and after Israel disrespected the Ark and broke the Covenant over and over again, there is some poetic justice, as it were, that Ethiopia may have been chosen by God for its safe keeping. Was the wife of Moses not an Ethiopian woman? And so, if the Ark is in Ethiopia, then it is in the safe hands of the other half of Moses' family!

But there are two relevant prophecies of Jeremiah which interest me. The first is that: "the place (of hiding of the Ark) is to remain unknown until God gathers his people together again and shows them his mercy. Then the Lord will bring these things once more to light, and the glory of the Lord will be seen, and so will the *cloud*, as it was revealed in the time of Moses, and when Solomon prayed that the Holy Place might be gloriously hallowed" (2 Maccabees 2-9). How interesting! It is believed by many that we are now in the time of God's *mercy* before His *justice* prevails.

"The glory of the Lord will be seen, and so will the *cloud*." Can this be interpreted that the *pillar of cloud* will be seen once more — that *pillar of cloud* which is sometimes called *The Shekinah Glory*?

The second prophecy of Jeremiah which is relevant to the Ark, was made when he was talking about the restoration of

Israel: "When you multiply and become fruitful in the land," says the Lord, "they will in those days no longer say, 'the ark of the covenant of the Lord!' They will no longer think of it, or remember it, or miss it, or make another" (Jeremiah 3:16). Generally speaking, Israel no longer remembers the Ark nor considers making another.

But the ancient Ark was only a herald of the new and living Ark. This new Ark is among us, appearing all over the world and calling us to renew and observe the Covenant with God. She is *truly* the living *Ark of the Covenant.* Her name is Mary.

80.

Above: The chapel in Axum said to contain the Ark of the Covenant (see p. 76)
Below: Pillar of cloud appears in front of the chapel

Above: An ancient Ethiopian papyrus portraying the Annunciation (see p. 76)
Below: Ethiopian Orthodox priests at the start of the procession in Axum (see p. 77)

Above: The Ark covered with brocade is carried by the custodian (see p. 77)
Below: The rich brocade embroidered with a dove

83.

Above: The crowds approaching the tent (see p. 77)
Below: A pillar of cloud is seen in a photograph taken when the Ark was placed in the tent (see p. 77 & 78)

## CHAPTER 10.

## *Mount Carmel and the Prophet Elijah*

"If the Lord is God, follow him; but if Baal, then follow him."

1 Kings 18: 21-22

But there was yet another great Covenant story in the Bible. We have already recalled how the Israelites, in spite of Yahweh's favours and miracles, were still seduced by Baal and other pagan gods. They continued to break the Covenant and it was the Prophet Elijah who admonishes them in a most dramatic way. Now, the story of Baal goes back to the Canaanites, and I will relate it in some detail as it explains why Mary looks with favour on Carmel and how she is linked to the Covenant.

Many years after the conquest and settling into Canaan by the Israelites under the leadership of Joshua in the 12th century BC, the Covenant-people disobeyed the Lord's commandments, and many of the Israelites did "what was evil in the sight of the Lord, their God, in serving the Baals" (Judges 3:7). The pagans believed that Baal was the master of the earth and agriculture, who controlled the weather and had the power to allow women to have children. He was called the son of Dagon (the god of agriculture). In Hebrew, Dagon means "grain."

The Canaanite religion was chiefly a fertility cult and its practice included ritual prostitution, both male and female, and sometimes child sacrifice. Throughout the centuries this ritual, which included music, magic and sex, offered a seductive challenge to the Israelites and it is documented that in the later years of his reign (965-926 BC), even the great King Solomon departed from fidelity to Yahweh.

Following the death of Solomon, the reign of King Jeroboam in Israel (931-910 BC) and Rehoboam in Judah (931-913 BC) put Israel deeper and deeper into apostasy. The House of

Jeroboam in Israel was succeeded by the House of Omri and King Omri's son, Ahab (874-853 BC), like his predecessors in office, tolerated the practice of Baalism in Israel. However, he angered the God of Israel more than all the other kings of Israel before him, as Baal worship came closer to becoming the religion of Israel.

King Omri arranged for young Ahab to marry the Phoenician princess, Jezebel, daughter of the king of Tyre, and when Ahab assumed the throne, Jezebel immediately embarked upon an ambitious programme to convert the Israelites to sole worship of Baal. Ahab was no match for Jezebel and he even built a temple to Baal and permitted cultic sacrifices to be performed on Baal's altar. In fact, we are told in I Kings 16:34 that Ahab even slaughtered his son Segub in sacrifice to Baal.

It is thought that the people had still not completely rejected Yahweh, but merely continued to burn incense to those idols at the same time. Likewise, Ahab, for political and economical reasons, tried to keep Jezebel and her Phoenician entourage satisfied. Yahweh, however, eventually moved to put an end to this apostasy and duplicity and He called on Elijah to summon Ahab and his people back to single-hearted devotion to Him.

The Prophet was ushered into Ahab's audience hall by a royal servant. The king was startled when his visitor was announced, but Elijah entered the room and wasted no time on formal greetings. Without hesitation, he began to condemn and threaten Ahab for the paganism which had breached Israel's sworn Covenant with the Lord: "As sure as the Lord God of Israel lives, before whom I stand, there will be neither dew nor rain in these years except by my word" (1 Kings 17:1). A long drought would obviously demonstrate that God and not Baal controlled the forces of fertility. Before Ahab could recover, Elijah was gone. So said, the most severe drought and famine befell the land while Elijah retired to the desert. The drought slowly began to ravage the land over which Baal was supposedly the almighty lord, and which he alone supposedly could keep rich and fertile.

After some three years, during which time the drought had taken its toll, Yahweh told Elijah that it was time to call the people to repentance and to single-hearted devotion to Him. Elijah then reappeared. When the Prophet entered the throne room, Ahab cried out: "Is it you, you troublemaker of Israel?" Elijah responded firmly: "I have not troubled Israel, but you have, and your father's house, because you have forsaken the commandments of the Lord and followed Baal.

Now, therefore, send and get all Israel to me at Mount Carmel and the four hundred and fifty prophets of Baal and the four hundred prophets of Asherah, who eat at Jezebel's table" (1 Kings 18: 17-19). The pagan idol Asherah was the mother goddess.

This large large cadre of Baal worshippers was luxuriously housed by the State and dined at the palace. Indeed, they were a heavy addition to the burden of Israelite taxpayers. Ahab agreed to a test of strength between the two gods, and issued a proclamation summoning all citizens of Israel to the mountain of Carmel which towered over the plain of Jezreel where they lived. The story is recorded in 1 Kings 18: 20-40.

Once they had gathered, Elijah admonished them saying: "How long will you go limping with a different opinion? If the Lord is God, follow Him; but if Baal, then follow him." The crowd remained silent, then Elijah said to the people: "I, I alone, am left the prophet of the Lord, but Baal's prophets are four hundred and fifty men. Let two bulls be given to us and let them choose one bull for themselves and cut it in pieces and lay it on the wood (of their altar), but put no fire to it. I will prepare the other bull and lay it on the wood (of my altar) and put no fire to it. You will call on the name of your god and I will call on the name of the Lord and the god who answers by fire — he is God indeed." The crowd answered: "It is well-spoken." This crowd then were not only spectators, they were called upon to judge the outcome of the contest and execute the sentence.

The prophets of Baal took the bull which was given to them and laid it on the altar, calling on the name of Baal from morning until noon, saying: "O Baal, answer us," but there was no voice and no one answered. Then the brazen and confident Elijah began to taunt them saying: "Shout louder for he is a god. Maybe he is in conversation or he has gone out. Perhaps he is on a trip or perhaps he is asleep and must be awakened!" So they shouted more loudly, and after noon they continued to rave until the time for the appointed evening sacrifice. But there was no sound, no answer, no recognition from their god.

Then Elijah took twelve stones according to the number of the tribes in Israel and built an altar in the name of the Lord, an implicit allusion to Moses who, after renewing the Covenant of Sinai, built an altar at the foot of the mountain with twelve standing stones (Exodus 24:4). Elijah then put the wood in order, cut his bull in pieces and laid it on the wood. Then, after pouring four jars of water (to make the miracle more impressive) over the holocaust and the crowd, he called upon the Lord saying: "O Lord, God of Abraham, Isaac and

Israel, let it be known this day that you are God in Israel and that I am your servant. Answer me, O Lord, that these people may know that you, O Lord, are God, that you have turned their hearts back." Note how he addressed Yahweh as the God of Abraham, Isaac and Israel (Jacob) — namely, as the *Covenant* God.

Then fire fell from heaven and consumed the burnt offering, even though it was soaked in water, and when all the Israelites saw it, they fell on their faces and said: "Yahweh is God! Yahweh is God!" Following this, at the command of Elijah, the awe-struck people seized the false prophets of Baal and brought them down to the river Kishon where they were slaughtered. Ahab could only watch helplessly.

And so, Mount Carmel was the mount of God's intervention through the Prophet Elijah in the 8th century BC. It was the mountain where hearts were turned and the Israelites returned to their one God. It was the mount of the renewal of the Covenant. Appropriately, the Hebrew name Elijah means "The Lord is my God."

## CHAPTER 11.

## *Our Lady of Mount Carmel*

"Flower of Carmel, tall vine, blossom laden...
none equals you."

Flos Carmel

There was another sequel to this victory of Yahweh over the satanic worshippers of Baal. Following the massacre of the prophets of Baal, Elijah now foresaw that the three year drought would end and he climbed towards the top of Carmel and sat with his face bowed between his knees, waiting. Seven times he sent a servant round the hill to look out over the Mediterranean Sea. It was not until the seventh time that the servant reported seeing a tiny *cloud* rising above the horizon *in the shape of a foot*. It was to be the bearer of the rain which would deliver the parched land. And so, Yahweh ended the great drought, thereby demonstrating that it was He who controlled rain, fertility and the powers of nature, and not the pagan god, Baal.

For centuries, many commentators on the Holy Scriptures have seen in this cloud a prototype of the Holy Virgin who bore in her womb the Redeemer of the world, the Mediator of the new Covenant, He who would bring the water of life to our arid souls. It was a foot-shaped cloud. It was the symbol of the Woman who was to arise immaculate from the sea of humankind to crush Satan beneath her heel as she brought forth the Saviour of the world. In fact, as far back as the 5th century AD, Chrysippus of Jerusalem greeted the Blessed Virgin: "Hail, cloud of rain, that offers drink to the souls of the saints." It was because of this belief that a sanctuary dedicated to the Virgin was built on Mount Carmel.

In August 1989 and again in November 1992 I stayed for a few days in this sanctuary dedicated to the Virgin. It is the *Stella Maris* Monastery on the north western promontory of

Mount Carmel overlooking the Bay of Haifa, about 30 miles from Nazareth. This monastery, the site of the origin of the Carmelite Order, was built in the 17th century but its history goes back to the time of Elijah (see p. 92).

Fr. Elias Freidman, once of the Jewish faith and a fellow doctor of medicine, and now a Roman Catholic priest of the Carmelite Order, has been living a contemplative life in the *Stella Maris* Monastery for decades. He is also the founder and spiritual advisor of the Association of Hebrew Catholics, a world-wide Association which works for the creation of a community of Israelites within the Church to develop a specific Catholic Israelite identity and spirituality. Pater Elias, as he is familiarly called, has been my friend and tutor on Carmel and I have spent many hours with him in *Stella Maris*, listening to his research on the cave of Elijah and the origin of the Carmelite Order.

In his booklet *Christian Legends of the Terrace of Mount Carmel*, he writes: "Crusader sources are unanimous in placing the abode of Elijah on Mount Carmel to the cave that bears his name, below the terrace within the present day monastery." He quotes, among others, Louis de Ste. Thérèse (1663), historian of the Carmelites in France, who preached that Elijah had founded an Order and built an oratory on Mount Carmel which was dedicated to the Mother of the Messiah yet to come. He also cites Giambattista di S. Alessio (1780), who claimed that, after contemplating the little cloud (symbol of the Virgin) from in front of his cave, Elijah gathered together his disciples and built for them a chapel on the spot.

After many centuries of changes and enlargement of the chapel, it was ruined by the Moslems in 1291, and in 1766, Giambattista, with a great desire to rebuild the chapel, supervised the construction of the large Carmelite monastery over the site of the first chapel ever built in honour of the Blessed Virgin Mary. On the foundation stone of the new monastery are inscribed these words: "Under the auspices of the Blessed Virgin Mary, our Holy Father Elijah and the entire Holy Family, the Vicar of the place laid the first stone on November 15, 1767, for the construction of her sanctuary, the first chapel in the whole Christian world, built on top of Carmel, in her honour during her lifetime, dedicated to the Most High by the followers of Elijah, and completely destroyed by the Saracens in 1290 of the Christian era."

And so, the Order of the Carmelites was founded by Elijah with the Blessed Virgin Mary as its Patroness. It was respected preeminently as the first Marian Order. It is apparently for this reason that the Virgin has a special predilection for Carmel and appeared as *Our Lady of Mount Carmel*, not only in her last apparition in Fatima on October 13, 1917, but also in Garabandal, Spain, in 1961-1965. It may not be her last appearance as *Our Lady of Mount Carmel!*

Carmel is the most beautiful mountain in the whole of Israel and, unlike the rest of the country, it remains green throughout the year, blessed by the heavy dew which falls on it. It is clothed with a verdure of small oak trees and shrubs, and from its summit one can see the great plain of Jezreel stretching away in the distance onto Nazareth, which is only about 35 miles away.

Undoubtedly, Mary frequently gazed upon the beauty of Carmel from her Nazareth home, and from there beauty beheld beauty, for as the Scripture reveals to us, Carmel, according to Catholic interpreters of the Bible, is a symbol of Mary's beauty.

Indeed, the Catholic Church has traditionally seen the Bride of the *Song of Songs* as a foreshadowing of the Church and of Our Lady. The *Song of Songs* compares this most beautiful of women to Carmel: "How beautiful you are, how charming, my love, my delight! Your head is held high like Carmel" (Song 7:5-6). But whereas Carmel has been likened to Mary, the Prophet of Carmel, Elijah, can also be likened to her Son, for just as Christ raised the son of a widow to life, as told in Luke 7:11-17, so did Elijah (I Kings: 17-24), and just as Christ fasted for forty days and forty nights (Matthew 4:2), so did Elijah (1 Kings 19:8). The living Christ ascended to heaven (Acts 1: 9-11); Elijah too was taken up to Paradise (2 Kings 2:11).

Over the centuries little of the colourful history of Carmel has been available to historians. However, after the Crusaders suffered a severe defeat at the hands of the Moslems, the Holy Land was overrun by the Saracens and groups of Carmelites started leaving Mount Carmel for Europe. In 1242 Sir Richard de Grey of England brought some "Brothers of *Our Lady of Mount Carmel*," as they were then called, to his estate of Aylesford in Kent. There they founded a religious house and in 1247 the Brothers elected a Prior General with authority over the Carmelites everywhere.

Tradition also has it that, facing many serious difficulties, Simon Stock, the Prior General, had begged the Virgin, as Patroness of the Order, to grant some privilege to the Brothers who bore her name. One day he was devoutly reciting the *Flos Carmeli (Flower of Carmel)* when the Blessed Virgin responded to his fervent plea and appeared to him, holding in her hand a brown Scapular. She then said: "Dear son, take the

**91.**

Scapular of your Order as the badge of my brotherhood and a special grace for you and all Carmelites. Whoever dies in this garment will not suffer everlasting fire. It is a token of salvation. It safeguards in danger. It pledges us to peace and the *Covenant*." This was on July 16, 1251, now celebrated as the feast of *Our Lady of Mount Carmel.*

The brown Scapular is the continuation of the most ancient gesture of consecration known to man. Elijah, the founder of the Order of Carmel, consecrated his successor Elisha by throwing a cloak over his shoulders, and when Elijah was taken away from this earth, his mantle fell upon Elisha to give him the "spirit of Elijah." Likewise, the Scapular, the symbol of the religious habit, is Mary's consecration cloak. Simply, it is the Woman of Carmel putting her cloak over her children to protect those who wear her habit faithfully and live with the spirituality it denotes. The choice of the colour brown, the colour of humility and of the earth from which we are made, appears to have been Mary's preference.

Carmel is Mary's mount because it is the mount of the Order dedicated to her, and it is also the mount of the *renewal of the Covenant* by the great Prophet Elijah. And so, in the spirit of Elijah, *Our Lady of Mount Carmel* has been returning to earth and is inviting us to encounter God and renew the *Covenant* with Him.

Above: The Stella Maris Monastery on Mount Carmel (see p. 89)
Below: Our Lady of Mount Carmel (see p. 90)

## Chapter 12.

## *The Covenants of The Bible: The New Covenant*

**"By speaking of a new covenant, he implies that the first one is already old."**
**Paul (Hebrews 8:18)**

Over the years, when the Israelites continued in their infidelity to the Covenant with Yahweh, they set up altar upon altar to the false gods of the pagans. It was then the harsh duty of the Prophet Jeremiah (640-587 BC) to predict misfortune, and it was also his unhappy fate to witness and lament its fulfillment. However, he did not leave the Israelites without hope.

He prophesied a new Covenant to come, a new religion of the *heart* and of inner sincerity: *"The days are coming,"* says the Lord, *"when I will make a new Covenant with the house of Israel and the house of Judah. It would not be like the Covenant that I made with their fathers the day I took them back by the hand to lead them forth from the land of Egypt; for they broke my Covenant and I had to show myself their master, but this is the Covenant which I will make with the house of Israel after those days. I will place my Law within them and write it in their hearts. I will be their God and they shall be my people"* (Jeremiah 31:31-35).

Whereas, therefore, the Old Covenant was conditional, was dependent upon man's faithfulness and was graven in stone, the New will be unconditional and will be written in the *heart*, as God's great object in salvation was to take possession of the *heart* of men. It was going to be, as it were, a *heart to heart* relationship.

The passage of time and the continual breaking of the Covenant on the part of the Israelites culminated in the destruction of the Temple which was built to house the *Ark of the Covenant.* The hope of Israel was then directed towards the great king of the Jews who was to come in the future. It was the Davidic Covenant, namely, that from David woul come an everlasting throne and kingdom. However, they did not realize that the Messiah was not to be a political figure who would bring greatness to Israel once more, but one who would free them from the slavery of sin and Satan and pay, with His life, the ransom for their transgressions.

With the entrance of Jesus into the world this prophecy "came to pass." The fullness of time had come and the Incarnation of Christ was God's most intimate step into human history. And so, the new Covenant was eventually struck, the Covenant which would also incorporate the Gentiles into the body of Christ as *spiritual* descendants of Abraham.

When God heard the cry of the Israelites and decided to free them from Egyptian bondage, He sent plagues on Egypt when the Pharoah refused to let His people go. However, it was the tenth plague which eventually won the day for Israel. God decreed that a young lamb without blemish, a one year old male, was to be slaughtered and some of its blood daubed on the door posts of the houses. The Israelites were to eat the lamb hurriedly that same night with unleavened bread and bitter herbs for the Lord was to pass through the land of Egypt that night and strike down every first-born: *"When I see the blood I will pass over you and no plague shall destroy you when I strike the land of Egypt"* (Exodus 12:1-13).

Now, in Old Testament times almost all things, according to the Law, were cleansed with blood and without the shedding of blood there was no remission. And so, by the sacrifice and blood of the paschal lamb the Hebrews were delivered from Egyptian slavery and God Himself laid down the ceremony of that sacrifice in keeping with His divine plan (Exodus 12:1-14).

In the new Covenant, however, the Blood of Christ was to replace the animal Covenant blood of Moses. Therefore, the lamb had to be male, for Christ, the true Paschal Lamb of God, was to be of that sex. It was one year old to foretell that Christ would be sacrificed in the early flower of His manhood. It had to be without spot, stain or blemish to foretell the sinlessness of Christ. The Hebrews fled from Egypt at night and were delivered from slavery to foretell how the Lord would be arrested at night to be sacrificed and to deliver the world from slavery to Satan.

The lamb's blood sprinkled on the doorposts pointed to Jesus' Blood sprinkled on the Cross, by which we were redeemed from sin, except that the killing of the unblemished lamb on that fateful night in Egypt was merciful when compared to the dreadful Passion and crucifixion of the true Lamb of God, who voluntarily chose for Himself the most painful and agonizing of deaths: *"The Father loves me, because I lay down my life in order to take it up again. No one takes it from me; I lay it down of my own free will"* (John 10:18).

Fr. James L. Meagher, D.D., in his book *How Christ Said The First Mass*, describes how the Mass was foretold in the Passover ceremony of the Israelites. The word "Passover" comes from the Hebrew "Pesach," because in Egypt the Lord "passed over" the Israelites' houses signed with the blood of the paschal lambs, when He killed the firstborn of every family and animal on the night of the Exodus. The Passover is still held by the Jews as their greatest religious feast, commemorating the anniversary of the delivery of their fathers from Egyptian bondage. It is their Easter, the key of their calendar, and regulates all their movable feasts and fasts, just as the Christian Easter to which it gave rise, ordains the feasts, fasts, and movable seasons of the Church Year.

In the time of Jesus everyday at nine in the morning and at three o'clock in the afternoon, the chief sacrifice was the lamb, and there were prayers sung by a choir of some five hundred priests. The lamb was killed by the priests in the Temple, foretelling how the Jewish priesthood would later demand of Pilate the execution of the Saviour.

This was the way the lamb was prepared centuries before Christ. They washed the animal, foretelling the Passover washing performed by Christ on His Apostles, and with a rope they fastened the right forefoot of the lamb to the left hindfoot and left forefoot to the right hindfoot, the cord making a cross, emblematic of Christ fastened to His Cross. It was then skinned just as Christ was scourged almost skinless, and then, without breaking any of the bones, they drove a pomegranate stick through the tendons of its forefeet. They called this operation *"The crucifying of the lamb,"* foretelling Christ crucified with His hands and feet nailed to the Cross. The victim they now named "the body of the lamb," to which Christ alluded at the Last Supper when He said: *"This is my body"* (Luke 22:19).

Yahweh also decreed to Moses and Aaron: *"This is what is ordered for the Passover... It (the lamb) is to be eaten in one house alone, out of which house not a single morsel of the flesh is to be eaten; nor must you break any bone of it"* (Exodus 12:46-47). This was to foretell that while they would break the legs of the two thieves, not one bone of the true Lamb was to be broken (John 19:33-34). And so, Christ became the Pascal

Lamb through whom we have been saved. He was killed, His blood was shed, His legs were not broken, His flesh was to be eaten.

The crucified lamb was placed in an oven lying on its cross. When cooked, the lamb was then placed on the table still lying on the cross. It was a striking prophetic portrait of the body of the dead Christ on the Cross, His skin all torn off by the flagellation, His blood and serum oozing out and then dried, making Him look as though He had been roasted. This was the real portrait of Jesus on the Cross, not the aesthetic and comfortable looking figure which is seen on crosses in churches and elsewhere.

It was 1300 years after the sacrifice of the paschal lamb in Egypt that Jesus was crucified, and at the moment the Cross was lifted up on Calvary, the Temple resounded with the blast of trumpets which were always blown to announce the sacrifice of the paschal lambs in the Temple courtyard. The sacrifice of Isaac will be renewed on Calvary. But, whereas on the Mount of Moriah God supplied the victim (a ram) to be substituted for Isaac, and spared both the life of the son and the heart of his father Abraham, on Calvary God fully accepted both the sacrifice of His Son and the broken heart of His Mother.

At three o'clock in the afternoon, the customary hour of the sacrifice and death of the paschal lamb in the Jewish ritual in the Temple, the true Lamb of God died. At that moment the Temple veil in front of the empty *Holy of Holies (the Ark of the Covenant* was since lost) was torn from top to bottom and an earthquake toppled the two pillars which held the veil, depicting the end of the old dispensation and the ushering of the new Covenant (Matthew 27: 51-54). Prophecy was fulfilled.

But about 740 years before the birth of Jesus, Isaiah did accurately prophesy the Passion of the Lamb of God: "He was pierced through for our faults, crushed for our sins. On him lies a punishment that brings us peace, and through his wounds we are healed. We had all gone astray like sheep; each taking his own way, and Yahweh burdened him with the sins of all of us. Harshly dealt with, he bore it humbly, he never opened his mouth, like a lamb that is led to the slaughter house, like a sheep that is dumb before its shearer, never opening its mouth" (Isaiah 53: 5-7).

Yet, even before the time of Isaiah, Psalm 22 also prophesied the type of death of the Messiah: *"My God, my God, why have you deserted me?... I am like water draining away, my bones are all disjointed, my heart is like wax, melting inside me, my palate is drier than a potsherd and my tongue is stuck to my* jaw... I can count every one of my bones, and there they glare at me, gloating; they divide my garments among them and cast lots for my clothes."

After reading the Scriptures I find it most inexplicable that Judaism refuses to recognize Jesus as the Messiah. In fact, Jesus Himself lamented for Jerusalem; *"Days will come upon you when your enemies encircle you with a rampart, hem you in, and press you hard from every side. They will wipe you out, you and your children within your walls, and leave not a stone on a stone within you, because you failed to recognize the time of your visitation"* (Luke 19:43-44).

And in Matthew 23:37-39 He tearfully admonishes Jerusalem: *"Jerusalem, Jerusalem, you who kill the prophets and stone those who are sent to you! How often have I longed to gather your children, as a hen gathers her chicks under her wings, and you refused! So be it! Your house will be left to you desolate, for, I promise, you shall not see me anymore until you say: 'Blessings on him who comes in the name of the Lord!'"*

This human sacrifice of the Son of the Most High was not God's reward to mankind for our faithfulness and virtue, for man's history was one of sin, disloyalty and ingratitude. What inspired the Incarnation and the sacrifice on Calvary was not man's merit, therefore, but God's love and infinite mercy.

Paraphrasing St. Thomas Aquinas in his *Summa Theologica*, Father Gerald Farfan, C.S.Sp. of Trinidad, in his textbook *A Biblical Course of Religious Instruction*, explains why God became man: "When man rebelled against God, God's justice required that adequate reparation be made; justice meaning 'giving to everyone his due.' But since God is infinite, an infinite insult was made to Him when man rebelled against Him, and if the reparation was to be adequate, that is, if justice were to be satisfied, such an insult required infinite reparation.

"Justice also required that the reparation be offered by man, but man is a finite being and incapable of making infinite reparation. Left to himself, therefore, man would forever be separated from God. The only solution to the impasse was that the infinite God should become man, and as man offer reparation to God. Since the person offering the reparation would Himself be infinite, the reparation would equal the crime and man could once more be united in friendship with God. So in His loving mercy, God sent His Son to make reparation for the sin of man: 'God so loved the world that He sent His only begotten Son...'" (John 3:16).

How perfect God is in everything He says or does! What, therefore, no thought of man or angel could have conceived, what even now surpasses all understanding, the eternal Son of God came into time, took flesh and blood, and then shed that Blood. It was the blood of the new and everlasting Covenant, shed for all men so that sins may be forgiven. Indeed, at that moment God made atonement not only for the sin of Adam and Eve, but also for all the sins of all men, not only for those committed before His coming into the world, but also for those which will be committed until the end of time. It was the Covenant by which God reconciled us with Himself and pledged His alliance with us forever.

But it was on the night before He was crucified, a Thursday night, that He instituted the Sacrament of the new Covenant, the Sacrament of Love, and before He died He left us two legacies of His Love. He left Himself in the Eucharist to be with us forever. It is Emmanuel, God dwelling with us in the Eucharist. He also bequeathed His Mother to be our Mother. She is the *Ark of the New Covenant*,

## CHAPTER 13.

## *The Medical Aspects of the Crucifixion*

**"They have pierced my hands and my feet;
I can count all my bones..."**

**Psalm 22:17-18**

It is not possible to research Mary without researching the Crucifixion for this was the greatest sorrow ever endured by any woman. Even to this day, Mary stands at the foot of the Cross.

It was the sorrow she showed when she appeared on January 17, 1871, to two boys, Eugene and Joseph Barbedette, in Pontmain, France, during the Franco-Prussian War. She presented a large red crucifix to the children and her sadness made such a deep impression on Joseph that he later wrote: "Her sadness was more than anyone can imagine. I saw my mother overwhelmed with grief when some months later, my father died. You know what such grief in a mother's face does to the heart of a child. "But, as I remember, what instinctively came to mind was the incomparable sadness of the most Blessed Virgin,which must have been the sadness of the Mother of Jesus at the foot of the Cross that bore her dying Son." Mary's face was contorted from sheer sorrow.

Crucifixion was one method of capital punishment commonly used among the ancient people around the Mediterranean basin from approximately the sixth century BC to the Christian century. It was considered by the first century BC statesman and philosopher Cicero to be the most horrible of deaths. Constantine the Great, the first Christian Emperor in 337 AD, abolished it as a token of respect to Jesus Christ, who chose to redeem the world through death on a Cross.

However, it was his mother St. Helena, who is credited with unearthing the true Cross in Jerusalem in 326 A.D. when she was 80 years of age. There are accounts of her and her servants finding three crosses in the excavations. A very sick woman was touched by two of them with no effect, however, when the third touched her body, she was instantly cured. It was considered to be the wooden tree upon which Christ had died.

No one can fully appreciate the anguish of crucifixion, neither can my inadequate pen fully describe it, and because of His divine humility the Gospels detail very little of the unspeakable suffering He endured. It was the most cruel, most shameful murder that has ever been seen in the world. Sr. Anne Catherine Emmerich (1774-1824), a mystic, stigmatist and visionary, bore the wounds of Christ towards the end of her life. She ate no food other than Holy Communion and was in ecstasy a great deal of the time. It was during these ecstasies that she witnessed in visions some of the details of Our Lord's life and His Passion.

According to her, during the scourging there were six executioners, swarthy men who appeared to be half drunk: "It is quite impossible to describe the cruelty shown by these ruffians towards Jesus, our loving Lord. The Son of God, true God and true Man, writhed under the blows of these barbarians: His mild but deep groans might be heard from afar: they resounded through the air, forming a kind of touching accompaniment to the hissing of the instruments of torture.

"Two ruffians continued to strike Our Lord with unremitting violence for a quarter of an hour, and were then succeeded by two others. His body was entirely covered with black, blue and red marks; the blood was trickling down on the ground... Two fresh executioners commenced scourging Jesus with the greatest possible fury and when they began to flag, two fresh executioners took the places of the last mentioned... They recommenced scourging him with even greater fury than before..."

"The body of Our Lord was perfectly torn to shreds — it was but one wound. He looked at His torturers with his eyes filled with blood, as if entreating mercy, but their brutality appeared to increase. The dreadful scourging had been continued without intermission for three quarters of an hour."

I will not detail here the great suffering He endured during the carrying of the heavy Cross for some six hundred yards, but when He reached Calvary (from the Latin *calveria* meaning skull; Greek, *golgotha*), according to the visions of Sr. Anne Catherine, they placed the Cross on the ground and then "seizing his right arm, they dragged it to the hole prepared for the nail, and having tied it down with a cord, one of them knelt upon his sacred chest, a second held his hand flat, and a third, taking a long thick nail, pressed it on his hand, and with a great iron hammer drove it through the flesh and far into the wood of the Cross. Our Lord uttered one deep but suppressed groan, and his blood gushed forth and sprinkled the arms of the executioners...

"When the executioners had nailed the right hand of Our Lord, they perceived that his left hand did not reach the hole they had bored to receive the nail, therefore, they tied ropes to his left arm and pulled the hand violently until it reached the place prepared for it. They drove the second nail into his left hand... (see p. 105).

"The whole body of Our Lord had been dragged upward and contracted by the violent manner by which the executioners had stretched out his arms, and his knees were bent. They, therefore, flattened and tied them down tightly with cords, but soon perceiving that his feet did not reach the bit of wood which was placed for them to rest upon, they became infuriated: 'He will not stretch himself out, but we will help him?' They accompanied these words with the most fearful oaths and imprecations, and having fastened the rope to his right leg, dragged it violently until it reached the wood.

"The agony which Jesus suffered from this violent tension was indescribable. The words *My God, my God*' escaped his lips... They then fastened his left foot onto his right foot... Next, they took a very long nail and drove it completely through both feet into the Cross below, which operation was more than usually painful on account of his body being so unnaturally stretched out. I counted at least thirty six blows of the hammer.

"During the whole time of the crucifixion, Our Lord never ceased praying and repeating those passages in the Psalms which he was then accompanying... In this manner he had prayed when carrying his Cross, and thus he continued to pray until his death. "It was a quarter past twelve when Jesus was crucified, and at the moment the Cross was lifted up, the Temple resounded with a blast of trumpets, which were always blown to announce the sacrifice of the Paschal lamb... Several men then shoved the foot of the Cross towards the hole prepared for its reception. The heavy Cross fell into this hole with a frightful shock. Jesus uttered a faint cry, and his wounds were torn open in the most fearful manner. His blood again burst forth, and his half-dislocated bones knocked one against the other.

"I contemplated his disfigured countenance, his head encircled with that terrible crown of thorns, which prevented his raising it even for a moment without the most intense suffering. His mouth was parched and half opened from exhaustion, and his hair and beard were clotted with blood. Blood constantly trickled down from the gaping wounds in his hands, and the flesh was so torn from his ribs that you might almost count them. The blood which flowed from his wounds was at first red, but it became by degrees light and watery, and the whole appearance of his body was that of a corpse ready for internment... He endured an anguish which no mortal pen can describe.

"It was towards three o'clock when he cried out in a loud voice:*'My God, my God, why have you forsaken me?'* ...His tongue was parched and he said: *'I thirst!'* Then before he died he said: *'It is consummated!'* And, raising his head, cried out in a loud voice: *'Father, into your hands I commend my spirit.'"*

Now, what was the actual cause of death of the Saviour? Like Dr. Pierre Barbet of Paris, France, I, too, researched the medical aspects of the Crucifixion. This was published in the Trinidad Guardian of April 15, 1984, and in Australia it was synopsized in a Sydney newspaper. If the world could only appreciate how agonizing, painful and shameful a death it was, perhaps man would be less ungrateful. It was not to be a killing by the sword nor by stones. These were, relatively speaking, too merciful. It had to be a prolonged and merciless agony. It had to be by crucifixion. It was His choice. He was to be the Lamb.

I believe that St. John described literally what he saw, in that the blood issued from the wound in His side before the water (serum). Much of the agony of crucifixions stems from the victim's incessant quest for air. As he is fastened by nails and stretched almost immobile, the muscles contract violently and cramps begin in the limbs and trunk. Severe muscular spasms ensue and the stomach muscles tighten to form a hollow cavity beneath the rib cage. Hours later, the chest cavity becomes distended because of the forceful and persistent inspiratory attempts to breathe, and the ribs become more prominent as the intercostal muscles contract.

The only means of delaying death is for the victim to raise himself up so that he could inhale. Unfortunately, the nail in his feet is the only fulcrum which he can use to elevate his torso, and this, in turn, evokes most agonizing pains each time it is attempted. In the case of Christ, these up and down and writhing movements were continuous for three hours. In fact, it was because of the use of the nailed feet to alleviate breathing that the soldiers customarily broke the legs of the victim so that he could no longer breathe.

Eventually, the heart muscle weakens and becomes flabby.

Heart failure ensues and fluid fills the lungs and also the space (the pleural space) between the tissue lining the lungs (the pleura) and that of the chest wall. In Christ's agony there was yet another reason for an effusion of fluid in the pleural space, albeit this time of blood. This could have been due to the severe trauma to His chest from the ruthless flagellation.

In the upright position on the Cross for three hours, the red blood cells would then settle at the bottom of the fluid in the pleural space, leaving the clear serum above. This would explain why when he was pierced between His lower ribs with the lance, a gush of blood preceded the "water," as testified by John (John 19:31-34) (see p. 105).

Such was the price the Redeemer paid and at His death the blood of the Lamb of God was almost totally "poured out" for us. With this blood the new Covenant was signed and sealed on the Cross.

It was the fulfillment of the prophecy made 1000 years earlier by King David: *"My God, my God, why have you forsaken me... But I am a worm, not a man; the scorn of men, despised by the people. All who see me scoff at me... I am like water poured out, all my bones are racked. My heart is like wax melting away within my bosom. My throat is dried up like baked clay, my tongue cleaves to my jaws... They have pierced my hands and my feet; I can count all my bones. They look and gloat over me; they divide my garments among them and for my vesture they cast lots"* (Psalm 22:2-19).

But standing at the foot of that Cross was the Co-sufferer, the *Ark of the Covenant*. History knows of no greater motherly love and of no greater suffering by a mother. It was the Redeemer and the Co-Redemptrix on a hill called Calvary.

When He was in the garden of Gethsemane Jesus knew and foresaw the great suffering He had to undergo, and according to the mystic the Venerable Catherine Emmerich, before He uttered these words: *"My Father, if it is possible let this cup pass from me"* (Matthew 26:39), He first exclaimed: *"My Father, can I possibly suffer for so ungrateful a (human) race?"*

Indeed, many in this world, especially those who are in a position to be "givers," can truly appreciate what *ingratitude* is. It is found in all walks of life and human endeavour, even in homes among parents and their children. William Shakespeare wrote about it. In his *Julius Caesar*, Anthony rebuked Brutus who was the last to stab his friend Caesar: "For Brutus, as you know, was Caesar's angel: Judge, O you gods, how dearly Caesar loved him! This was the most unkind cut of all: For when the noble Caesar saw him stab, *ingratitude*, more strong than traitors' arms, quite vanquished him: then burst his mighty heart."

But Jesus had previously experienced ingratitude many times during His ministry. Luke relates one such example when Jesus cured ten lepers: "One of them realizing that he had been cured, came back praising God in a loud voice. He threw himself on his face at the feet of Jesus and spoke his praises. This man was a Samaritan. Jesus took the occasion to say, 'Were not all ten made whole? Where are the other nine? Was there no one to return and give thanks to God except this foreigner?'" (Luke 17:15-18). This is also a common experience among doctors and nurses. Perhaps this is why this quote of Our Lord was penned by Luke, the physician!

Sr. Faustina Kowalska, in her diary of her conversations with Jesus in 1935, quoted Him as saying: "My Heart drinks only of the ingratitude and forgetfulness of souls living in this world. Oh, how indifferent are souls to so much goodness, to so many proofs of love!"

Only God's unlimited mercy and love surpass the dimension of man's ingratitude. But there was one Woman who is forever grateful to the Lord for the gifts He has bestowed upon her: "My soul magnifies the Lord, and my spirit rejoices in God my Saviour, because he has regarded the lowliness of his handmaid..." (Luke 1:46-48). She is the *Immaculate Conception*.

The hand is nailed (see p. 100)

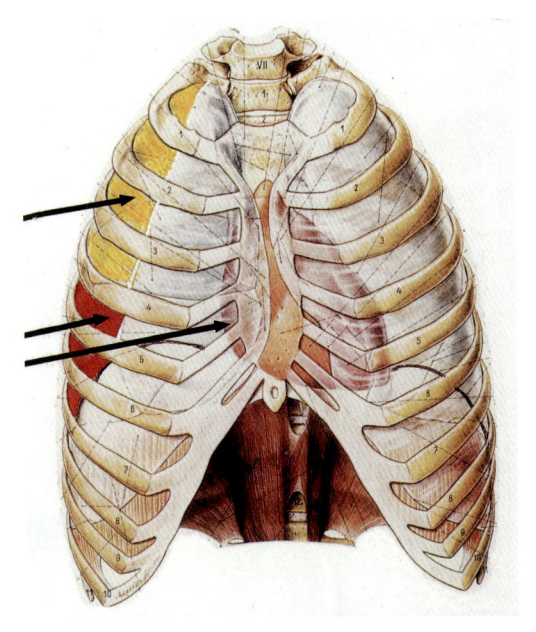

The author's theory of the issuance of blood and water (see p. 102)

## CHAPTER 14.

## *I Am The Immaculate Conception*

"Qué soy l'Immaculado Conceptiou."

Mary to Bernadette, 1858

In researching the literature, I discovered that in the Eastern Church the feast of the Immaculate Conception was celebrated as early as the 7th century AD. For the Greeks, the initiators of the feast, the expression *"Immaculate Conception"* meant that Mary, from the very first moment of her life, was preserved from sin.

It is taught that whereas actual sin is a deliberate personal transgression of God's law, original sin is inherited and transmitted at conception to the descendants of Adam and Eve, who as father and mother of the human family, sinned. We, their children, were then deprived of the supernatural destiny and of the gift of sanctifying grace, and Christ demands that a man be born again of water and the Spirit in *baptism* (John 3:6). The inherited stain of original sin thus differs from the stain of personal sin which is committed, not contracted.

The first Adam was born sinless. Christ was the second Adam. He too was immaculate and sinless. Why then is it so difficult to suppose that Mary, the second Eve, had an immaculate conception when the first Eve was also immaculate at birth? Surely, God's logic would demand that the second Eve should also be immaculate.

That Mary was also preserved from personal sin, theologians admit without question, for as Augustine said: "The honour of Christ forbids the least hesitation on the subject of possible sin by His Mother." Indeed, what true believer in the perfection and purity of the Godhead could ever accept that He would select a Mother who was anything but immaculately conceived like the first created woman! As the great Franciscan St. Bonaventure once said: "It was becoming that the Blessed Virgin Mary by whom the devil was to be conquered should never, *even for a moment*, have been under his dominion."

The Son, the God-Man, was never under Satan's power and never succumbed to his temptations. How is it possible that the Holy Spirit, that "Eternal Sigh" of the mutual love of the Father and His Son, could have as His Bride one who was under Satan's dominion, if even for a moment. Surely, to think otherwise would be an insult to God.

Accordingly then, God so prepared the body and soul of the Blessed Virgin to be a worthy temple on earth for the God-Man, for Purity itself could not abide in a sinful womb. He could not enable Lucifer to reproach Him with the shame of having a Mother who had once been his slave and the enemy of God. The Virgin was therefore called *Immaculate*, for in nothing was she corrupt. St. John Damascene put it this way: "The serpent never had any access to this Paradise!"

But the actual revelation by the Queen herself that she was *immaculately* conceived began with her apparition in Guadalupe in Mexico on a December morning in 1531. It was then that a humble Mexican peasant Juan Diego saw a strikingly beautiful young woman on Tepeyac hill. She identified herself thus: "I am the ever Virgin Mary, the Mother of God." It was a Saturday, the day dedicated to Mary in the Church. It was December 9, which in those days was the feast of *the Immaculate Conception*.

On November 27, 1830, 300 years after her apparition in Mexico, the Blessed Virgin appeared as Queen of the Universe to Catherine Labouré, a nun of the Sisters of Charity in the Rue du Bac in Paris. It was the Saturday before the first Sunday of Advent at 5:30 in the evening. Her feet rested upon a globe, crushing a serpent with her virginal foot, signifying her victory over Satan as prophesied in Genesis 3:15, and in her hands she held, at the level of her breast, a smaller globe surmounted by a Cross.

Soon afterwards an oval-shaped tableau formed around the Virgin and on it were written in letters of gold: "O Mary, *conceived without sin*, pray for us who have recourse to thee." Then a voice was heard to say: "Have a medal struck after this model. Those who wear it will receive great graces; abundant graces will be given to those who have confidence." Suddenly the oval seemed to turn and Catherine saw the reverse of the medal. It was the letter "M" surmounted by a Cross, and below it were *two Hearts*, one crowned with a crown of thorns, and the other pierced by a sword. She seemed then to hear a voice which said to her: "The 'M' and the two Hearts say enough."

All the mysteries of Mary are found in the symbols on this medal, symbols to which biblical theology gives the key:

The Virgin, the new Eve, who crushes the serpent's head; the Cross and the two Hearts, one which bled from a lance, and the other pierced with a "sword"; and the twelve stars signifying the Woman of the twelve tribes of Israel, the Woman of the Apocalypse. The invocation on the medal "O Mary, *conceived without sin*" helped to start the immense movement of faith which impelled Pope Pius IX to define the dogma of *the Immaculate Conception* 24 years later in 1854. In fact, the medal was originally called the "Medal of the Immaculate Conception," but because of the many miracles associated with those who wore it in faith, it was later called the "Miraculous Medal" (see p. 111).

Catherine Labouré died on December 31, 1876. On April 11, 1988, 111 years later, I visited the Rue du Bac in Paris and saw the *incorrupt* body of this saint lying behind the altar rail in the chapel where she was privileged to see the Virgin Mary.

Some 28 years after the apparitions ended in the Rue du Bac, Bernadette Soubirous was the chosen visionary for the apparitions in the grotto of Massabielle in Lourdes, France, which began on February 11, 1858. The following month, on March 25, the feast of the Annunciation, the Virgin confirmed the dogma of Catholic faith as defined by Pope Pius IX in 1854 in a most unexpected manner. She announced to Bernadette these words which still echo across the valleys and hills of Lourdes to this day: *"I am the Immaculate Conception."*

She did not say: "I am the result of an immaculate conception," or "I am she who was conceived immaculate." She made a most authoritative, definitive and personalized statement: *"I am the Immaculate Conception."* As W. R. Ainsworth once said: "To those who might question this manner of identifying herself, one could reply that it seems to run in the family since her Son Jesus also declared: *"I am the Resurrection and the Life."*

The Virgin chose the date for her last apparition to Bernadette. It was July 16, 1858, the feast of *Our Lady of Mount Carmel*. Mount Carmel is the mount in Israel where the Israelites, through the Prophet Elijah, renewed the Covenant with Yahweh.

The ancient *Ark of the Covenant* was made of "incorruptible" acacia wood, so was Mary incorrupt, incorruptible and immaculate, neither was she allowed to experience the corruption of the grave. If Bernadette, to whom *the Immaculate Conception* appeared, did not experience corruption in the grave, how is it "conceivable" that God would allow the body of *the Immaculate Conception* herself to corrupt! And so, in 1950 Pope Pius XII proclaimed it a dogma that the Blessed Virgin Mary was assumed bodily into heaven. It was not only theological sense. To me, it was also common sense!

On Saturday, March 9, 1979, Archbishop Anthony Pantin of Trinidad invited me to assist in the restoration of the Cathedral of the Immaculate Conception in Port of Spain in time for the 150th anniversary of its construction and blessing, which was to be celebrated in February 1982. As large and historic as it was, there were no stained glass windows in the cathedral, and among the sixteen new stained glass windows which I designed in collaboration with Mr. William Earley of the Abbey Stained Glass Studio of Dublin, Ireland, is one depicting the apparition of *the Immaculate Conception* to Bernadette in the grotto in Lourdes (see p. 112).

It was more than thirty years after seeing and being moved by the film *The Song of Bernadette*, and after the renovation of the Cathedral was completed that I eventually felt spiritually motivated to go to Lourdes. It was July 12, 1982, when I arrived and it was raining heavily that night. However, I could not wait until the next morning to see the grotto where Bernadette heard the Virgin say those words which she did not understand at that time: *"I am the Immaculate Conception."* There was only one other pilgrim in the grotto that night. We were not "singing," but "praying in the rain."

The following day I visited the Medical Bureau where the medical records of approved miracles are available for study. Of course, there are many claims of miraculous cures from all over the world and in divers "miracle crusades," but relatively few have been so thoroughly investigated and examined by panels of distinguished scientists as in Lourdes. At Lourdes the claims or miraculous cures are documented and investigated by a commission of medical specialists, some even without religious belief, and since the apparitions ended in 1858, almost 40,000 doctors have participated in these investigations.

The medical commission at Lourdes does not use the word "miracle" in its reports. It declares that the healing under investigation cannot be explained by any of the laws and knowledge of medical science. Also of immense scientific interest is the claim that the water of the spring at Lourdes has a unique quality. Bacteria cannot live in it.

That first visit to Lourdes in 1982 was to be the first of four, one in the company of my daughter Maria. In 1987 and again on July 22, 1992, with a friend from Australia, I visited the Convent of St. Gildard in Nevers, France. There lies the incorrupt body of St. Bernadette with her beautiful and serene face, in a glass casket behind the altar rail (see p. 18).

She, who was given the privilege by God to relay to the world the words of the incorrupt and incorruptible *Ark of the Covenant:* "*I am the Immaculate Conception,*" was herself exempt from the corruption of the grave. It was God's logic.

111.

Above: The Miraculous Medal (see p. 108)
Below: Pope John Paul II in Lourdes

Above: The Shekinah appears on a photo of Our Lady of Lourdes grotto in Crystal Stream, Trinidad

Below: Apparition of Lourdes on stained glass in the Cathedral of the Immaculate Conception in Trinidad (see p. 109)

## CHAPTER 15.

# Mary, The Living Ark of the New Covenant

**"While the New Testament lies hidden in the Old, the latter is revealed in the New."**

St. Augustine

The ancient Ark was the most sacred object in the Old Testament, but according to Catholic theology, it was only a herald of the great living Ark to come, Mary. The title of the Immaculate Virgin in the Litany of Loreto, *Ark of the Covenant*, has always appealed to me ever since I was a child, and there was a certain ring to it that fascinated me. This title originated at the occasion of the Annunciation.

After the fall of Adam and Eve man lived in a world of "great expectation" of the Redeemer, and in the fullness of time, God eventually sent His ambassador to deliver a message to a maiden, with a deference and respect which a subject would show to his Queen. The glad tidings were that the second Person of the Blessed Trinity wished her to "prepare a body" for Him (Heb. 10:45). "Hail Mary," he greeted her.

### The Holy House of Loreto

That opening greeting by the angel, which is repeated every time we say the Rosary in memory of that great moment, took place in the Holy House of Nazareth, which historians and researchers firmly believe to be the Holy House of Loreto in Italy. On August 11, 1993, I visited this Holy House of Loreto. Its measurement is said to be 31 feet long by 13 feet 4 inches wide by 28 feet high (see p. 119). It was 11 a.m. and I arrived just in time for the start of the only Mass celebrated in that Sacred House that day.

I studied in detail the research which was done on this miraculous event, namely the seemingly impossible transportation of the Holy House of Nazareth, which was the scene of the Annunciation, during the Saracen invasion of the Holy Land in 1291. It is said that it was first transported from Nazareth to Croatia (then called Illyria) in Yugoslavia. For unknown reasons, it was miraculously removed a second time, three years later on December 10, 1294, this time to Loreto in Italy. It is only in the past two years that I probably understand why. Hundreds of Catholic churches have already been destroyed in the recent ethnic and religious war in what was previously called Yugoslavia. Was this not foreseen several hundred years ago?

At first very skeptical, I was eventually convinced of the authenticity of this miracle, which is obviously beyond scientific explanation. The House stood on the ground. There was no foundation! Its bricks are as old as the time of Christ.

St. Francis of Assisi once said: "Someday, the Holy House of Loreto will be known as the holiest place on earth." The ancient *Ark of the Covenant* was the holiest object in the whole of Israel and I see St. Francis' statement in relation to this. The Holy House of Loreto was the site of the Annunciation. It was there that Mary became the living *Ark of the Covenant* when she said "Yes" to the angel's invitation. In like manner, this living Ark is also the holiest creature ever created.

Hundreds of saints have since visited this Holy House, including, St. Teresa of Avila, St. Francis de Sales, St. John Bosco, St. Thérèse of Lisieux, St. Maximilian Kolbe, to name a few. On October 4, 1962, Pope John XXIII went to Loreto the day before he convened the Second Vatican Council. It was on the feast of St. Francis of Assisi. Pope John Paul II has also visited the Holy House twice, spending much time in prayer there (see p. 118).

The event of the Annunciation in this Holy House is recorded in Luke 1:35, *"The Holy Spirit will come upon you, and the power of the Most High will overshadow you."* The Holy Spirit is frequently represented in the form of a dove. It was in this house that Mary became the *Ark of the Covenant.* How can anyone describe the emotion of believing that one is standing in the very room of the Annunciation!

I took two quick photographs during the Mass without using the flash unit, and when the films were developed seven bright dove-like figures in flight appeared in profile from right to left in front of the altar (see p. 119). Seven is the perfect number!

The angel's flight to earth meant the dawn of a new day, the beginning of a new Covenant and the fulfillment of God's long awaited promise to mankind in Genesis 3:15: *"I will put enmity between you and the woman, and between your seed and her seed; (s)he will crush your head..."* He was speaking of the Woman, the second Eve, and her Son Jesus.

Undoubtedly, the Annunciation was the starting point of the world's greatest love story, for it was at the Annunciation or the feast of the Incarnation that God who is Love, in an act which humbled humility itself, united Himself to mankind and became like us in all but sin. To do this He had to obtain the consent of a young Virgin to be His Mother, one more beautiful in body and soul than the rest of humanity and with a plenitude of graces greater than all the angels combined. God chose the tabernacle of Mary's body within which to dwell. He came to restore mankind to the innocence lost in Eden and His arrival on earth was truly the high point in human history.

The mystery of the Incarnation has surely revealed to us how important man is to God; how intimately God wants to be united with His creation, man. The Annunciation was the beginning of the 'Good News' that God will dwell among men, for without the Annunciation and Mary's consent there would be no Gospel; there would be no "Good News." But while the Annunciation was "Good News" for the world, it was bad news for Satan. The Woman had consented. With her consent, she played her part in what may be called "God's conspiracy" to save the world from the dominion of Satan, the prince of this world.

Just as the cloud is described in Exodus as *overshadowing* the Tent of Meeting which housed the Ark, the Angel Gabriel tells Mary: "The Holy Spirit will come upon you and the Most High will *overshadow* you" (Luke 1:35). Immediately following her consent she conceived the God-Man. She was the sole human parent. A human father is not mentioned. As M. Basil Pennington in his book *Mary Today* states: "Christ chose to identify Himself as the Son of Man, but He was not the Son of any man. He was the Son of Man, a member of the human family, because he was the Son of a woman, and through a woman he received His human nature."

It was at the Annunciation that Mary then became the living *Ark of the Mediator of the New Covenant*, the Ark who sheltered and contained the Uncontainable. She was the womb of God and like the ancient Ark of Noah which saved his family, she became the new Ark of salvation. It was at that moment that not only was she the daughter of the Father, but she became the bride of the Holy Spirit and the mother of the Son.  At that moment another wonder of wonders took place — a woman became the mother of her own Creator.  Yet another great mystery took place at that instant — a virgin without ceasing to be virgin became a mother, and God without ceasing to be God became man.  The *Cause of our Joy* conceived the Incarnate Word.  God left *eternity* to dwell in *time.*

Now, just as the ancient *Ark of the (Sinai) Covenant* was made of incorruptible acacia wood, so was the Virgin immaculate and incorrupt.  Indeed, it was Hypolitus of Rome who first compared the ancient *Ark of the Covenant* to Our Lady: "Now the Lord was without sin, being in His human nature from the incorruptible wood, that is, from the Virgin." There is also the indication that the incorruptible wood of the Ark would eventually signify the Virgin's immunity from the corruption of the grave.

According to the great mystic Mary of Agreda: "Among the titles of the most holy Mary none was more expressive than the *Ark of the Covenant*... The ancient Ark was a prototype of this Lady and of what she was to do in the new church of the Gospel... The finest and purest gold which was on the outside and inside of this ancient Ark certainly indicated the most perfect and exalted graces and gifts which shone forth in her heavenly thoughts, in her works and activities, so that in no exterior or interior of this mystical Ark could be discerned anything which was not entirely covered by the gold of the most explicit and finest carat." St. Alphonsus Liguori added his touch.  He declared that Mary was the "House of Gold which eternal Wisdom chose for His dwelling on earth." No wonder she always wears a gold dress on her feast days in Medjugorje!

Just as the ancient Ark contained the Law, namely, the Ten Commandments or Decalogue, Mary contained in her virginal womb the Lawgiver Himself.  As David brought the Ark with the tablets of the Law to Jerusalem from Kiriath-Jearim, so did Mary carry her God from Nazareth to Jerusalem.  David leapt with joy in front of the Ark before it was brought to Jerusalem, so did the unborn John the Baptist leap with joy in his mother's womb when Mary arrived at the house of Zacharias (Luke 1:44).   Elizabeth's exclamation at the appearance of the living *Ark of the Covenant* at her doorstep: "Who am I that the Mother of my Lord should come to me?" (Luke 1:43) recalls David's query in 2 Samuel 6:9-10 when the Ark came to him from Kiriath Jearim: "How can the ark of the Lord come to me?"  The analogies do not stop there.  The Ark remained in the house of Obededom for three months and God blessed Obededom. Likewise, Mary brought blessing to the house of Zacharias and Elizabeth, and stayed for three months until John the Baptist was born. As the beautiful Ark was terrible to its foes (1 Samuel 5) or to those who treated it with disrespect (1 Samuel 6:19), so is Mary fair as the moon but terrible as an army set in battle array (Song 6:10). According to Alphonsus Liguori: "She is called terrible because she well knows how to array her power, her mercy and her prayers, to the discomfiture of her enemies and for the benefit of her servants who in their temptation have recourse to her most powerful aid."

Finally, just as the ancient Ark contained a ciborium with some of the manna which fell from heaven and which fed the Israelites in their trek through the desert, Mary contained in her womb the true Bread of Life come down from heaven to nourish our immortal souls. John quotes the words of Jesus Himself: *"I tell you most solemnly, it was not Moses who gave you bread from heaven, the true bread; for the bread of God is that which comes down from heaven and gives life to the world"* (John 6: 32-34). *"I am the bread of life... Your fathers ate manna in the desert and they are dead; but this is the bread which has come down from heaven. Anyone who eats this bread will live forever ..."* (John 6: 48-51).

The plan unfolds. The Old Testament is fulfilled in the New. As Augustine of Hippo once said: *"Novum Testamentum in Vetere Latet et Vetus in Novo patet."* — "While the New Testament lies hidden in the Old, the latter is revealed in the New." In fact, he was so impressed by the way in which the Old Testament foreshadowed Christ that he compared it to a mother in labour and said it was "pregnant with Christ."

In the time of Christ and Mary the *Holy of Holies* was empty. The ancient Ark was not there. However, little did the priests of the Temple know that at the "presentation" of the child Mary in the Temple, the living *Ark of the New Covenant* had entered. In the Book of Revelation, the Ark is eventually seen in heaven: "Then the sanctuary of God in heaven opened, and the *ark of the covenant* could be seen inside it... Now a great sign appeared in heaven: A woman adorned with the sun, standing on the moon, and with twelve stars on her head for a crown" (Rev. 11:19; 12:1).

According to Catholic theologians, this certainly could not be the ancient Ark in the desert since that Ark lies hidden somewhere on earth. It can only be the Blessed Virgin, the God-bearer.

The Ancient Ark was the most holy object in all of Israel. In like manner, the new and living Ark is the most holy of

God's creatures. And so the Church says: "Holy Mary, Mother of God, pray for us sinners..."

*The Holy Father praying in Loreto before the statue of Our Lady there (see p. 114)*

119.

Above: Inside the Holy House (see p. 113)
Below: A profile of seven dove-like figures in flight appear on a photograph taken inside the Holy House (see p. 114)

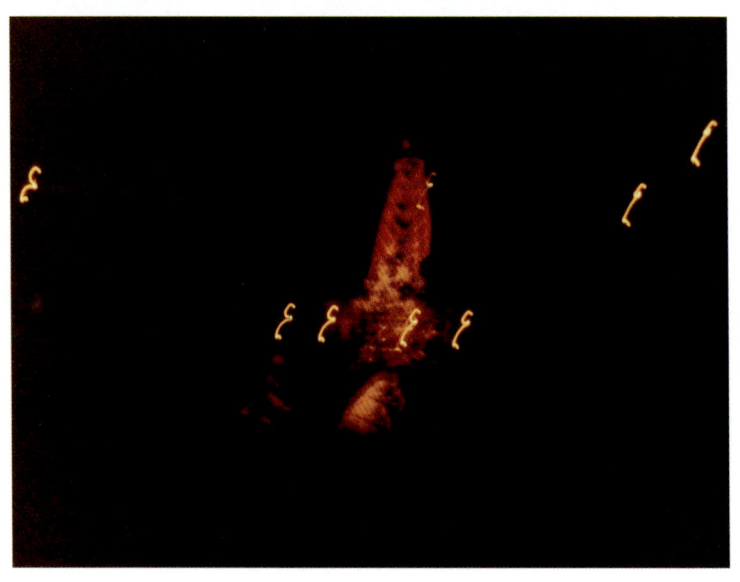

## CHAPTER 16.

# *The Ark At Kiriath-Jearim*

**"The men of Kiriath-Jearim came and, taking up the ark of Yahweh, brought it to the house of Abinadab on the hill."**
**1 Samuel 7:1**

I first became aware of a church dedicated to *Mary, Ark of the Covenant*, when I read Graham Hancock's book *The Sign and The Seal*, and although I had been to Israel five times since 1983, once with my whole family, I had never heard of this church as it is not included in the popular brochures for pilgrims touring the Holy Land.

I immediately rang the telephone operator in Jerusalem for the telephone number of the church, and after several attempts he eventually traced it for me. The church is cared for by the Sisters of St. Joseph of the Apparition, a congregation founded by Blessed Emille de Vialiar in 1832.

Within a week I arrived in Tel Aviv. It was 6 o'clock in the morning of Saturday, November 20, 1994, when I was met at the airport and driven to Kiriath-Jearim, a half an hours drive away. There, on the summit of a hill, was a large basilica and on its broad steeple was a statue of the Blessed Virgin with the Child Jesus on her left arm, while He, in His right hand, held a Host. She was standing between the cherubim on the ancient *Ark of the Covenant* which was carved in stone (see pp. 123-4).

The town of Kiriath-Jearim was one of the most hallowed places in the Old Testament because the *Ark of the Covenant*, the most precious possession of the Hebrews, had rested there for nearly a century before it was taken up to Jerusalem by King David. According to history, the first Christians wanted to consecrate the memory of the "dwelling of God" on that hill and around 444-460 AD a basilica was built there. A liturgical calendar of the seventh century, *Ordo de Fiflis Grego-Palestino*, recorded July 2 as the feast of the *Ark of the Covenant* in the territory of Kiriath-Jearim.

This basilica was destroyed by the Persians in the year 614 AD. It was rebuilt but was again totally destroyed under Hakem Kalife, the Egyptian Caliph, in 1010 AD. There it remained desolate for centuries until Sr. Josephine Rumebe of Jerusalem arrived to rescue it from oblivion. Sr. Josephine's life was centered on the *Ark of the Covenant* and on Mary. She was born on October 18, 1850, and we are told that her first spoken word was "Jerusalem!" She joined the Sisters of St. Joseph, and when she was only eighteen she made her vows in January 1868.

At the beginning of the twentieth century she bought the plot of land at Kiriath-Jearim and excavations began. One day one of the workmen unearthed part of an ancient church. There emerged from beneath the ground the well-preserved remnants of a Byzantine basilica which was estimated to have been erected as far back as the fifth century. In 1906 all the remains of the old basilica were uncovered and Sr. Josephine was determined to erect a new sanctuary worthy of this holy place. However, it was not until January 8, 1920, that the foundation stone of the new basilica was laid by Cardinal Dubois, Archbishop of Paris. At last, on August 31, 1924, the great day of the consecration of the basilica dedicated to *Mary, Ark of the Covenant*, arrived, and Archbishop Barlassina, Patriarch of Jerusalem, in the presence of a large crowd, consecrated the church. Pope Pius XI sent a telegram of blessing.

The basilica, *Mary, Ark of the Covenant*, is just thirteen kilometers outside Jerusalem on the road to Tel Aviv. The large statue of Mary overlooks a beautiful village and from the height of this magnificent hill in the heart of the Judean mountains can be seen the highway leading to the holy city, Jerusalem. That there was a church dedicated to *Mary, Ark of the Covenant* in Israel was a most exhilarating discovery for me.

I toured the basilica and examined the fifth century Byzantine ruins. A most beautiful tapestry in the basilica attracted my attention. It was a magnificent icon, depicting the story of the *Ark of the Covenant*. At the centre of the icon was Mary and on her left arm was the Child Jesus who, in His left hand, held the scroll of The Law (The Torah), which, as a Jew, He respected and observed, and which He came to accomplish: *"Do not think that I have come to abolish the law and the prophets. I have come, not to abolish them, but to fulfill them"* (Matthew 5:17). With His right hand He gave His blessing.

On the head and shoulders of the Virgin were three stars, signifying the virginity of Mary before, during and after the birth of Jesus. Behind the Virgin and Child were the walls of the old Jerusalem and at its top was a rainbow, the symbol of God's Covenant with His people and with humanity (Genesis 10:15-17). To the right of the Virgin was a depiction of King David playing the harp, and to her left was the High Priest Melchizedek offering incense, for the Lawgiver was a High Priest like Melchizedek and a descendant of David. At the bottom of the icon were the Hebrews carrying the *Ark of the Covenant* towards the Promised Land (see p. 125).

I took several photographs of the basilica and when the films were developed, to my happy surprise, a prominent white *pillar of cloud* appeared at the side of the steeple and the statue of *Mary, Ark of the Covenant*. It was called in Old Testament days, the *Shekinah*. It was a *pillar of cloud* by day and a *pillar of fire* by night, which preceded the Ark on the journey to the Promised Land (see p. 124).

It was not the first, but one of many photographs in which the *pillar of cloud* mysteriously appeared in front of pictures of *Mary, Ark of the Covenant*, and for which, like many other people who have recently been receiving mystical photographs of one kind or another, I am very grateful, so utterly undeserving as I am.

123.

The basilica of Mary, Ark of the Covenant in Kiriath-Jearim

Above: A side view of the basilica and the steeple (see p. 120)

**124.**

Left: A close up view of the statue of Mary standing on the Ark of the Covenant on the steeple of the basilica in Kiriath-Jearim in Israel. Note the "Baby" holds the Eucharist in His right hand.
(see p. 120)

Right: The pillar of cloud appears beside the ancient Ark and the new Ark
(see p. 122)

125.

The tapestry depicting the history of the Ark of the Covenant in the basilica in Kiriath-Jearim
(see pp. 121-2)

## CHAPTER 17.

## *The Eucharist —*
## *The Sacrament of the New Covenant*

"**Unless you eat the flesh of the Son of Man and drink his blood, you have no life in you.**"

John 6:53

The ancient Ark of the Covenant contained some of the miraculous manna which fell from heaven, and just as Yahweh did in Old Testament times, Jesus, in His time, performed many miracles so that people would believe. When John the Baptist sent a message asking Him if He was the Messiah, Jesus calmly and with great authority replied to the messenger: *"Go back and tell John what you hear and see; the blind see, the lame walk, lepers are cleansed, the deaf hear, and the dead are raised to life..."* (Matthew 11:2-6). These are the signs which He provided to authenticate His divinity.

In Capernaum there are excavations of the ruins of the synagogue where Jesus once preached. It stands impressively on a little hill close to "Peter's house," overlooking the sea of Galilee. I have visited this historic site on two occasions and walked among the ruins of this synagogue where the crowd once asked Jesus: "What miracle will you perform so that we may see and believe you? What will you do? Our ancestors ate manna in the desert, just as the Scripture says: He gave them bread from heaven to eat" (John 6:28-32).

It was at that most historic moment that Jesus prepared His apostles for the Passover meal on Maundy Thursday: *"I tell you the truth,"* he replied,*"what Moses gave you was not the bread from heaven; it is my Father who gives you the real bread from heaven. For the bread that God gives is he who comes down from heaven and gives life to the world."* To which they exclaimed: "Sir, give us this bread always." It was then that they received the reply that astounded and confused them (and still to this day confuses many people of other faiths and even some Christians): *"I am the living bread come down from heaven. If anyone eats this bread he will live forever, and the bread that I shall give him is my flesh for the life of the world"* (John 6:30-40).

Not surprisingly, this statement started an angry argument among the crowd: "How can this man give us his flesh to eat?" But Jesus calmly persisted: *"I tell you the truth; if you do not eat the flesh of the Son of Man and drink his blood, you will not have life in yourselves. Whoever eats my flesh and drinks my blood has eternal life and I will raise him up on the last day, for my flesh is real food and my blood is real drink. Whoever eats my flesh and drinks my blood lives in me and I live in him..."* This teaching was "too hard" for his followers and "many turned back and would not go with him anymore" (John 6:52-66).

What is most significant, however, is that Jesus did not attempt to call them back. He did not say: *"Come back. You have misunderstood me. I did not mean it to be literal."* He had nothing to retract. He meant what He said! He obviously did not wish to repeat the words He previously said to His distressed disciples when He calmed the storm: *"Where is your faith?"* (Luke 8:22-25).

That there is a crisis of faith in the world today is partly exemplified by a poll of American Catholics conducted by the *New York Times* and *CBS News* in April 1994. According to this poll, only 29% of Catholics aged 18-29 believe in the True Presence as opposed to 51% of those aged 65 and older. The statistics are interesting, but I am yet to see an analysis of these figures. However, among the several factors responsible for these results, the suppression of religious education in the schools and the lack of such instructions in the home and, in some cases, even in the churches, must certainly play a significant role. But it was also Jesus Himself who questioned: *"When the Son of Man comes, will he find any faith on earth?"* (Luke 18:8).

The Roman Catholic Church, the Greek Church, the Russian Church, the Copts, Armenians, Syrians, Chaldeans and, in fact, all the Oriental Churches still hold fast to the teaching of the Real Presence of the Body and Blood of Our Lord in the Holy Eucharist. Even Martin Luther, who defended the literal interpretation of this sixth chapter of St. John against Zwingli, Carlstadt, and Oecolampadius, confessed that he was initially tempted to deny the Real Presence in order "to give a great smack in the face of Popery," but the Scriptures were too overwhelming in its favour. He eventually confessed: "I am caught. I cannot escape. The text is too forcible."

Three years before Jesus made that stunning and authoritative statement and at a time when He thought that

His hour "had not yet come," His Mother initiated His ministry, and at her request He performed His first public miracle, changing water into wine at the wedding banquet in Cana. I say "public" because I believe that He must have performed "private" miracles which were known to His Mother. It was as though protocol demanded that His Mother should be the one to open the chapter of His public ministry.

Three years later, on a Thursday night at around 8:30 p.m. in the Cenacle, He performed His greatest and last miracle of all, this time changing bread into His Body and wine into His Precious Blood. In so doing, He instituted the Sacrament of the new and everlasting Covenant.

On that night before He was crucified, He changed the Jewish Passover ceremony into the Christian Mass of the new dispensation, and as it was the head of the Jewish household who broke the bread at the Passover meal, Christ, as Head of the Church, took bread, broke it, and gave it to His disciples, saying: *"Take this and eat, this is my body which will be given up for you."* Then he took the cup, gave thanks to God and said: *"This is the cup of my blood, the blood of the new and everlasting Covenant which will be shed so that sins will be forgiven. Do this in memory of me"* (Luke 22:20 — The Roman Missal).

Just as the Passover meal was eaten in memory of the exodus of the Israelites from slavery, He was in effect saying: "Do this in memory of Me and of your 'exodus' from the slavery of sin." However, instead of the lamb of the ancient Hebrews, in future they would feed on His own Body and Blood, the new sacrifice and the new meal for Christians. It was to be the *perfect sacrifice.*

In other words, in saying: *"Do this in memory of me,"* He was asking us to celebrate the Passover, no longer in memory of what God did for us in the past, but in memory of the shedding of His Blood on Calvary the next day. This new Covenant is perpetuated and made present in an unbloody manner in the Eucharist. How easy it is for humanity to forget! And so, He pleaded: *"Do this in memory of Me."*

Catholic theologians agree that the Eucharist is truly the greatest Sacrament of them all. It is the perpetual sacrifice of the true Lamb of God. It is the Manna come down from heaven, not for forty years, but forever. It is Emmanuel — "God with us" forever. It is the new Covenant of love between God and man. It is a spiritual banquet, for whereas bread is the nourishment of the body, the Eucharist is food for the soul, and just as material food is necessary for life and one cannot live without it, so too, spiritual food is necessary for life and spiritual life cannot be well nourished without it.

But why bread and wine? Bread has always been the basic and staple food of man over the millennia. It is a food which sustains our life day by day: *"Give us this day our daily bread"* (Mark 6:11). Bread is simple and humble. Wine, on the other hand, is joy: "Joy of the heart and joy of the soul is wine drunk daily and in moderation" (Sirach 31:28); "Wine and music gladden the heart" (Sirach 40:20). Three times the Old Testament refers to wine as "the blood of the grape." Wine is love and because it signifies love and has the colour of blood, it also represents sacrifice, especially sacrifice done *out of* love.

As L. Alonso Schökel in his book *Celebrating the Eucharist* concludes: "So, bread and wine are what we offer you, Lord. You have chosen them, simple and humble, yet loaded with meaning. You have taught us to bring them together to your table. You have given them to us in your goodness, and now we present them to you. And so we say: 'Blessed are you, Lord, God of all Creation, through your goodness we have this bread to offer, which earth has given and human hands have made. It will become for us the bread of life... and this wine, fruit of the vine and work of human hands. It will become our spiritual drink.'"

However, the Holy Spirit, the often silent God, as greatly active as He is little known, works continually as Love who gives prominence to the Father and the Son. It is through Him that the Word became flesh in the womb of Mary, and it is through Him that the bread and the wine become flesh and blood in every Mass.

I cannot end a discourse on the Eucharist without linking it to the great Queen, for there is no secret how the Blessed Virgin is related to the Eucharist. It is very simple. It was she who gave Him His Body and His Blood, and she is the channel of divine grace who draws men to her Son. As Pope John Paul II says in his Encyclical *Redemptoris Mater*: "Mary guides the faithful to the Eucharist." Indeed, in a decree dated September 12, 1963, his predecessor Pope Paul VI declared the Most Blessed Virgin Mary as *"Our Lady of the Most Blessed Sacrament,* the principal and heavenly Patron of the Congregation of the Fathers of the Blessed Sacrament." This Congregation was founded by St. Peter Julian Eymard (1811 - 1868).

Significantly, it was on that feast day, the feast of *Our Lady of the Blessed Sacrament,* that she chose to open her apparitions in Fatima. It was on May 13, 1917. The Eucharist is the Sacrament of the new and everlasting Covenant and *Our Lady of the Blessed Sacrament* is the *Tabernacle of the Most High.* She is the *Ark of the Covenant.*

The ancient *Ark of the old Covenant*, which was kept in the *Holy of Holies* in Soloman's Temple, contained some of the miraculous manna which fell from heaven. But the Tabernacle on the altars of Catholic churches houses the Eucharist behind small doors, frequently covered by a veil like in the days of old. This is the new *Holy of Holies* which contains the true Bread of Life, the Law giver Himself, the Mediator of the new and everlasting Covenant.

**CHAPTER 18.**

## *Eucharistic Miracles — The Confirmation*

**"The Eucharist is the wonder of wonders, the greatest of miracles."**
St. Thomas Aquinas

Controversy over the presence of Jesus in the Eucharist has been with us since the days of Capernaum, and around the year 1517 the Protestant Reformation denied the adoration of the Eucharist and the sacrifice of the Mass. Even today, there are those who question, there are those who "protest," including some professed Catholics, some of them even clergymen.

Questions of all sorts are raised. Does the bread and wine really become the Body and Blood of Christ? Is the Host not a symbol rather than Jesus Himself? And so, we are living in a divided Church in which the Body of Christ is so divided that a common Eucharist cannot be celebrated. However, the Eucharist is the backbone of the Catholic Faith (including the Orthodox Church) and the Church insists, as Christ Himself insisted in Capernaum, that His words are to be taken literally.

But how difficult must it be for the proud to fathom the humility of God! That Jesus would humble himself to the extent that He comes to us under the simple appearance of bread is frequently beyond human comprehension. Moreover, He chooses to come not only as humble bread, but unleavened bread, bread which does not rise, bread which is not 'puffed up!'

Indeed, He revealed His Eucharistic abode from the very beginning. He chose Bethlehem for His birthplace. Bethlehem means *"House of bread."* He did say *"Learn from me, for I am meek and humble of heart"* (Matthew 11:29). As St. Francis of Assisi once exclaimed: "O sublime humility, O humble sublimity!"

The great apostle of the Eucharist, St. Thomas Aquinas, in his *Summa Theologica*, put it this way: "The consecrated Host still looks like bread, feels like bread, and tastes like bread;

the wine that has been consecrated into the Blood of Christ still looks like wine, and tastes like wine. On the other hand, neither the Host nor the Precious Blood looks like the Body and the Blood of Christ. We can only say that the whole substance of the bread has been changed into the substance of the Body of Christ, and the whole substance of the wine has been changed into the Blood of Christ, but that the appearances of bread and wine still remain. Theologians call a change of this kind *transubstantiation."*

To draw a parallel, in modern medicine we use a product, a salt substitute, as a therapeutic measure in hypertension and liver failure. It looks like salt, feels like salt and tastes like salt — but it is not salt. So it is with the bread and wine. But the God we worship is also a God of 'good taste.' He is the God of etiquette and aesthetics. Would he then choose to change the bread and wine into visible raw flesh and fresh blood for us to eat and drink? Would this not be aesthetically undesirable? In His supreme Wisdom, therefore, He chose to perform the change imperceptibly, and in so doing also required that we have *faith*.

I have had the privilege of visiting three shrines of Eucharistic miracles. In 1989, I journeyed to Daroca, a little village in Spain, which is one of the many historic homes of a Eucharistic miracle. The miracle occurred on February 23, 1239, when there was a great battle being waged between the Spaniards and the invading Moors. As was the custom at that time, the commanders went to confession, and Mass was celebrated at the camp by the chaplain, Fr. Mateo Martinez. However, before the six commanders were able to receive the Eucharist, word came to them that the Moors had launched a surprise attack. The Mass was interrupted as the commanders had to return to the field of battle immediately. The priest then wrapped the consecrated Hosts in the corporal and hid them under rocks some ten yards away.

Victorious in battle, when the commanders returned to the camp, they asked the priest to give them Communion in thanksgiving to the Lord for their victory over the Moors. Fr. Mateo then ran to the spot where the Hosts had been buried, took the corporal from under the rock and unfolded it. He gasped at the sight before his eyes. The six Hosts were bleeding and stuck to the corporal, leaving six spots of blood on the cloth. This miracle confirmed that in receiving the Holy Communion under the form of bread, the communicant also receives the Blood of Christ as proclaimed in 1415 when the Council of Constance defined that Christ is present under either appearance of bread or wine.

A contingent from Daroca then went to Rome in 1261 to inform Pope Urban IV of the Eucharistic miracle. He was the Pope who later instituted the feast of Corpus Christi, and it is believed that he accepted the news of the Eucharistic miracle in Daroca as one more sign from the Lord that He wanted this feast instituted.

On Sunday, October 22, 1989, when I travelled to Daroca, by fortunate coincidence, the village was celebrating the 750th anniversary of the miracle of the Hosts. It was about 1:00 p.m., and two gracious nuns opened the beautiful reliquary for me to see the miraculous corporal with the stains of blood from the consecrated Hosts, still intact after seven centuries. The blood on the corporal has been analyzed and determined to be of human origin (see p. 136).

But the first of all recorded Eucharistic miracles occurred in the eighth century AD in a town in Italy now called Lanciano. In ancient days it was called Anxanum and at the beginning of the thirteenth century its name was changed to Lanzanum. According to tradition, Longinus, the Roman Centurion who pierced his lance into the side of Christ, originally came from Anxanum. It is said that he had poor vision, but regained perfect sight after touching his eyes with his hand dripping with the Blood of Jesus. As a consequence of this, he became a convert and died a martyr. His feast day is celebrated on March 15.

A document of 1631 gives some data on this miraculous event in Lanciano: "About the year 700 of Our Lord, in the Monastery of St. Longinus, today under the care of the Franciscans, where the monks of the Order of St. Basil lived, there was a monk, not very firm in the faith, well versed in the sciences of the world, who went on from day to day doubting whether in the consecrated Host was the Body of Christ, and also whether the wine was the real Blood. Nevertheless, not abandoned by the divine grace of continuous prayer, on one occasion he begged God to remove from his heart this wound which kept on invading his soul, when the most kind God, Father of mercy and of our every consolation, from so dense a fog granted him that grace, which He once imparted to St. Thomas, the Apostle. While, therefore, one morning in the midst of his sacrifice, after having pronounced the most holy words, and finding himself more immersed than ever in his persistent error, he saw the bread change into Flesh and the wine into Blood."

The Host turned Flesh and the wine turned Blood (five clotted pellets), without the use of any form of chemical, have been preserved in an artistic silver reliquary (see p. 136). A number of authentications have been performed through the centuries, but the last authentications were the most scientifically complete, They were in 1970-71 and again in 1981. These scientific investigations were performed by an illustrious scientist, Professor Odoardo Linoli, Professor of Anatomy and Histo-pathology and Chief Physician of the United Hospitals of Arezzo in Italy. He was assisted by Professor Ruggero Bertelli, Professor of Anatomy of the University of Sienna. With the permission of the Archbishop, Monsignor Pacifico Perantoni, they examined two tiny fragments from the edge of the Holy Flesh and the Holy Blood. The analyses were performed with unquestionable scientific precision and were documented by a series of microscopic photographs.

These scientific studies showed that the "Flesh is real Flesh and the Blood is real Blood," and that the Flesh and the Blood belong to the human species. The Flesh consisted of the muscular tissue of a *Heart*, as seen in the microscopic examinations of the histology slides, and showed the myocardium, the endocardium, and sections of the vagus nerve. The Blood type was AB. The committee's report was published in the Vatican's daily *L'Osservatore Romano* of April 3, 1971, and on November 3, 1974, Pope John Paul II, at that time Cardinal of Krakow, visited the Shrine of the Eucharistic Miracle in Lanciano, a sign of his great devotion to the Holy Eucharist.

In a letter written on March 7, 1976, Fr. P. Lewis Della Zizza, O.F.M., Superior of the Eucharistic Shrine, wrote: "This miracle, as you well know, is the greatest and most perfect of our Catholic Faith and for twelve centuries stands out as uninterrupted proof of Christ's love and irrefutable proof of the Real Presence of Jesus in the Eucharistic Mystery. Here at Lanciano, Christ made us a gift of Himself to remain with men until the consummation of the ages, by changing Himself into living Flesh and living Blood. This stupendous and marvelous reality was confirmed by a rigorous scientific documentation which guarantees its authenticity."

On Friday, November 16, 1989, over 1000 years after the miracle, I visited the Church of St. Francis in Lanciano, Italy, and with the guidance of a Franciscan priest, I was led to the reliquary where the Host-Flesh and the clotted Blood can still be distinctly seen. I then visited the museum annexed to the Church and examined the microscopic photographs of the Heart muscle. I did not realize at the time that November 16 was the feast of St. Gertrude, Patroness of the West Indies! According to *The Lives of the Saints*, Catholic

Book Company, she was characterized by a great devotion to the Blessed Eucharist and by a tender love for the Blessed Virgin.

In the light of these and many other indisputable proofs of the *transubstantiation* given to us by God, I find it totally inexcusable that anyone would deny the miracle of the Eucharist, especially the clergy who should have more access to this information than most. After these experiences, it was the beginning of a new era of deeper devotion to the Real Presence of Jesus in the Eucharist.

Later on, I will describe a more recent miracle of the Eucharist which occurred in Betania, Venezuela, on December 8, 1992. There is also a great devotion to the Eucharist in Lourdes which was the first shrine I visited in 1982, however, Medjugorje in Yugoslavia was the first modern-day shrine that I ever visited. My first visit there was in 1986. There too you will find a great devotion to the Eucharist. But first, a very brief history of Yugoslavia.

136.

Above: The bleeding Hosts of Daroca in Spain (see p. 133)
Below: The reliquary in Lanciano with the Host turned flesh and the wine turned blood (see p. 133)

## CHAPTER 19.

### Medjugorje: Mary's School of Prayer

**"With prayer and fasting you can prevent war and suspend natural laws."**

**Gospa**

Yugoslavia is a mosaic of religious denominations and faiths which is unique in the world. Five nationalities are recognized: Serbs, Croats, Slovenes, Macedonians and Montenegrans. There are six republics and two autonomous provinces: Bosnia-Hercegovina (Capital: Sarajevo), Croatia (Zagreb), Macedonia (Skopje), Montenegro (Titograd), Slovenia (Ljubljana), and Serbia (Belgrade). Serbia includes the two autonomous provinces, Kosovo and Vojvodina.

The major religious identification of the population is Serbian Orthodox 34%, Roman Catholics 26% and Moslems 10%. The Croats were the first Slavic people to accept Christianity dating from 626 AD. However, paganism still prevailed among most of the people until the second half of the ninth century, and Bosnia was the last of the South Slavic provinces to be christianized.

The Moslem Turks made their first incursion into Bosnia in 1386, and into Hercegovina after 1400. Eventually, the Turks gained complete control in 1478. The Roman Catholic Church in Bosnia was abandoned by the hierarchy and slid into schism, following which, to save their lives and livelihood, there was a mass Islamisation of Catholic Croats. The task of reviving the Church in Bosnia was then given to the Franciscans, who distinguished themselves during the Islamic occupation, and still enjoy to this day great prestige in the region. They arrived in Bosnia in 1399 and in Hercegovina twenty years later, in 1419.

However, over the decades Turkish rule gradually weakened and Turkish occupation of Bosnia-Hercegovina finally ended in 1878 after a reign of 400 years. That year (1878), at the Berlin congress, the decision was made that the Austro-Hungarian monarchy should occupy Bosnia-Hercegovina. Then, in 1908, the Hapsburg dual monarchy annexed Bosnia and Hercegovina. This caused quite a political turmoil and an international crisis.

Balkan nationalism eventually culminated in the assassination in Sarajevo on June 28, 1914, of the Austrian Archduke Franz Ferdinand, the heir to the Austro-Hungarian empire, and his wife Sophia. The assassin, Gavrilo Princip, belonged to the Serbian nationalist secret society. One month later, World War I (1914-1918) started.

After the war the influence of the Axis powers grew in Yugoslavia during the 1930s, but Yugoslavia remained neutral at the outbreak of the Second World War. However, when German troops invaded Yugoslavia on April 6, 1941, resistance militants were soon formed and General Draza Mihajlovic assembled the loyalist "chetniks," while Josip Broz or Tito organized the "partisans." Eventually, after a bitter internal struggle, Tito formed the government in March 1945, and the November elections gave 90 percent of votes to his Communist-directed party.

At the end of World War II (1939-1945), the newly adopted constitution of January 31, 1946, closely resembled that of the Soviet Union. Yugoslavia was declared a federal people's republic, and was recognized by the western powers, although its leanings were decidedly pro-Soviet. Tito, however, refused to align himself with a strict Stalinist policy, preferring to make Yugoslavia a neutral socialist state, independent of the USSR.

Now, when Tito set up Communist Yugoslavia, he included in the constitution a clause whereby the six republics, which had joined the federation were free to leave at any time they chose. Forty years later, in 1989, with Communism caving in everywhere else, the Communist parties in four of the republics, faced with the increasing domination of the Communist party in Serbia and its ally, Montenegro, forced a national referendum. The people rejected Communism resoundingly in the provinces, except in Serbia and its ally, Montenegro, and on June 25, 1991, the two northernmost republics, Croatia and Slovenia, declared their independence from the Communist central government. It was the date chosen ten years earlier by the Madonna of Medjugorje (Gospa) for the feast of *Our Lady, Queen of Peace.*

Suddenly, war in Yugoslavia was the lead story in all the newspapers of the world, and the federal government authorized the Communist-controlled federal army to crush the dissidents. Yugoslavia's army used planes and tanks to keep Croatia from leaving the federation. The general staff and core of the Yugoslavian army were almost certainly hard-lined Communists, and as such they regarded the Church as their most dangerous long-term enemy. A record number of churches were deliberately destroyed, some four hundred and more.

The Serbs apparently wished to drive the Croatian people away from their provinces in order to amalgamate them into Serbia. The plan is to create a "Greater Serbia." This is nothing new. As far back as 1849, there was an elaborate Great Serbian Plan for the annexation of Croatia and Bosnia-Hercegovina, which was outlined in an essay called "The Serbs altogether and everywhere." It was published in Vienna by Vuk Karadjic.

The atrocities then became a tripartite conflict with Orthodox Serbs, Catholic Croats and Moslems, maiming and killing one another on an unimaginable scale which has astonished the world, and a scenario then unfolded where former neighbours and friends became bitter enemies. The senselessness of it all was illustrated by a remark of Nikifor Simsic, a journalist from Sarajevo, who, referring to his own family as an example, once said: "My father is a Serb, my mother is a Catholic, my wife is a Moslem. So what are my children?"

However, while all around it is being bombarded, pillaged and destroyed, Medjugorje, just fifty miles away from Mostar, is still untouched by the war. Indeed, since her first apparition there in 1981, the Blessed Virgin has been calling the nation and the world to prayer and fasting, but only Medjugorje and its immediate environs took her messages seriously.

Fr. Kenneth Roberts in his book *Up On The Mountain* records this miraculous preservation of Medjugorje, which is attributed to Mary's protection: "In Medjugorje itself, the church, the rectory, the sisters' retreat house, are all untouched; in fact, damage to the village has been so slight that it is a testimony to the prayers of the faithful all over the world. Doubly so, when one considers the testimony of a Yugoslavian Army pilot who defected: they had been given orders to bomb Medjugorje, concentrating on the church (of St. James), but when they flew over, they couldn't find it; it was as if someone had drawn a screen over the buildings. Even if that were not so, even if the village had had been obliterated and every person that we knew and loved had been killed,they could not have killed Medjugorje. For it is no longer a place or a particular people. It is a spirit — a flame in the hearts of millions all over the world, growing brighter day by day."

Medjugorje has been for me *the* most important influence in my "conversion." I have been a pilgrim there on seven occasions, and my close friendship with the visionary Marija Pavlovic was a singular blessing. It was always a great joy to return there. Soon, Fr. Slavko Barbaric and Fr. Svetovar Kraljevic were to be my close friends and spiritual advisors. What committed clergymen, these Franciscans!

Medjugorje is situated in the Republic of Bosnia-Hercegovina. Hercegovina has always been deeply religious and is known as one of the most faithful pockets of Catholic faith in Communist Yugoslavia. As Fr. Michael O'Carroll says: "Medjugorje is a centre of Croatian piety outside Croatia." The estimated population is about 2500 people, some 450 families. They are Croats, mainly Catholic, and their livelihood is based on vine and tobacco plantations. The name of the village is of Slav origin, and it is called Medjugorje because of its position among the hills. Medjugorje means "between the mountains."

The main mountain overlooking the church is about 2000 feet high and is known as Krizevac or "Hill of the Cross," for in 1933 the people of the parish erected a great concrete Cross, 14 meters high on its summit, to celebrate the nineteen hundredth anniversary of the Passion of Our Lord. The other smaller mountain is called Podbrdo.

Before 1981, Medjugorje was virtually unknown throughout the world. However, on June 24 of that year, the feast day of John the Baptist, six young witnesses maintained under oath that they saw the Blessed Virgin. The apparitions began in the hamlet of Bijakovici, one of the four hamlets which make up the village of Medjugorje. The visionaries relate that the Madonna or "Gospa," as they call her in Croatian, has an indescribable beauty. Her eyes are blue and her feet are always covered by a little grey cloud. She wears a luminous grey dress, while on her head is a crown of twelve stars in suspension. This first encounter was one of total silence as she covered and uncovered the Child she held in her arms.

On the second day, June 25, she appeared and signalled with her hand that the visionaries should come closer. They were Vicka Ivankovic, Mirjana Dragicevic, Marija Pavlovic, Ivan Dragicevic, Ivanka Ivankovic, and Jakov Colo, all youngsters between 15 and 17 years of age, except Jakov who was 10 years old. On June 26, the third day of the apparitions, she identified herself: "I am the Blessed Virgin Mary."

It was on August 6 that she declared: *"Ja sam kraljica mira."* — *"I am the Queen of Peace."* Later on, she requested that June 25 be remembered and celebrated every year as the feast of *Our Lady Queen of Peace.* Since then she has appeared everyday in Medjugorje. As Fr. Richard Foley, a Jesuit priest in London, once said: "Medjugorje is a virtual Mariapolis, a city of Mary!"

She always begins her conversation with the phrase: "Praised be Jesus Christ," an old Franciscan greeting since the days of St. Francis, and she usually ends by saying: "Go in the peace of God." When asked on the third day, June 26, why she had come and what she wanted, she replied: "I have come because there are many believers here. I want to be with you to *convert* and *reconcile* everyone."

On the fourth day the children pleaded with her to show some sign to prove to the world that she was truly appearing. She replied that those who do not see her should believe as though they were seeing her. She was thus echoing her Son's remark to Thomas: "Blessed are they who have not seen and have believed" (John 20:29). On the fifth day, when the visionaries asked the Madonna what she wanted of them, she responded: "Faith and respect for me!" On another day, one of the visionaries asked her: "Gospa, how is it that you are so beautiful?" "Because I love! Love, and you too will be beautiful," she replied.

She told the children that she would impart *ten* confidential revelations (secrets) to them. Two of the girls have already received all the secret prophecies and no longer see Our Lady daily. The other seers have so far received nine secrets. She has promised to leave a visible sign on Podbrdo after the apparitions have ended. It is meant particularly to convert those who do not believe. She also warned: "You faithful must not wait for the sign to convert yourselves. Do not delay in converting yourselves... When the sign comes it will be too late for many." We are told that the ninth and tenth secrets are particularly grave. They concern a chastisement for the sins of the world, and the visionaries say that after these ten events "life in the world will change. Afterwards, men will believe like in ancient times."

In Old Testament times it took *ten* plagues from God to free the Hebrews from Egyptian slavery — the turning of water into blood, the frogs, the mosquitoes, the gadflies, the death of the livestock, the boils, the hail, the locusts, the three days of darkness, and finally, the death of the first-born.

it that history will repeat itself? Is it that it will also require *ten* chastisements in this era before we decide to free ourselves from Satan's control?

On March 1, 1984, the Virgin continued her "School of Prayer" in Medjugorje through the "Thursday messages." However, on January 8, 1987, these weekly messages ended and the Madonna began to give monthly messages on the twenty-fifth day of every month. As nothing is done haphazardly by heaven, I wondered why she chose the twenty-fifth day of the month.

The number 25 is certainly significant in the Christian calendar. The twenty-fifth of December is the celebration of the birth of her Son; the twenty-fifth of July is the great feast of the parish, the feast of St. James; the twenty-fifth of March is the feast of the Annunciation, and the twenty-fifth of June is the day she has requested to be designated the feast of *Our Lady Queen of Peace*. One must wonder whether her last apparition will also be on the twenty-fifth?

Mirjana said that in 1982 the Virgin gave in substance the following message: "You must know that Satan exists. One day he asked to test the Church for a certain time. God gave him leave to try the Church for one century. Satan then chose the twentieth century. When the secrets confided to you are revealed, his power will be destroyed. Even now he is beginning to lose his power and has become aggressive. He is destroying marriages, creating divisions among priests, and is responsible for obsessions and murder. You must protect yourself against these things through fasting and prayer, especially community prayer. Carry blessed objects on yourself. Put them in your houses. Bring back the use of holy water."

Here we recall the vision of Pope Leo XIII in 1884, when he had a frightening apocalyptic vision of the future of the Church, and heard Satan boasting to God that he would destroy the Church if he were given full rein. It was then that Pope Leo introduced the prayer to St. Michael which priests used to recite after Mass up to the time of the Second Vatican Council. Indeed, this twentieth century has truly been the century of Satan. It is the century of the great wars — World War I in 1914 and World War II in 1939, both instigated by the author of rebellion and war, the fallen angel, Lucifer.

This century has seen more lives lost in wars than in all the wars of human history. The Church has had more martyrs since 1900 than in all the nineteen centuries since the first martyrdom of the founder of Christianity on Calvary.

Apart from finding many believers there, one wonders why the Madonna chose Yugoslavia in which to appear in Europe. Perhaps it was also because it was straddled between the Communist East and the West. Notably, it was the events in Yugoslavia that ignited the spark which started World War I. Now World War III looms threateningly over our heads.

It is recorded in Fr. Kraljevic's book *Apparitions of Our Lady at Medjugorje* that the Madonna told the children: "In God differences do not exist among His people; and religion need not separate people. Every person must be respected, despite his or her particular profession or faith. God presides over all religions as a king controls his subjects, through his priests and ministers. *The sole mediator of salvation is Jesus Christ.* However, it is not equally efficacious to belong to or pray in any church or community, because the Holy Spirit grants His power differently among the churches and ministers for all believers do not pray the same way. It is intentional that all apparitions are under the auspices of the Catholic Church." So testify the visionaries.

Fr. René Laurentin's book *Is the Virgin Mary Appearing at Medjugorje?* was first published in 1984, and in it he said: "*Reconciliation* is possible. It can be brought about within families that are divided... Still more, we may hope for *reconciliation* between the Croatians and the Serbians..." This was written 10 years ago! In fact, in 1987, the Virgin of Medjugorje also made this plea in one of her apparitions there: "Love your Serbian Orthodox and Moslem brothers and the atheists who persecute you."

Four years later, the tenth anniversary of the apparitions, I was in Medjugorje with two friends from Australia for this celebration. There was a quiet joy in Medjugorje for it was on that day, June 25, 1991, the day which Mary had requested the Church to celebrate the feast of the *Queen of Peace*, that Croatia and Bosnia-Hercegovina declared their independence from the central Communist government. Suddenly, war in Yugoslavia escalated just as we left for Rome on June 26. Since then, a war, in certain ways more atrocious than the massacres of Hitler's war, erupted in what was formerly Yugoslavia. "With prayer and fasting you can prevent war and suspend natural laws," the Virgin had said in Medjugorje in 1984. But how many prayed? How many fasted? War broke out.

According to the visionaries, these apparitions of Mary are her last apparitions on earth in this era. Indeed, she once said to them: "I came to Lourdes in the morning, to Fatima at noon, and to Medjugorje in the eveningtime." Although this is interpreted in a figurative sense, meaning that she came to Medjugorje in what may be called "the final hour" of time, it was also literally true in that in Lourdes her first appearance to Bernadette was at 7 o'clock in the morning; in Fatima she appeared to the children just after noon, and to the visionaries in Medjugorje at 6:15 p.m. in the evening.

    That Mary chose to appear in Medjugorje for the first time on June 24, the feast of John the Baptist, is also not without relevance and significance. Just as the Baptizer prepared the way for the First Coming of Jesus, by fasting and preaching penance and conversion, Louis Marie Grignion de Montfort and other Marian scholars teach that Mary's role is to prepare the world for the Second Coming of her Son, and that she is preaching the same message of John — conversion, penance and reconciliation.

    It took the Church thirteen years to approve the apparitions in Fatima, and the Church has not as yet given its official approval of Medjugorje. However, in 1989 Bishop S. Treinen of Boise, Idaho, USA, had a private conversation with Pope John Paul II during his Ad Limina visit to Rome. He said to the Pope: "Holy Father, I have just come from Medjugorje. There are wonderful things going on there." The Pope replied: "Yes, it is good for pilgrims to go to Medjugorje and pray and do penance. It is good" (Extract from Bishop Treinen's Mass homily, Notre Dame Conference, May 14, 1989).

    Bishop Paul Hnilica, auxiliary Bishop of Rome, has also testified that on August 1, 1989, while the Pope was addressing a group of Italian physicians who had just conducted scientific studies of the visionaries in Medjugorje during a state of ecstasy, he paid the following tribute: "Today's world has lost its sense of the supernatural. But many are searching for it — and find it in Medjugorje, through prayer, penance and fasting."

## CHAPTER 20.

## St. James and Mary — El Pilar

"Spain was with good reason called 'La Tierra de Maria.'"
John Paul II

Looking for a connection between the Blessed Virgin and St. James, to whom the church in Medjugorje is dedicated, among the many books I researched was *The Mystical City of God*. According to the great mystic, the Venerable Mary of Agreda, whereas his brother John was the beloved apostle of the Lord, James, she says, was the favourite of the Mother of the Lord.

It is said that she loved St. James with a special tenderness and that he deserved this favour on account of his piety and his great affection for her. He was a fiery man but a humble apostle and was known as "the Thunderer," allegedly because of his temper. He is also called James the Greater to distinguish him from James, the son of Alphaeus. He is not the James who wrote the "Epistle of James."

Mary of Agreda relates that the Blessed Virgin appeared to St. James in Saragossa while he was evangelizing in Spain. However, my interest to visit Saragossa was kindled by Conchita Gonzalez (now Keena), the visionary of Garabandal. It happened at her home in May 1989 when I told her that my second visit to Medjugorje was on October 12, 1987. It was then that she exclaimed excitedly that in Spain, October 12 is the feast of *El Pilar* or *Our Lady of the Pillar*, a feast for which all Spanish-speaking countries have a very special devotion. She then gave me a gift of something which was very special to her. It was a small replica of the famous statue of Mary as *"El Pilar."*

I arrived in Saragossa on a special day. It was October 16, 1989, the feast of St. Margaret Mary Alacoque, to whom Jesus appeared as the Sacred Heart in Paray le Monial in 1673. It was four days after the great Marian feast of El Pilar, but the thousands of fading flowers around the outside walls of the Basilica of El Pilar testified to the recent festive occasion.

The importance of Saragossa as a shrine of Our Lady dates back more than 1900 years and centers around St. James. Mary of Agreda relates how the apostles, desirous of accomplishing the mandate of the Lord to *"go out to the whole world and proclaim the Gospel to all nations"* (Mark 16:15), were praying in the Cenacle for ten continuous days to discern the wish of the Lord with respect to the provinces to which each of them should go to evangelize. At the end of this time, Peter, by divine inspiration, assigned James to the land of Spain.

Hesiquio, Bishop of Salona in the 5th century AD, also testifies that James was sent by Peter to Spain and that he spread the Christian faith there, building churches and ordaining bishops. It is said that James was the first apostle to leave Jerusalem in the year 35 AD, one year and five months after the Passion of Our Lord, eight months after the martyrdom of Stephen and five months before the conversion of Paul.

According to an ancient and venerable tradition, while she was still living in Jerusalem, the Virgin Mary bilocated to Saragossa to console and encourage her beloved apostle who was evangelizing in this Spanish city beside the river Ebro. While he was praying with his disciples on the night of January 2 in the year 40 AD, the Madonna appeared and told him that the Lord wished him to return to Jerusalem where he was to be the first apostle to be martyred.

It was obviously the fulfillment of the challenge of Jesus in reply to the request of Salome, the mother of the sons of Zebedee: "Promise that these two sons of mine (James and John) may sit, one at your right hand and the other at your left in your kingdom." *"You do not know what you are asking,"* Jesus answered,*"Can you drink the cup that I am going to drink?"* They replied,"We can." *Very well,"* he said, *"You shall drink my cup"* (Matthew 20: 20-23). James was the first apostle to drink the cup!

As the legend goes, a great number of angels accompanied the Virgin and formed a royal throne of a most resplendent cloud and placed her on it. The angels then made a pillar of jasper and upon it they placed a small image of their Queen, made of another substance. The Virgin also informed James that God wished the construction of a house of prayer under her patronage and name, in which He was to be glorified and magnified. She promised great favours and blessings from the pillar, stating that the temple to be built for her would remain and be preserved until the end of the world. Indeed, anyone can see the wonderful preservation of this pillar and statue in Saragossa for it remains intact for more than 1900 years. After the apparition, it is said that St. James spent over a year in building the small chapel to house the pillar.

As requested, James returned to Jerusalem at a time when the whole city was very much incensed against the disciples, but he continued to preach there with great fervour, converting many. Eventually, however, by order of Herod Agrippa, the grandson of Herod the Great, he "drank the cup" and was martyred in Jerusalem around Easter in the year 44 AD.

The small oratory built by the apostle in Saragossa was enlarged over the centuries. It was then destroyed by a fierce fire in 1434, but interestingly, the Virgin's pillar was miraculously "respected" by the flames. The idea of building the present great basilica occurred in 1677, and the cornerstone of the basilica was laid on July 25, 1681, the feast of St. James. The Holy Chapel in the basilica houses the pillar and the venerated statue of the Virgin. In fact, of such an age is this pillar that, although it is made of a very hard and precious stone and is at least 12 inches in diameter, through the many kisses of veneration over the centuries, there is a deep hollow in the pillar from nineteen centuries of gentle kissing from millions and millions of pilgrims.

The Marian title of "El Pilar" is the most venerated throughout Spain, and was the starting point of the great devotion to Our Lady in that country, and subsequently in her territories abroad. It was a Spanish expedition led by Christopher Columbus which discovered the New World and it was not by coincidence that the discovery of the island of El Salvador in the Caribbean was on October 12, 1492, the feast of "El Pilar."

The island was named *San Salvador* after "The Saviour," but among the ships which led the crew to the New World was the flag ship of Columbus, the *Santa Maria*. It may well be said that this was but one more symbolic example of Mary leading us to Jesus, the Saviour.

This is why the Virgin of the Pillar is the Patroness of the Hispanidad, that commonality of language and civilization which links the Spaniards of the Old and New Worlds. As a symbol of religious communion between Spain and the countries of the New World, the flags of all the Spanish-American peoples of the New World can be seen hanging on the walls inside the great basilica in Saragossa. Mary was claiming the New World and in 1900, nearly 400 years after the *Santa Maria* landed in San Salvador, the Virgin was declared Patroness of the Americas, both North and South.

On November 6, 1982, for the first time in history, a Pope went as a pilgrim to the Basilica of *Our Lady of the Pillar* in Saragossa. John Paul II entered the basilica, knelt in front of the pillar and image of Our Lady, kissed it and, as a testimony of his personal devotion to the Virgin, he placed a special and precious Rosary at her feet.

In his homily on that day, he called Saragossa the Marian city of Spain and the Sanctuary of *Our Lady of the Pillar*. He said that on that day he had accomplished a desire which he always had, namely, to prostrate himself as a devoted son of Mary before the sacred pillar. "Spain," he said, "was with good reason called *'La Tierra de Maria.'* I come as the first pilgrim Pope to Pilar, and to place myself under the protection of Our Lady. The pillar and its tradition evoke for you the first steps of the evangelization of Spain... It was what impelled afterwards the transplant of Marian devotion to the New World discovered by Spain."

## CHAPTER 21.

## *The Medjugorje Miracles*

"It is impossible for us not to speak of
what we have seen and heard."

Acts 4:20

Throughout the history of mankind, God has sometimes chosen to manifest His presence by physical signs and miracles so that people will believe. And so, while it is often stressed that the importance of Medjugorje does not lie in the physical signs which are not infrequently seen there, nonetheless, I do believe that these signs are important or else God would not have allowed them. Like in the days of old, they are meant to strengthen our feeble faith.

One of the earliest physical signs in Medjugorje was the appearance of the word *"MIR" (PEACE)* which was seen one evening in large bright letters in the sky above the Cross on Mount Krizevac. This was witnessed by many people, including the priests from the village. It was an important early phenomenon to identify the mission of Our Lady as *Queen of Peace*.

A number of other unusual phenomena have occurred on Krizevac and many people, for example, have seen the Cross change into a bright white column of light. Father Svetozar Kraljevic, a Franciscan priest who served a neighbouring parish at Ljubuski, has testified in one of his books on Medjugorje: "I, who am writing this, have seen the Cross on the hill called Krizevac turn into a beautiful pillar of light, and I swear to this here and now. Many other people, moreover, have seen the same thing."

Yet another miraculous sign of great importance which occurred very early in the history of the apparitions took place on October 28, 1981. On that day a fire of unknown nature broke out on the bushy hill at the site of the first apparition on Podbrdo. It lasted for about fifteen minutes and was seen by several hundred people. At that time the hill was still under guard by the Communist authorities and one guard, who had been stationed at the foot of the hill to prevent the pilgrims from climbing to the top, later investigated the site. The burning bush was brightly lit, yet there was no trace that the fire had burnt the bush. During the evening apparition it is recorded that Mary said to the visionaries: "This is one of the heralds of the great sign (to come)."

I was deeply curious about the significance of this statement and recalled that in his book *St. Mary in the Orthodox Concept*, Father Tatrous Malaty lists some of the titles given to Mary in the Coptic Orthodox Church, and among the many symbols of Mary in the Old Testament is that of the *Burning Bush*. The Roman Church also identifies the *Burning Bush* as a Marian symbol (Dictionary of Mary, Catholic Book Publishing Company).

Mary as the *Burning Bush* relates to Moses' encounter with God at Horeb, the mountain of God (Exodus 3:2-6): "There the angel of Yahweh appeared to him (Moses) in the shape of a flame of fire, coming from the middle of a bush. Moses looked; there was the bush blazing but it was not being burnt up. 'I must go and look at this strange sight,' Moses said, 'and see why the bush is not burnt'... and God called to him from the middle of the bush. *'Come no nearer. Take off your shoes for the place on which you stand is holy ground. I am the God of your father, the God of Abraham, the God of Isaac and the God of Jacob.'* At this Moses covered his face, afraid to look at God." Here once more we see God identifying Himself as the *Covenant God*, the God of the Covenants He made with Abraham, Isaac and Jacob.

Father Malaty also quotes part of the Theotokia or Coptic Orthodox hymns, singing praise to Mary: "The bush which Moses saw in the wilderness was flaming, but the branches were not consumed. It is a type of Mary, the spotless Virgin. The Word of God came and He was incarnated of her but the fire of His divinity did not consume her womb, and she was virgin even after her childbirth." He then recalls the words of St. Ephrem (306-373 AD): "She bore Christ in her virginal womb as the bush on Mount Horeb bore God in its flame."

In his book *The Admirable Heart Of Mary* St. John Eudes also speaks of the *Burning Bush*: "Mary's heart became inflamed with the love of God to such an intensity that this sacred flame would have consumed her corporal life if she had not been miraculously preserved in the midst of such heavenly fervour. It was, therefore, a greater wonder to behold Our Lady living surrounded by heavenly fire, without being annihilated, than to watch the burning bush of Moses in the midst of fire without being consumed." And so, the *burning bush* on the hill of Podbrdo was not only a symbol of Yahweh, the *Covenant God*, but also of the Virgin, the *Ark of the Covenant*.

The visionaries revealed that Our Lady said that the fire which was burning on the hill of Podbrdo is "one of the heralds of the great sign to come," and which will be left on the hill permanently.

At her apparitions in Lourdes when she appeared with a Rosary for the first time, the beads were described by Bernadette as white and the links were golden. More recently, many people have had the links of their own Rosaries turn into a similar golden colour, at first in Medjugorje and then in various parts of the world. I have personally seen several of these Rosaries. In all cases the change in colour has remained permanently. Surely, this must be Mary's stamp of approval of and love for the psalter that is her Rosary.

In the early period of the apparitions, on August 2, 1981, the feast of *Our Lady Queen of the Angels*, some people saw the Sun spinning, then a large heart was seen and under it six small hearts. Hundreds of people have since witnessed diverse solar phenomena in Medjugorje. On my second visit to Medjugorje on October 12, 1987, I myself witnessed an extraordinary phenomenon which defied the laws of science and nature, and as Father Svetozar testified to what he saw on Krizevac, in like manner, I, too, testify to what I saw on that day, the eve of the anniversary of her last apparition in Fatima, when seventy thousand people witnessed the famous miracle of the Sun there in 1917.

I had just returned from Podbrdo hill where Mary first appeared to the visionaries in 1981. It was raining heavily there and I was the only person at the top of the hill. It was the same occasion when I took two photographs of the Cross and the hill as described in Chapter 4. As my clothes were drenched with rain, I did not stay long on the hill and returned to the church after a slow and careful trek down the slippery slope of Podbrdo. At 2:10 p.m., just as I was about to enter the church in my wet clothes, I saw about seven people standing at the right side of the church, looking up at the sky. I approached them just in time to hear one American pilgrim exclaim: "Look at the Sun!" (see p. 156).

It was then that I saw the Sun spinning rapidly and changing colours as it disobeyed all the cosmic laws of nature. Occasionally, the various colours of the Sun would be reflected on the faces and clothes of the spectators of this great miracle. Within three minutes my clothes felt quite dry. On that day, the miracle of the Sun continued for longer than one hour, and we all looked steadily at it for that period of time without hurting our eyes in the slightest. This is not possible under ordinary circumstances as the retina can easily be damaged after a brief period of staring at the Sun.

But as in Fatima, the colours of the Sun on that day were white, gold, red, purple and green, and it changed its colourful coat at varying intervals. However, the most beautiful and dramatic change was to the colour gold, and then all the clouds nearby would also turn into a beautiful golden colour. Whenever that panorama occurred there was a spontaneous shout of joy from the crowd: "Oh, it is all gold now!"

On the other hand, the most frequent change of colour was to green, so much so that one pilgrim said to me: "I wonder what is the significance of the green?" I too wondered. But it was not until several weeks later that it occurred to me that the colours of the Sun, as we saw them that day, were the colours of the veil in front of the *Holy of Holies* containing the ancient *Ark of the Covenant* in the Jewish Temple in Jerusalem (according to Fr. James Meagher in his book *How Christians Said The First Mass*). Significantly, these are now the liturgical colours of the Church — white, gold, red, purple and green!

White is the symbol of purity and triumph. Gold vestments, however, are permitted in place of white for great solemnities, and this undoubtedly accounts for the fact that on her major feast days in Medjugorje, Mary always appears in a beautiful gold robe. Red is the colour of fire and of blood. Accordingly, it is used for Pentecost, marking the Holy Spirit's descent on the apostles in the form of red fiery tongues. Red is also used for feasts commemorating Our Lord's Passion, His Cross and His martyrs. Purple is used during the season of penance and, finally, green is the symbolic colour of hope.

One interpretation could well be that the *Ark of the Covenant* is calling us to turn completely to God and to renew the Covenant with Him; that she is calling us to purity (white), and to the fire of love of God (red); that she is inviting us to do penance (purple) and encouraging us, in the face of all the anxieties and calamities around us, to have hope (green) in her. Alexander Pope (1688-1744) once said: "Hope springs eternal in the human breast." There is one compassionate Woman who the Church addresses in the words of the great eleventh century canticle, the *Salve Regina*. It says: "Hail, holy Queen, Mother of Mercy; hail, our life, our sweetness and our *hope*."

The Virgin comes to Medjugorje as the *Queen of Peace*, and in her lies the world's greatest hope of peace for, as stated in one of Our Lord's messages in Fatima, *"the peace of the world has been entrusted to her."* And so, Medjugorje's *ultimate* message is not one of destruction but of resurrection, not one of war, but of peace. It is not one of despair, but of hope.

That night when I returned to my friend Jozo Vasilj's home, Margaret Leonard, a nurse from Aberdeen, Scotland, and a very close friend of Maria Pavlovic, invited me to accompany her to Podbrdo hill as Marija had told her that Gospa requested the visionaries to meet her on the hill at 10 o'clock that night.

I immediately accepted the invitation, and after dinner we hurriedly set out for the summit of the hill with a small torchlight as our "pillar of fire" to lead us up the dark hill which was without any electricity. When we arrived at the hilltop, the prayer group were already there singing the most beautiful songs in Slavic, while awaiting the arrival of the Virgin. A most gently drizzle fell and the light of the new Moon barely allowed us to see one another.

I brought a special candle about five inches high and three inches wide, with an embossed figure of the Virgin on it. I wedged this candle in a space between two large boulders upon which we sat. Then at about a half hour later, close to the appointed time, the visionaries arose and we followed them some hundred yards away to the foot of the metal Cross, erected at the site of the Virgin's first apparition in Medjugorje on June 24, 1981. It was in front of this Cross that the Virgin appeared.

The apparition lasted for about seven minutes and the forty or so pilgrims on the hill that night stood in reverent silence as the visionaries conversed with the Madonna. Ivan then told us that Our Lady blessed the crowd, was very happy and was accompanied by two angels. She ended her message by asking us to "pray, pray, pray."

As we started our downward trek I suddenly recalled that I had forgotten to remove the candle from between the boulders. However, the night was so dark that it seemed impossible to identify which two of the rocks were our chosen seats. Margaret and I were aimlessly shining the torchlight to the left and right when suddenly out of nowhere a lady appeared in front of us. The darkness of the night was there with her Son wherever the Blessed Sacrament is such that we could not recognize her facial features. "What are you looking for?" she asked in a soft and soothing voice.

I really could not identify any particular accent in her voice. "Oh, just a candle." I whispered, not wishing to involve anyone else in this personal search. "*I* will find it for you," she calmly said. Then she opened the palms of her hands upon which the candle rested. Absolutely astounded, I gently took the candle from her hands and before I could say, "Thank you. How could you have found it?" she disappeared. Margaret, in amazement, then said with great emotion: "Let us pray to decide whether we should leave the candle among the others at the foot of the Cross or take it back to your home." A candle with the embossed figure of the Virgin is now the most precious object in my home.

I have been to Medjugorje seven times, and on several occasions I have been privileged to be asked to be present with the visionaries during the apparitions of the Virgin in the choir loft of the church. They see and speak to her, but words cannot describe the emotion of those moments when one believes that the Mother of God is but an arm's length away!

On one occasion Marija invited me to her home along with Archbishop Philip Hannon of New Orleans, Mary Lou McCall and Wayne Weible. Marija is a most amiable hostess and it was a joyous occasion. We must have been together for about half an hour when she suddenly stopped speaking and after a brief pause, she said: "Gospa is coming." This unexpected announcement was too much for me and I became somewhat nervous.

With a quick rearrangement of the furniture, we all knelt down as Marija walked over to one corner of the room where there was a small statue of Our Lady (Gospa). Within a minute it was obvious to us that a conversation was taking place. It lasted about two minutes, then Marija made the sign of the cross and looked upwards as the Virgin left. I well remember telling Archbishop Hannon that I could not help feeling somewhat apprehensive throughout the whole event. He consoled me: "Don't worry, I too was apprehensive" (see p. 156).

On October 16, 1988, I returned to Medjugorje following a conference on AIDS in San Marino, Italy. That evening my colleague Dr. William Blattner of the National Institutes of Health, Bethesda, Maryland, USA, and I were invited by Fr. Slavko Barbaric to be present with Marija, Ivan and Jacov during the apparition, and later in the night to speak in the Church of St. James during the occasion of the exposition of the Blessed Sacrament. The church was packed to capacity.

The theme of my short talk was on AIDS and that while God hates the sin, He loves the sinner. It was once more on the feast of St. Margaret Mary Alacoque, that privileged nun of the Visitation Order who was chosen by God to reveal to the world the devotion of the Sacred Heart of Jesus. It was an appropriate night for adoration of the Blessed Sacrament.

But the saints have frequently said that Mary is always there with her Son wherever the Blessed Sacrament is exposed, and that she always leads us to Jesus in the Eucharist. She is *Our Lady of the Blessed Sacrament* and the *Tabernacle of the Most High*. That night, after the "adoration" was over, Margaret Leonard who was also in Medjugorje on this occasion, came to me all excited: "There was a strong aroma of roses in the church," she exclaimed. The ancient *Ark of the Covenant* was made of *sweetly-smelling* setim wood, and many pilgrims have sometimes experienced the sweet scent of roses whenever the Virgin appears.

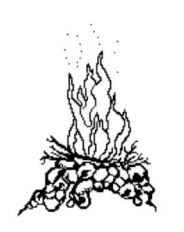

156.

Above: With Wayne Weible, Marija and Archbishop Phillip Hannon at Marija's home (see p. 154)

Left: "Gospa" suddenly appears there (see p. 154)

Right: Witnessing the miracle of the sun in Medjugorje (see p. 151)

## CHAPTER 22.

## *"You Are On Mount Tabor"*

"Jesus took with him Peter and James and
his brother John and led them to a mountain
where they could be alone."

Matthew 17:1

On Krizevac Hill is the great concrete Cross, the symbol of the faith of the people of Medjugorje in the face of an atheistic government. The Cross was so meaningful to the people that they changed the name of the hill from Sipovac (Rose-hip Hill) to Krizevac (Cross Mountain). "Kriz" is the Croatian word for "Cross." It was erected on the top of this huge mountain in 1933 to celebrate the 1900th anniversary of the crucifixion of Our Lord. Since the erection of the Cross, it has been the custom to celebrate Mass there each year on the feast of the Exaltation of the Cross (September 14). Not too far away from the Cross there is a large copper plaque depicting the fifteenth station of the Cross, the Resurrection.

On Krizevac, at about 11:30 p.m. on June 24, 1986, the fifth anniversary of the apparitions, the Virgin appeared and the visionaries relayed her message to the pilgrims who were on the mountain: "You are on Mount Tabor," she said. "Here you receive *blessings, strength* and *love*. Carry these gifts home with you when you go. To each of you a special *blessing*. May you grow in *joy* and in *prayer*, and in the spirit of *reconciliation*."

Researching this message, I was so utterly fascinated by the "Taboric" relevance of her words, especially those which I have highlighted above in italics that, two years later, en route to my first visit to the *Stella Maris* Monastery on Mount Carmel, the site where Elijah lived and prayed, I visited the Church of the Transfiguration on Mount Tabor. It was by sheer coincidence that I arrived in Israel on August 6, the feast of the Transfiguration. It is that great feast which celebrates the divinity and glory of Jesus. It commemorates that great night when Jesus took with Him Peter, James and John, and went up the mountain to *pray*, and as He prayed, His face became resplendent as the Sun and His garments as white as snow (Matthew 17:1-6).

At the Incarnation, Jesus had hidden himself in flesh, and now they saw Him unclad and in His "glory." Moses and Elijah appeared at His side and conversed with Him about the death He was to suffer in Jerusalem and to which He had *reconciled* Himself. Peter was so overcome with *joy* that he exclaimed: "Lord, it is wonderful for us to be here; so let us make three tents, one for you, one for Moses, and one for Elijah." While he was still speaking, a luminous cloud enveloped them, and a voice was heard proceeding from it with these words of *blessing* and *love*: "*This is my beloved son in whom I am well pleased; hear him*" (Matthew 17:1-6).

But what do Moses and Elijah have in common? Elijah was responsible for the renewal of the Covenant by the Israelites on Mount Carmel after the defeat of the worshippers of the pagan god, Baal. Moreover, just as Jesus fasted in the desert for forty days and forty nights, He too walked for forty days and forty nights to Mount Horeb (Sinai), the place where the true God, Yahweh, revealed Himself to Moses and where the old Covenant had been concluded with Moses as the mediator (1 Kings 19:1-14). There, like Moses, Elijah was allowed to see God, and he saw his own mission as that of continuing the work of Moses, namely, the maintenance of fidelity to the Covenant.

It was fitting that those three apostles, who would soon behold Jesus in the depth of His humiliation in Gethsemane, should catch a glimpse of His glorified humanity and of His divinity, so that their faith should be *strengthened* during the trial to follow. Appropriately, the opening prayer of the liturgy of the feast of the Transfiguration reads: "God our Father, in the transfigured glory of Christ, Your Son, you *strengthened* our faith by confirming the witness of your Prophets." Now I completely understood the message of the Virgin on Krizevac that night.

In Medjugorje, millions climb up to Mount Krizevac to pray and to receive *blessings*, *strength* and *love*, to transform their lives and to "reconcile" themselves to God. Each one seeks a personal *transfiguration*. Indeed, a dear friend from Jamaica, May Lowe, once sent me a letter about her pilgrimage to Medjugorje. In it she says: "How wonderful it is to climb Mount Krizevac and then to Podbrdo Hill! Life is a continual mountain climbing. As we ascend with our vision fixed on top of the mountain, a new vista is revealed to us and we seem to encounter God more easily. At the same time, many of our worldly interests become far away. Each climb challenges us to a fuller commitment and a fuller involvement with the Lord. Each time we climb a spiritual mountain, a transformation takes place. We grow and mature spiritually."

However, whereas Our Lady herself has likened Mount Krizevac to Mount Tabor, I see a parallel between the other hill called Podbrdo and Carmel. I see Krizevac as the "Mountain of the Lord," the Cross mountain, and Podbrdo as the "Mountain of Mary," and just as in Israel Tabor is a higher mount than Carmel, so is Krizevac in Medjugorje higher than Podbrdo. Mary first arrived at Podbrdo with the Infant Jesus in her arms, just as ancient tradition relates that she used to visit the hermits of Carmel with the Infant Jesus from her Nazareth home nearby. Carmel is the mount where, after the victory over the worshippers of Baal, Elijah saw the little cloud in the shape of a foot.

The Church has interpreted this cloud as a symbol of the Virgin who was to bring "the water of life" to this arid desert, our world. In Medjugorje, Podbrdo is the mount where the Virgin appears on a little *grey* (not white) cloud. But is it not the *grey* cloud which brings rain? Her beautiful feet were hidden in this little *grey* cloud and it is as though the cloud is her foot. Marian commentators have also seen the little cloud above Mount Carmel as the symbol of the Woman who was to arise immaculate from the sea of humankind to crush Satan beneath her foot.

The Virgin first came to Podbrdo on June 24, 1981, the feast of John the Baptist, the "Elijah who has come already." And so, Mary comes to Podbrdo in the *spirit of Elijah* and in the *spirit of John the Baptist*, calling for prayer, fasting, and conversion, and to urge us to renew the Covenant with God. Like Elijah, this *Ark of the Covenant* is "inviting" us "to take a side." She frequently says in Medjugorje: "Dear Children, I am inviting you to abandon yourselves completely to God."

## CHAPTER 23.

## *"Dear Children"*

**"Come, O children, listen to me."**
**Psalm 34:11**

Mary's messages have a beauty which lies not only in their simplicity and tenderness, but also in their supplication and concern which betray her immense motherly love. In her school of prayer in Medjugorje she always begins her messages, saying: "Dear children," and ends them ever so graciously: "Thank you for your response to my call." I have selected only a few of her weekly and the later monthly messages from April 1, 1984, without interrupting their chronological sequence. These are her words, and as simple as they are, they dwarf a thousand sermons.

"Dear children,"
 "I have chosen this parish in a special way and I wish to lead it. I am guarding it in love and I wish everyone to be mine... This evening I am especially asking you to venerate the Heart of my Son Jesus, and make atonement for the wounds inflicted on His Heart, that Heart which has been offended by all sorts of sins. I continually need your prayers. You may wonder for what are all these prayers. Look around, dear children, and you will see how much ground sin has gained in the world. Therefore, pray that Jesus conquers... Without prayer there can be no peace. Therefore, I say to you, pray at the foot of the Cross for peace... The Cross was in God's plan when you built it. I ask you to read the Bible in your homes everyday. Let it be in a visible place there, so that it always encourages you to read and pray... I call you to renewal of family prayer in your homes. Let prayer take the first place in your family... I want you to open your hearts to God like flowers in spring yearning for the Sun.

"Satan has manifested himself in this parish in a particular way these days, so pray that God's plan is carried out, and that every work of Satan is turned to the glory of God. I love you, and in a special way I have chosen this parish which is dearer to me than all the others where I have gladly been when the Almighty has sent me... I ask you to ask everyone to pray the Rosary. With the Rosary you will overcome all the troubles which Satan is trying to inflict on the Catholic Church. Let all priests say the Rosary. Give time to the Rosary...

"I beg you to put more blessed objects in your homes, and that every one carry blessed objects. Let everything be blessed so that Satan will tempt you less, because you are armed against him... I call you to prayer, especially now when Satan wants to make use of the grapes of your vineyards. Pray that he does not succeed... In particular, live the messages regarding fasting, because your fasting gives me great joy.

"I am tireless, and I call you even when you are far away from my heart. I feel pain for everyone who has gone astray. But I am your Mother and I forgive easily, and I rejoice over every child who comes back to me... I ask you to show me your love by coming to Mass, and the Lord will reward you abundantly... Do not allow Satan to reign in your hearts. Do not be an image of Satan, but my image.

"I am calling you to prayer so that you may be witnesses of my presence. God cannot fulfill His will without you, but He gave everyone a *free will* and it is up to you to be so disposed... Meditate on the Passion of Jesus, and be united with Him in your lives. Dear children, surrender yourselves completely to me so that I can lead you. Do not preoccupy yourselves with material things... Only by prayer are you able to overcome every influence of Satan in your place. I am with you, but I cannot take away your *free will*... Without your prayers, I cannot possibly help you to realize the mission given to me by the Lord for you.

"I want you to understand that this life lasts only a little while when compared to that of heaven; therefore, dear children, decide today anew for God... Today again, I want to invite you to prayer, for when you pray you are so much more beautiful, like flowers which after the snow show all their beauty, and all their colours become indescribable. So also, you, dear children, after prayer, show in God's sight all the beauty which makes you more dear to Him. For this reason, pray and offer your innermost heart to the Lord, so that He may make of you a harmonious and beautiful flower for heaven.  I want to appeal to all of you to start living a new life from today.

"Pray, lest Satan seduces you with his pride and power to deceive... If you pray, he cannot hinder you even in the least, because you are God's children and He keeps an eye on you.  Pray, and may the Rosary be ever in your hands as a sign to Satan that you *belong* to me... I am again inviting you to abandon yourselves completely to God.  You do not realize, dear children, with what great love God loves you.  For that reason He allows me to be with you so that I may instruct you and help you to find the road to peace.

"Never forget that your life is as transitory as a springtime blossom; all beautiful it is today, no trace of it will be visible on the morrow... Fear not, little children, because I am at your side even when you may feel that there is no way out and that Satan is prevailing.  It is peace that I bring you for I am your Mother and the *Queen of Peace*... Know that this peace does not come from you but from God... It is for this peace that I come as your Mother and as *Queen of Peace*.  Today I give you my special blessing, bear it to all Creation that it may know peace.

"I invite you to make yourself open to God.  See how nature makes herself open, yielding life and fruit.  I invite you to do likewise with God.  I call upon you to live the messages I have been giving you over the past eight years.  This is a time of grace... Resolve as from today to consecrate some time each day as a meeting-point, in silence, with God.  Thus you will be enabled, with God on your side, to bear witness to my presence here in Medjugorje.

"Today as never before I call you to pray for peace, for peace in your hearts, peace in your families, and peace in the whole world, because Satan wants war, not peace. He wants to destroy all that is good.  Therefore, dear children, pray, pray, pray.  I intercede before God for each one of you, because each one of you is important in my plan for salvation.  These years I have been calling you to pray, to live what I tell you, but you hardly live my messages.  You talk but do not live.  That is why, dear children, this war is lasting so long.  I love you and wish to protect you from every evil, but you do not desire it.

"I cannot help you if you do not live God's commandments, if you do not live the Mass, if you do not abandon sin. I invite you to become apostles of love and goodness. In this world without peace give witness to God and God's love and God will bless you. Dear children, I invite you now in this time, like never before, to prepare for the coming of Jesus. Thank you for responding to my call."

Words of the Queen herself. Who can put it more succinctly, more tenderly, more lovingly? Who will dare to attempt "to gild refined gold, to paint the lily?"

Chapter 24.

## *Mary In The Old Testamant*
## *The Column of Smoke*

**"The New Testament lies hidden in the Old."**
**St. Augustine**

Ark of the Covenant, Mystical Rose, Tower of David, House of Gold! — all these are but some of the symbols applied to Mary. But another Marian symbol which is not as well known to many Catholic yet well recognized in both the Roman and Eastern Churches, is the title *"Column of smoke."* The *Dictionary of Mary* lists it among other less well known Marian symbols as "The flower of Sharon" (Song 2:1), "The sachet of myrrh" (Song 1:12) and "The best myrrh" (Sirach 24:15).

I, too, was unacquainted with this Marian title and symbol until yet another lesson on Mary in the Old Testament was taught to me through other mystical photographs. Once more the schoolyard was Medjugorje. I was there for the feast of the Exaltation of the Cross on September 14 which is so special to the Croatians of Medjugorje, and on September 13, 1988, having scaled the circular iron railing surrounding her statue in the courtyard of the church, I placed a bouquet of seven roses at the feet of the statue of *Our Lady of Medjugorje*. These beautiful roses were given to me to take to Medjugorje by a medical colleague, Dr. Laverne Lee. She chose seven roses in honour of the feast of the Seven Sorrows of Our Lady, which is celebrated on the day following the feast of the Exaltation of the Cross.

It was a bright sunny day when I took a photograph of the statue of the Madonna. Then, after placing the flowers, I took three other photographs in rapid succession. Once more, when the film was developed certain unusual phenomena were seen. The first photograph showed the statue of *Our Lady of Medjugorje* against the bright and sunny background with the crucifix on the iron railing directly in front of her. The second was a close-up photo of the seven roses at her feet. The third photograph was most unusual in several aspects. Suddenly, the background was no longer bright and sunny. There was a cloudy haze in the sky and a black *column of smoke* with blue tinted edges appeared in front of the upper portion of the statue. In the fourth photograph the black *column of smoke* was fully formed, *leaning* obliquely from above the head of the statue down to the arm of the crucified Christ (see p. 166).

I did not understand the significance of this curious imposition on the photograph and thought that perhaps the carrying-cord of the camera had moved in front of the lens. However, several commentators on the photographs did not favour this interpretation. Nonetheless, should there be a recurrence, and to avoid any possible debate in the future, I cut off the carrying-cord of the camera. I now had, as it were, a bob-tailed camera!

One month later, on October 13, the anniversary of the Virgin's last apparition in Fatima, I was once more in Medjugorje en route to a medical conference in Tanzania, and I climbed Krizevac Hill in the cool, early hours of the morning to spend an hour there. Just as I was about to begin the downhill journey to the home of my host Jozo Vasilj, I took a few photographs of the large concrete Cross and the huge copper plaque nearby, depicting the fifteenth station of the Cross — the resurrected Christ.

What appeared on that print left no doubt that the previous black column seen in front of the statue was not an artifact, for coursing across the arm of the Cross on Mount Krizevac and *leaning* towards the "resurrected Christ" was a similar black *column of smoke* with a blue tint at its edge, this time horizontally not vertically (see p. 167).

Seeking an explanation for this *column of smoke*, I mysteriously experienced an inner call to "go to Francis de Sales." In my home library are several books on St. Francis de Sales (1567-1622), whose shrine in Annecy, France, I had visited on April 8, 1988, when I was participating in a medical seminar there. He was the founder of the Order of the Visitation nuns and because of his scholarship and his writings, he is the patron saint of writers and journalists. The Basilica of the Visitation houses the sacrophagus which contains the body of the saint. His incorrupt heart, however, lies at Travise. I took two photographs of the sacrophagus from different angles and in one photo two pillars of cloud appeared in front of the casket (see p. 168).

Some of the sermons preached by this great Marian Doctor of the Church between 1602 and 1622 were faithfully recorded by his Visitation nuns. Dramatically enough, it was in the first sermon of the first book that I selected from my library, entitled *The Sermons of St. Francis de Sales on Our Lady*, that I found what certainly appeared to be the explanation of the photographic phenomena.

This sermon in the book was given nearly four hundred years ago on the feast of the Assumption, August 15, 1602. He started with a quotation from the *Song of Songs*, betraying his well known predilection for a Marian mystical interpretation of Solomon's *Song of Songs*. It was a quotation of Song 8:5: "Who is this coming up from the desert, flowing with delights, *leaning* upon her Lover?" Later on, he quoted another passage: "Who is this coming up from the desert like a *column of smoke*, perfumed with myrrh and frankincense?" (Song 3:6).

According to the Catholic Encyclopedia, Vol. 7, incense, with its sweet-smelling perfume and high-ascending smoke, is typical of prayer which rises up as a pleasing offering in God's sight. As prescribed by Yahweh Himself, an altar of incense was positioned directly in front of the curtain which separated the *Holy of Holies* containing the sacred *Ark of the Covenant* from the outer court.

Psalm 141:2 also says of incense: "My prayers rise like incense, my hands like the evening sacrifice." In fact, incense is mentioned no less than seventy-five times in the Bible, beginning with the Book of Exodus. Here Yahweh said to Moses: *"...Compound an incense, such a blend as the perfumer might make, salted, pure, and holy. Crush a part of it into a fine powder, and put some of this in front of the Testimony (Ark of the Covenant) in the Tent of Meeting, the place appointed for my meeting with you. You must regard it as most holy... You must hold it to be a holy thing reserved for Yahweh."* (Exodus 30:34-37). Incense is Yahweh's favourite perfume!

With this background, let us now return to Francis de Sales. Following his quotation from the *Song of Songs*, he began his sermon with this account: "The *Ark of the Covenant* had been kept under tents and pavilions for a very long time when the great King Solomon placed it in the rich and magnificent Temple which he had prepared for it (1 Kings 8). The rejoicings in Jerusalem were so great at this time that the blood of the sacrifices flowed in the street, *the air was filled with clouds from so much incense and perfume."*

This, therefore, seems to be the explanation for and interpretation of the cloudy haze of the atmosphere which appeared on the third photograph of *Our Lady of Medjugorje* in the courtyard of the Church of St. James, taken on September 13, 1988. It was meant to be the result of the smoke from the incense burnt in front of the *Ark of the Covenant*.

"But, O God!" St. Francis de Sales continues, "if the reception of that ancient Ark was so solemn, what must we not think to have been that of the new Ark? I speak of the most glorious Virgin Mother of the Son of God on the day of her Assumption. O joy incomprehensible! O feast, full of marvels which makes devout souls, the true daughters of Zion, cry out in admiration: 'Who is this coming up from the desert...?'

"She comes up from the desert of this lower world, but nevertheless, so perfumed with spiritual gifts, that excluding the Person of her Son, heaven has nothing comparable. She comes up like a *column of smoke* laden with myrrh, with frankincense; Who is this, it is asked in the *Song of Songs,* coming up from the desert like a *column of smoke,* laden with myrrh, frankincense and with the perfume of every exotic dust?" (Song 3:6).

Francis de Sales adds: "But let us look at the remainder of the sentence we have chosen for our subject. It says that this holy Lady coming up from the desert flowing with delights, is *leaning* upon her Lover... All the saints do the same, and particularly the Virgin. All her perfections, all her virtues, all her happiness are referred, consecrated and dedicated to the glory of her Son, who is their source, their author and finisher... If you call her a rose because of her most excellent charity, her colour will only be the blood of her Son. If you say that she is a *column of smoke,* sweet and pleasing, say at once that the fire of this smoke is the charity of her Son; the wood is His Cross. In brief, in all and through all, she is leaning upon her Lover."

This, then, appears to be the reason why the blue tinged *columns of smoke* in the photographs were both obliquely positioned. Blue tinged it was, because blue is her colour. They were meant to be symbolic of Mary *leaning* on the arm of her beloved Son. It was a photographic lesson on *Song of Songs* 3:6 and 8:5 for which I am ever so grateful.

Indeed, both the great mystic the Venerable Mary of Agreda and the stigmatist and visionary Anne Catherine Emmerich have seen in their visions that Our Lord accompanied His Blessed Mother when she was bodily assumed into heaven. In the chapter in the *City of God* on the Assumption of the Blessed Virgin, Mary of Agreda wrote: "Christ our Saviour came back up to heaven, and at His right hand the Queen, clothed in the gold of variety, was so beautiful that she was the admiration of the heavenly court. All of them turned toward her to look upon her and bless her with songs of praise. Then were heard those mysterious eulogies recorded by Solomon: 'Who is she that comes from the desert like a column of all the aromatic perfumes? Who is she that rises like the aurora, more beautiful than the moon, bright as the sun, terrible as many serried armies? Who is she that comes up from the desert *resting* upon her Beloved and spreading forth abundant delights?'"

Now, what is little known is that just before the Virgin appeared to the young children on October 13, 1917, in Fatima, a bluish-tinted *column of smoke* was seen above the heads of the visionaries in the dull, grey atmosphere of that rainy day. This phenomenon was witnessed by many people, and is recorded in Francis Johnston's book *Fatima: The Great Sign.*

He quoted the testimony of another scientist, Dr. Joseph Garrett, Professor of Natural Sciences, at Coimbra University in Portugal: "It must have been about half past one when there rose up, on the precise spot where the children were, *a column of smoke, a delicate, slender, bluish column* that went straight up to about two metres and then evaporated. The phenomenon lasted for some seconds and was perfectly visible to the eye... It was repeated yet a second and third time. On these three occasions, and especially on the last one, the slender posts stood out distinctly in the *dull grey atmosphere."* It was the calling card of the Virgin, the column of smoke.

There was yet another imposition of the *column of smoke* in another photograph. This time I was in Jerusalem for the Friday procession on the Via Dolorosa in memory of the "Way of the Cross" on Good Friday. I first took photographs of the crowd assembling in the courtyard of the Fort of Antonio at the first station of the Cross. On the second photograph which showed the start of the procession a prominent *column of smoke* appeared (see p. 169). Was it not a symbol of the Blessed Virgin, the Mother of the Crucified One, who accompanied her Son to Calvary and who started the devotion of the stations of the Cross, as testified by several holy mystics?

Now, Podbrdo (meaning "sub" or "under the hill") is part of the great mountain in Medjugorje called Crnica, and it grows out of it like a hump. In fact, the twin mountain is correctly called Crnica/Podbrdo. The word "Crnica" means "something black" (like smoke), and I immediately recalled the testimony of Dr. Joseph Garrett of Coimbra University, Portugal, about the sign which preceded the appearance of the Virgin of Fatima on October 13, 1917: "There rose up, on the precise spot where the children were, a *pillar of smoke*, a delicate, slender, bluish column that went straight up to about two metres above their heads and then evaporated."

I cannot help but wonder, therefore, if the great sign to be left in Garabandal and Medjugorje may not be the Marian sign, the *burning bush* or the *column of smoke*, or perhaps the *pillar of cloud* by day and the *pillar of fire* by night, which always preceded the *Ark of the Covenant* in the Sinai trek.

170.

Above left: The crucifix on the railing in front of
Our Lady of Medjugorje (see p. 165)
Above right: Statue of Our Lady there on a sunny day
Below left: Note the cloudy change in the photograph. A
column of smoke begins to form (see p. 165)
Below right: The column of smoke leaning on the arm of
her beloved (Song 3:6; 8:5) (see p. 165)

Above: The Cross on Mount Krizevac in Medjugorje (see p. 165)
Below: The column of smoke leaning on the arm of the crucifix (see p. 165)

172.

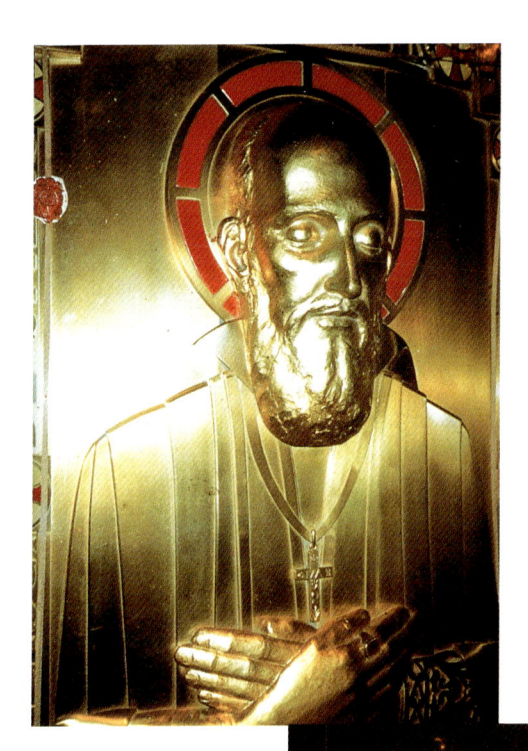

Left : Image of St. Francis de Sales on the lid of his sacrophagus in Annecy, France (see p. 165)

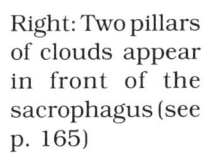

Right: Two pillars of clouds appear in front of the sacrophagus (see p. 165)

173.

Above: The start of the procession in the Via Dolorosa in Jeresalem (see p. 168)
Below: A column of smoke appears on the film in Jerusalem — the symbolic presence of Mary (see p. 168)

## CHAPTER 25.

## *A Brief History of the Copts*

**"We have been living with Christ for more than 1800 years."**

**Archbishop of Asiut**

On my return journey to Trinidad after my second visit to Medjugorje in October 1987, I read a booklet *When Millions Saw Mary* by Francis Johnston. It was an account of the apparitions of the Blessed Virgin Mary in the Coptic Orthodox Church of St. Mary in Zeitun, Egypt.

In Egypt there is a population of about 40 million, predominately Moslem, some ten million are Christians, most of whom are of the Coptic Orthodox faith. Nearly five centuries after the discovery of the New World, the Virgin Mary chose the dome of a Coptic (Egyptian) Orthodox Church in Zeitun, Egypt, to appear over a two year period to crowds of people of all religions.

Now, when the apostles established the Church throughout the ancient world, St. Paul founded the Church of Antioch; St. Peter and St. James the Church of Jerusalem; St. Andrew the Church of Constantinople; and St. Peter and St. Paul the Church of Rome. St. Mark the Evangelist, on the other hand, is the recognized founder and first Patriarch of the Coptic Christians. He entered Egypt around 43 AD, 10 years after the death of Christ, and stayed in Alexandria where he started his mission of evangelization. He was martyred in 68 AD after he had established the Coptic Church, also known as the Church of Alexandria. Presently, His Holiness Pope Shenouda III is the 117th in apostolic succession following St. Mark.

Thus, the Orthodox Church, like the Roman Church, is apostolic and can trace its existence historically through the ordination of bishops directly back to the apostles, and through them to Christ. This is called "Apostolic Succession." Obviously, not all Churches are apostolic.

In 451 AD, at the Council of Chalcedon, the See of Alexandria suffered a great defeat. According to Timothy Ware (Bishop Kallistos of Diokleia): "Chalcedon was more than a defeat for Alexandrian theology: it was a defeat for Alexandrian claims to rank supreme in the East. The Copts maintained that in Christ there was not only a unity of person but a single nature (Monophysitism). The Council reacted strongly against Monophysite terminology and stated that while Christ is one person, there is in Him, not one nature but two. Following this defeat, the See of Alexandria separated from the other Churches and the Patriarch of Alexandria became the Coptic Pope and continues to bear this title to this day. However, according to Timothy Ware, "one must conclude that... there is an ambiguity of concept and an underdeveloped terminology rather than a factual error in the Coptic teaching of one nature in Christ."

Professor Aziz Atiya, Professor of history in the University of Utah, U.S.A., in the introduction to his booklet *The Copts and Christian Civilization*, opens his treatise with this paragraph: "The Copts occasionally have been described as a schismatic eastern Christian minority, a lonely community in the land of their forebears. They have been forgotten since they chose to live in oblivion after the tragedy of Chalcedon (451 AD)... Though they were not unknown to medieval and early modern travellers from Europe, western Christianity appears to have lost sight of the Copts until 1860 when a Presbyterian mission came to convert them to Christianity. The Coptic Archbishop of Asiut asked them a rhetorical question: 'We have been living with Christ for more than 1800 years. How long have you been living with Him?'"

It was in 1054 that the "great schism" in the Christian Church took place. The main body of Christians then became divided into two communions; in western Europe, the Roman Catholic Church under the Pope of Rome; in the Byzantine Empire, the Orthodox Church of the East. Nonetheless, the Orthodox Church still believes that among the five Patriarchs a special place belongs to the Pope in Rome. But while Orthodoxy does not deny to the Holy and Apostolic See of Rome a *primacy of honour*, to Orthodoxy it is a 'primacy,' not a 'supremacy.' Moreover, while the Pope of Rome claimed infallibility on doctrinal matters, the Greeks held that in matters of faith the final decision rested not with the Pope alone, but with a Council representing all the bishops of the Church.

The second great difficulty was the so-called *filioque*. This dispute revolved around the words about the Holy Spirit in the Nicene-Constantinople Creed, composed by the Coptic Athanasius, the great Alexandrian theologian. Originally, the Creed read: "I believe... in the Holy Spirit, the Lord, the Giver of Life who *proceeds from the Father*..." This, the original form, is recited unchanged by the Eastern Church to this day. But the West inserted an extra phrase 'and the Son' (in Latin, *filioque*), so that its Creed now reads: "I believe... in the Holy Spirit who proceeds from the Father and the Son."

According to Ware, besides these two major issues, the Papacy and the *filioque*, there were certain lesser matters of Church worship and discipline which caused trouble between East and West. For example, the Greeks allowed married clergy while the Latins insisted on priestly celibacy; they had different rules of fasting and the Greeks used leavened bread in the Eucharist while the Latins insisted on unleavened bread.

In recent years an attempt to heal the Chalcedonian rift of 451 AD between Rome and the See of Alexandria was initiated when in a Common Declaration issued at the Vatican and dated May 10, 1973, Pope Paul VI and Pope Shenouda III sidestepped the age-old difficulty by declaring a common belief in the humanity and divinity of Jesus Christ: "We have, to a large degree, the same understanding of the Church founded upon the Apostles!"

According to Francis Johnston, two years later Cardinal Krol of Philadelphia, former president of the National Conference of Catholic Bishops in America, visited Pope Shenouda III in Egypt and declared that the Coptic Patriarch might be the key pivotal figure to bring about Christian reunion in this time of godlessness and secularism. The Cardinal declared: "We cannot afford these divisions among Christians, and I pray that Pope Shenouda, under the guidance of the Holy Spirit, will be the person to reverse this 15-century division between the Coptic Orthodox and Roman Catholic Churches." He then added: "The root causes of the religious divisions in the 5th century were political and personal."

Relations between the Coptic Orthodox Church and Rome were further enhanced by the return of the major part of St. Mark's relics by Pope Paul VI from Venice to Egypt. These were then enshrined in a crypt beneath the high altar of the new Coptic Orthodox Cathedral of St. Mark in Abbasia, Cairo. It seems that the stage was set for this act of fraternal charity by the extraordinary apparitions of the Mother of God at Zeitun in 1968.

In May 1973, two years after the end of the apparitions, His Holiness Pope Shenouda III was invited to Rome by Pope Paul VI. This historic event was the first meeting of these two bishops, the Bishop of Rome and the Bishop of Alexandria, which had taken place in 1600 years. They celebrated the anniversary of St. Athanasius, the 20th Pope of the See of Alexandria, and during this visit Pope Shenouda told Pope Paul all about the visit of the Holy Virgin Mary to Zeitun in 1968 —1971.

*Mark*

## CHAPTER 26.

## *Mary Returns To Egypt*

**"Out of Egypt have I called my son."**
**Matthew 2:15**

Soon after the birth of Jesus, Mary and Joseph had to flee to Egypt to save Jesus' life from the hands of King Herod, and so Egypt played an important role in the lives of the Holy Family. Now, at the intersection of Tumanbay Street and Khalil Lane in Zeitun, in a suburb of Cairo, there is a small Coptic Orthodox church. It is called St. Mary's Church, in honour of the Blessed Virgin (see p. 183). Khalil Lane is named after the Khalil Ibrahim family, known to be very devout Copts.

It is said that the Virgin Mary appeared in a dream to a wealthy member of the family at the end of World War I in 1918. She asked him to build a church in her honour on a piece of land which he owned, and that in *fifty years* she would bless the church in a special way. In obedience to this vision, the church was built and completed in 1924.

Zeitun borders on the vicinity which was once a part of ancient Heliopolis, and tradition has it that St. Mary's Church lies close to the route taken by the Holy Family during their flight from Herod into Egypt. The first apparition of Mary occurred on the night of Thursday, April 2, 1968, at 8:30 p.m. She was first seen by a group of Moslem workmen opposite the church, appearing as a luminous being, dressed in a shimmering robe of light, and her radiance was so intense that it was almost impossible to discern her features. She was *kneeling* beside the Cross at the top of the dome of the church. This was most spectacular because the dome has a round smooth sloping surface and no human being would dare stand on it, yet the luminous figure was seen moving and walking on the dome (see p. 183).

One of the workmen, Farouk Mohammed Atwa, had a gangrenous finger which was scheduled for amputation the following day. He was startled at what he saw and leapt from his chair, pointing his bandaged finger to the lady on the dome: "Lady, don't jump!" But as she rose, several women on the street cried out loudly: "Our Lady, Mary!" The next morning when Farouk Atwa arrived at the hospital for his operation, the surgeon was astonished to find that the finger was completely healed. It was the first of many healings that followed.

As Francis Johnston in his booklet *When Millions Saw Mary* acknowledged: "Pearl Zaki has devoted her life to spreading the story of this sublime event and has earned the blessings of Pope Paul VI and Pope Shenouda III for her indefatigable apostolate. Her book *Our Lord's Mother Visits Egypt* is the best researched literature on the apparitions." She reported that on many occasions the Blessed Virgin was seen *bowing* to the vast crowds down below. His Excellency Anba Athanasius, the Bishop of the Beni-souef Diocese, testified that he personally saw the apparition walking on the dome, sometimes moving her hands as she blessed the crowds, and sometimes *bowing* her head repeatedly. Frequently she would hold out an olive branch to the multitudes which then evoked a loud cry of ecstatic joy from the crowds. Incidentally, the Arabic word Zeitun means "olives."

The apparitions, which took place at night between April 2, 1968, and May 2, 1971, rank among the most astounding manifestations of the supernatural in modern times, yet they were hardly publicized in the West. However, soon after the apparitions began, news of the extraordinary phenomena spread like wildfire across Egypt, attracting immense crowds of Moslems, Christians and Jews to Zeitun. Within a few weeks the crowds reached an estimated 250,000 nightly, resulting in traffic congestions of unusual proportions in Cairo. Great numbers of Moslems were frequently seen kneeling on their prayer mats, reciting verses from the Koran in praise of Mary. Other Moslems would pray in unison with Catholics, Copts and Protestants. They were rare events in history when Christians and Moslems prayed together in such large numbers.

Her visits were twice or three times weekly, but the time of her appearance was always unpredictable, however, she did appear more frequently on her feast days or the eves of them. There are thirty-two feast days in the Coptic Calendar in honour of the Holy Virgin, and on the eve of the feast of the Assumption in 1968, the first year of her apparitions, she was seen for ten minutes over the church "as bright as a million Suns."

Notably, it was at the Assumption of the Blessed Virgin that this living *Ark of the Covenant* was taken up to heaven by her Son. John speaks about this glorious event: "And the sanctuary of God in heaven opened, and the *ark of the covenant* could be seen inside it... Now a great sign appeared in heaven: *a woman clothed with the sun*, standing on the moon and with twelve stars on her head for a crown" (Rev. 11:19, 12:1).

Incense was always burnt in front of the ancient Ark, and so, it was quite significant that a frequent accompaniment of the Virgin's apparitions in Egypt was a fragrance of *incense*, described by one of the bishops as "a fragrance so great as if from a million incensors." In fact, the smoke of incense frequently poured out of the domes of the church in large quantities.

Another enthralling phenomenon was the appearance of luminous white doves which flew and vanished suddenly, either before the Virgin appeared, accompanying her, or after she had disappeared. Whenever they appeared they were always in a certain formation and would disappear and reappear in the same formation. For example, sometimes there were three in the form of a triangle or seven in the formation of a cross. The triangle is a symbol of the Trinity. The Cross is a symbol of the crucified Christ, both of which Moslems deny.

Computer enhancement studies have been done by scientists on some of the photographs capturing all these phenomena and they were declared to be free of "trickery." It is not without some justification, therefore, that Bishop Gregorius, Prelate for Higher Studies, Coptic Culture and Scientific Research, has remarked: "The events (in Zeitun) have no equal in the past, neither in the East nor in the West." However, while the Egyptian newspapers, *The Egyptial Gazette*, *Al Ahran*, *Wantani*, *Al-Akhbar* and *Al Goumhouryia* headlined the apparitions, only a few overseas newspapers carried the events. Among them were *The Times* (May 6, 1968), *Le Figaro* of Paris (May 5), and *The New York Times* (May 5). You may well ask: "Who controls the press?"

On May 5, 1968, just one month after the beginning of the apparitions, the Coptic Pope Kyrillos VI issued a Papal statement authenticating that it was truly the Virgin Mother Mary, Mother of God, who was appearing there. He firmly believed that Mary came because she had found refuge in

Egypt with her Son Jesus and Joseph. The statement of Pope Kyrillos VI was followed by one from His Eminence Cardinal Stephanos I, Patriarch of the Catholic Copts, who are in union with Rome: "It is undoubtedly a real apparition, confirmed by many Coptic Catholic members of the highest integrity and reliability."

That she never spoke a word after nearly two years of her manifestations in Zeitun, is unique in the history of Marian apparitions. What then was the reason for her silence? Quoting Fr. Jerome Palmer, Pearl Zaki in her book wrote: "One can only speculate on the reason for this silence. Some see in it the necessary means of avoiding friction among the various classes witnessing the apparition. If Our Lady were to declare herself as "Mother of God," the Moslems, who do not regard Christ as God, would no longer be interested. If she referred to herself, as she did at Lourdes, as the "Immaculate Conception," the Copts, who believe that Mary was sanctified only at the time of the Annunciation (and not at birth), would possibly reject the visions as not authentic. Whatever message Our Lady has brought can be read in her silent gesture of holding out the olive branch, of kneeling at the Cross and of blessing and encouraging her people in their bitter struggle with poverty and war."

Now, Islam teaches that Mary is the "Immaculate," that Jesus was miraculously born of the Virgin Mary, and that God chose Mary, purified her and raised her above all other women of the world (Koran 3:42,43). The Koran also teaches that Mary remained a virgin. Indeed, the Koran (Penguin Classics) actually ends with these words: "But to the faithful Allah has set an example in Pharoah's wife... And in Mary, Imram's daughter, who preserved her chastity and into whose womb We breathed of Our spirit; who put her trust in the words of her Lord and His scriptures and was truly devout" (Koran 66:12).

However, Islam also teaches that Jesus was not the Son of God, and was never crucified, thus denying the Resurrection. According to Islam, it was the intention of His enemies to put Him to death on the Cross but God saved Him from their plot. Someone else took His place.

The Koranic text states: "And because of their saying: 'We slew the Messiah Jesus, Son of Mary, Allah's Messenger.' They slew him not, nor crucified him, but it appeared so unto them; and behold!... those who disagree concerning it are in doubt thereof; they have no knowledge thereof save pursuit of a conjecture; they slew him not for certain. But God took him up unto Himself. God is ever Mighty, Wise" (Koran 4:157-158).

Now, Chapter 3 in the Koran reads: "O Mary, worship the Lord devoutly; prostrate thyself and bow down in prayer with those who bow..." Significantly, in her book *Our Lord's Mother Visits Egypt*, Pearl Zaki records that Mary was seen on many occasions *prostrate* before the *Cross* or with her hands held in *prayer*. Indeed, from the first moment she was seen, she was *kneeling* and *worshipping the Lord devoutly* and *bowing down* in prayer with those of the Moslem faith who were bowing down below on their prayer mats!

It should seem obvious to all, therefore, that the Virgin would not prostrate herself before a mere cross, and that she was prostrating herself before the symbol of *"the Lord on the Cross."* At the same time it was also the enactment of the Judeo-Christian Psalm 95:6: "Come in, let us *bow, prostrate* ourselves, and *kneel* in front of the *Lord our Maker*, for this is our God." Could it not be said that her actions never spoke so loudly?

But she did actually speak in Egypt. However, it was not during her apparitions to the multitudes, but privately to a single individual. Francis Johnston quoted this event in his book. He said that an Anglican correspondent, Ronald Bullivant, writing in the Spring 1970 edition of the *Eastern Churches Review*, gave a graphic account of his visit to Zeitun the previous year. He was taken to the house of one of the leading Moslems in the district adjacent to the church. Initially, this man was very antagonistic and attacked the pilgrims who had to pass close to his house. He would throw stones at them and call on the police to have them arrested.

Mr. Bullivant testified that the Virgin appeared to the man and asked why he behaved in this way. She begged him not to continue in this fashion and commanded him to paint *the sign of the Cross* on his house. Although remaining a practicing Moslem, he then became convinced of the authenticity of the visions and forty huge white crosses were painted all around the walls of his house. This is of such importance that it should behoove unbelievers and skeptics to research this testimony of Mr. Bullivant. If confirmed to be true, then, she certainly has never spoken so loudly.

183.

Above: The Church of St. Mary in Zeitun, Egypt (see p. 178)
Below: An Egyptian newspaper photograph of the illuminated silhouette of Our Lady on the dome of the church.
A dove-like figure appears above her (see p. 178)

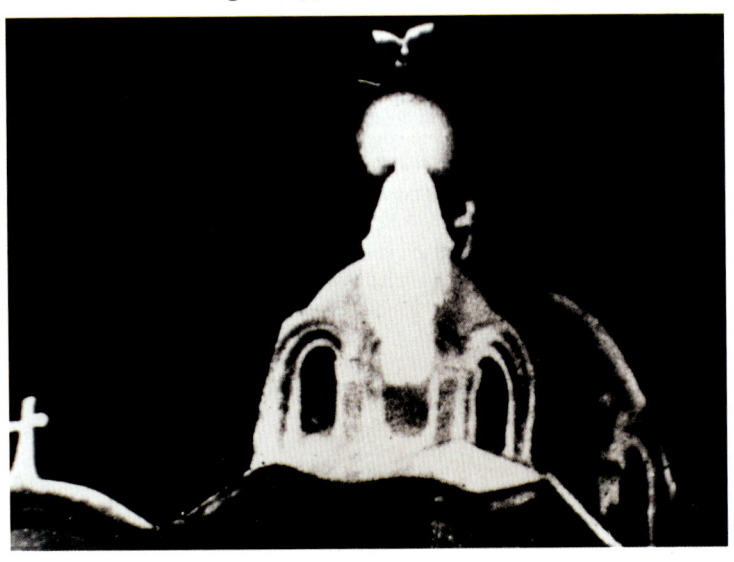

CHAPTER 27.

## *The Ark and the Shekinah in Egypt*

**"The Lord in the pillar of fire and cloud looked down upon the Egyptian army."**
**Exodus 14:24**

Fr. Slavko Barbaric and the visionary of Medjugorje, Marija Pavlovic, once gave me a photograph taken on December 7, 1987, by a Canadian pilgrim from Quebec. It was a photograph of a rose growing out of a stone wall in a house in Medjugorje at a time of year when roses do not bloom, reminiscent of the miracle of the roses in Guadalupe. In the centre of this red rose was the beautiful face of a lady with a veil on her head. This is one of Fr. Slavko's favourite photographs, depicting one of the symbols of Mary — the Mystical Rose.

However, one of the earliest symbols which I received was a prominent white pillar which appeared on a photograph of Podbrdo Hill. At that time I did not appreciate its biblical significance until I received another similar imposition on one of my films taken in Egypt. It all began on my return flight home after my second visit to Medjugorje in October 1987, when I read *When Millions Saw Mary*.

I was so impressed with the testimony in the book that I had a strong urge to visit the church where these apparitions took place. By a most unusual coincidence, when I returned to my office on the following day, among the many letters on my desk was an invitation from the Egyptian Medical Society to participate in a medical conference on AIDS in Cairo three months later. I immediately accepted the invitation.

I arrived in Cairo on March 2, 1988, and on March 4, I visited the Coptic Orthodox Church of St. Mary in Zeitun. By yet another coincidence, the present Coptic Pope, His

Holiness Pope Shenouda III, was visiting the church that morning and I was privileged to have a long audience with him during which he confirmed the authenticity of the apparitions which he personally witnessed (see p. 188).

On March 5, 1988, I attended evening Mass in the Armenian Church of the Annunciation in Cairo (see p. 188). It was an Armenian Church "in union with Rome" and the service was very similar to the Latin Rite. Significantly, the small congregation was reciting the Rosary before Mass. At the end of the Mass, at about 7 p.m., I was attracted by a beautiful arch and two pillars which were at the entrance of an alcove or tabernacle, containing a statue of Our Lady close to the vestibule of the church. It was the traditional statue of *Our Lady of Lourdes* with the inscription above her head: "I am the Immaculate Conception" (see p. 189).

I took a few quick photographs with a small automatic camera and the roll of film was developed in London two days later. It was then that I saw something remarkable on two of the photographs. However, it was the Jesuit theologian and well-known apostle of Medjugorje, Fr. Richard Foley of Farm Street Church in London, who first interpreted the unusual phenomena which were seen on the photographs. Independently, this same interpretation was repeated by His Grace the Archbishop of Port-of-Spain, Anthony Pantin, when I returned to Trinidad two days later.

In the first photograph the statue of Our Lady was seen to be centrally placed in the tabernacle, but with only the left pillar at the entrance to the tabernacle in view. At the top right-hand corner there was what appeared to be a little cloud. However, in the second photograph, the pillar on the right side now "descended," as it were, totally covered with a white cloud, the upper portion of which *leaned* towards "the Immaculate Conception" (see p. 189).

"My dear Courtenay," Fr. Foley exclaimed in discernment and appreciation of the photographs, "This is a symbol of the *Shekinah*, the divine Presence! It is in Exodus 33:9." It relates that whenever the people of Israel set up camp, Moses would take the sacred Tent and put it up some distance from the camp. It was called the Tent of the Lord's presence (containing the *Ark of the Covenant*), and anyone who wanted to consult the Lord would go out to it. Whenever Moses went out there, the people would stand at the door of their tents and watch Moses until he entered it. After Moses had gone in, the *pillar of cloud* would come down and stay at the door of the Tent, and the Lord would speak to Moses from the cloud.

It was interpreted, therefore, that what the photograph depicted and symbolized, was the *pillar of cloud* in front of the image of the living *Ark of the Covenant* in the tabernacle or tent. In addition, the photograph showed the cloud *leaning* towards Mary and was also interpreted as the *Shekinah leaning* affectionately towards His dove, just as the *column of smoke* was seen to *lean* towards Christ on the Cross as previously described in Chapter 24. These unusual photographs were taken in the Church of the Annunciation. It was at the Annunciation, and immediately following her consent, that Mary conceived and became the *Ark of the Covenant*.

Now, whereas the feast of the Annunciation celebrates the beginning of Mary's Motherhood, the great feast of the Assumption celebrates the end of her earthly sojourn in this "desert" and her bodily assumption into heaven. During the week preceding this feast on August 15 of that same year, I felt a profound call to be in Medjugorje for that great occasion. The Marian Year which began on the feast of the Annunciation on March 25, 1987, was due to end on that August 15. My busy schedule at that time only allowed me to be able to stay in Medjugorje for one full day.

I arrived in Medjugorje on the evening of August 14, and at 4 p.m. on the feast day, to my surprise, I was invited by Fr. Slavko Barbaric to be with the visionaries, Marija, Ivan, and Jakov for the apparition in the church at 5.40 p.m. At the appointed time, the visionaries walked over to the corner of the choir loft where the apparitions took place, and after a short prayer they suddenly knelt down in unison. She had appeared.

There was an indescribable sense of awe and excitement. Her psalter, the Rosary, was being loudly recited with great devotion by the large congregation downstairs in the church, and as the visionaries knelt facing the wall upon which hung a canvas painting of *Our Lady of Medjugorje*, I silently asked the Madonna: "I know I am not allowed to see you, but I wonder if you would be so kind as to show me, as you did in Egypt, the *pillar of cloud* in front of you." I then quickly took four photographs of the hallowed corner where she was standing.

The apparition lasted for about five minutes and it was an unforgettable experience and a great privilege to be so close to the invisible (to me) Queen on that day of her great feast. Immediately afterwards Drew Mariani, who was also invited to be in the choir loft that day, interviewed me for his famous videos *Transforming Your Heart* and *Marian Apparitions of the 20th Century*.

I started my long return journey to Trinidad on the following day. This time the roll of film was developed in Trinidad. All the thirty-plus photographs which were taken of various scenes in Medjugorje developed as expected. However, on the photograph taken in the choir loft at the time of the apparition, a *pillar of cloud* which was obviously not on the original painting of *Our Lady of Medjugorje* appeared in front of the image of the Madonna (see p. 190).

In Egypt the photographic symbol of the *pillar of cloud* in front of the new *Ark of the Covenant* was seen in photographs taken in the Church of the Annunciation, the church in honour of the moment when she became the living *Ark of the Covenant*. This last photographic repetition of the *pillar of cloud* on her image occurred on the feast which celebrates the end of her sojourn on earth and the assumption of the Ark into heaven. The Book of Revelations records her presence in heaven: "Then the sanctuary of God in heaven opened, and the *ark of the Covenant* could be seen inside it... Now a great sign appeared in heaven: a woman adorned with the sun, standing on the moon, and with twelve stars on her head for a crown" (Rev. 11: 19, 12: 1).

Above: His Holiness Pope Shenouda III and Hegomenos
Boutross Gayed, Rector of the Church of St. Mary of Zeitun
(see p. 185)
Below: A painting of the Annunciation in the Armenian Church
of the Annunciation in Cairo, Egypt (see p. 185)

A statue of Our Lady of Lourdes in the Church of the Annunciation (see p. 185)

A pillar of cloud appears in front of the "Ark," leaning towards her (see p. 185)

190.

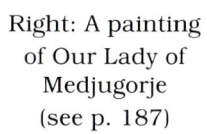

Right: A painting of Our Lady of Medjugorje (see p. 187)

Below: Note the pillar of cloud on the painting in the photograph taken when Our Lady appeared.

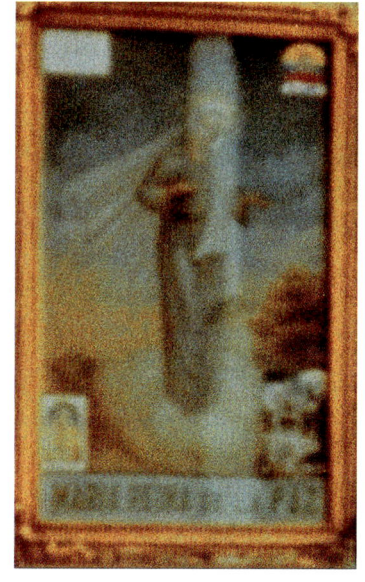

## CHAPTER 28.

## Guadalupe: The Year Was 1531

"Am I not here? I who am your Mother...
Am I not of your kind?"
The Virgin of Guadalupe

The statue of *Our Lady of Lourdes* in the Church of the Annunciation in Cairo bore the inscription "I am the Immaculate Conception" above her head, but it was in Mexico that she first acknowledged that title in a subtle way.

It was Good Friday in the year 1519 when the great Spanish explorer Hernán Cortés stepped ashore on a beach near present-day Vera Cruz. He would soon discover cities larger than any in Spain, volcanoes reaching into the clouds, armies so vast that they stretched out of sight, and bloody rituals of human sacrifice.

Pagan worship was the central element of Aztec life and there were many deities, most of whom represented aspects of nature. Human sacrifice was one of the main religious expressions of the Aztecs, and the killings were on a considerable scale, sometimes reaching thousands in a single day. The sacrifices were carried out on the top of huge stone temples and an almost universal symbol of the Mexican religion was the serpent. As Warren H. Carroll said in his book *Our Lady of Guadalupe and the Conquest of Darkness*: "Nowhere in history has Satan so formalized and institutionalized his worship with so many of his own actual titles and symbols."

The mightiest god was Quetzelcoatl, the feathered or stone serpent, and the temple of the great mother god Tonantzin stood on the summit of a small hill called Tepeyac. Tearing out the hearts of living victims was a common form of sacrifice and in the library records of Mexico of 1487, it is recorded that in the most spectacular sacrificial display ever seen in the Aztec capital Tenochtitlan (later Mexico City), twenty thousand people lost their hearts to Huitzilopochtli, the war god.

This was the environment in which Cortés and his men found themselves. Cortés had two banner standards made for his expedition to Mexico, with the royal arms of Spain on one side and a Cross on the other. In Trinidad he picked up many new recruits and then gathered more men and supplies in Havana. After many violent battles the Mexican empire began to fall to the Spanish conquerors in 1521. In 1523 an evangelical team of Franciscan friars left Spain to found a Christian mission in Mexico, however, the deep-rooted traditions of paganism was hard to eradicate and conversions to Christianity were few. Enter the Virgin Mary! It was twelve years after the landing of Cortés. The year was 1531.

"Know for certain, dearest of my sons, that I am the perfect and perpetual Virgin Mary, Mother of the True God, through whom everything lives, the Lord of all things who is Master of heaven and earth. I ardently desire a temple to be built here for me where I will show and offer all my love, my compassion, my help and my protection to the people.

"I am your merciful Mother, the Mother of all who live united in this land, and of all mankind, and of all those who love me, of those who cry to me, of those who have confidence in me. Here, I will hear their weeping and their sorrows and will remedy and alleviate their sufferings, necessities and misfortunes. Therefore, in order to realize my intentions, go to the house of the Bishop of Mexico City and tell him that I sent you and that it is my desire to have a temple built here. Tell him all that you have seen and heard."

These were the words of the Virgin Mary on Tepeyac Hill to a humble Aztec Indian, Juan Diego, who was recently converted to Christianity by the Franciscan evangelists in Mexico. What he saw was a most beautiful young woman clothed in a light *brighter than the Sun*, and dressed in the robes of a royal Aztec princess (see p. 197). It was the beginning of the most extraordinary events of Marian apparitions, and occurred in Guadalupe, Mexico on December 9, 1531. It was at that time the feast of *the Immaculate Conception*, and it was the first of four apparitions of Mary in Mexico between December 7 and December 12, 1531.

Juan Diego nervously relayed the message to Bishop Zumarraga who, understandably so, was incredulous of the story and requested him to ask the apparition for a sign to prove her authenticity. On Tuesday, December 12, the Virgin said to Juan Diego: "Listen and be sure, my dear son, that I will protect you; do not be frightened or grieved, or let your heart be troubled... Am I not here?... I who am your Mother, and is not my help a refuge? *Am I not of your kind?*"

The Virgin then told him: "Climb to the summit of Tepeyac, to the spot where you saw me previously. There you will find many flowers growing. Gather them carefully, assemble them together and bring them back and show me what you have." On reaching the hill he was amazed to find a profusion of flowers, including Castilian roses which were neither grown nor known in Mexico at that time. Not only were they blooming out of season, but it would be quite impossible for flowers to grow on such a stony terrain. Spreading out his tilma like an apron, he filled it with the colourful flowers and ran down the hill to where the Lady was waiting for him. When he showed her the colourful heap of flowers, with her own hands she rearranged them carefully inside his tilma before he journeyed to the bishop.

When he saw the flowers, the bishop could not believe his eyes. But he was more awe-stricken when another phenomenon was seen inside the tilma of Juan Diego. Miraculously painted on the inside of his tilma was the image of *Our Lady of Guadalupe*. This was the beginning of the greatest mass conversions in religious history. In a few years nine million Aztec Indians were converted to Christianity.

The image of *Our Lady of Guadalupe* on the tilma of Juan Diego remains one of the greatest Marian miracles in history. To the Aztec indians, the image was much more than a mere portrait. It was a pictograph which they were able to read and understand. The Lady stood in front of the Sun and this signified to them that she was greater than the dreaded Sun-god Huitzilopochtli. Her foot rested on a crescent Moon which signified one of their foremost deities, Coyolxauhqui, the goddess of the Moon. This was a sign that God had given her power over all of nature. The blue-green hue of her mantle was the colour worn by Aztec royalty; therefore, she was a Queen.

The stars strewn across her mantle told them that she was greater than the stars of heaven which they also worshipped as gods. Yet she could not be a god since her hands were joined in prayer, her head bowed in reverence, clearly to One greater than herself. The black Cross on the gold brooch on her neck was identical to the Cross on the banners and helmets of the Spanish conquerors, telling them that her religion was that of their conquerors. The sash around her waist with tassels signified that she was pregnant, and her right foot stood on the head of a serpent. She was mightier than the dreaded serpent god!

This miraculous image is there in the Basilica of *Our Lady of Guadalupe* in Mexico for all to see (see pp. 197-8), skeptics as well as believers. Scientists too have seen and have remained silent, being unable to offer any scientific explanation for its existence. The image is a painting on a tilma made of fibers from the maguey cactus which is known to disintegrate after twenty years, yet this image is as new as ever for over 460 years. For more than a century the image hung above an altar with no protection whatsoever. It was also exposed to the smoke from thousands of votive candles placed under it and in spite of this it shows no damage over the years.

On November 14, 1921, a bomb which was concealed in a bouquet of flowers placed under the sacred image, exploded during Mass. The force of the explosion twisted a heavy metal Cross on the altar into a semi-circular shape, but the sacred and beautiful image of *Our Lady of Guadalupe* was miraculously untouched.

The hypothesis that the sacred image is simply a painting was discredited in 1946 when a microscopic examination surprisingly revealed that there were no brush strokes. Further studies revealed other inexplicable qualities. For example, the colours used for the image are of unknown origin for they are neither animal, vegetable nor mineral dyes as known on this earth. Then, in May 1979 two American scientists, Professor Philip Callahan of the University of Florida and Professor Joddy Smith of Pensacola, Florida, took infra-red photographs to study the image: "I am interested in doing what William James said a hundred years ago — to bring together religion and science," stated Professor Smith. These infra-red photographs showed that the image was made without any underdrawing sketch, an essential first step for portraits made during that era.

In recent years over twenty scientists have looked at the eyes of the image under high magnification. Dr. Enrique Graue, Director of the Ophthalmology Hospital, Nuestra Señora de la Luz, in Mexico City had this to say: "I was dumbfounded. The eyes displayed depth and curvature and reflected light exactly like living eyes. In the eyes of the image were reflected twelve people who were present in the courtyard on the day Juan Diego opened his cloak, and the amazing fact is that the same figures appeared in both eyes at precisely the positions expected by the law of optics and twin-eyed physiology."

Under high magnification the image also shows no detectable signs of cracking — an inexplicable occurrence after 450 years of existence. "It may seem strange for a scientist to say this," concluded Professor Callahan, "but studying the image was the most moving experience of my life. Just getting that close, I got the same strange feeling that others did, who worked on the Shroud of Turin... I believe in logical explanations up to a point, but there is no logical explanation for life. You can break life down into atoms but what comes after that? Even Einstein said — God!"

On April 25, 1754, Pope Benedict XIV issued a bull approving *Our Lady of Guadalupe* as Patroness of Mexico, and on Saturday, October 12, 1887, almost the entire population of Mexico City seemed to have assembled in the vicinity of Guadalupe for the solemn occasion of the coronation of the sacred image.

In his sermon on that joyous occasion, the bishop of Yucatan said: "In choosing the Mexicans as a people Our Lady constituted herself as Empress and Patroness of America. O happy America! O fortunate West Indies! O blessed Mexico!" Finally, in 1900, the beginning of the twentieth Century, *Our Lady of Guadalupe* was proclaimed Patroness of the Americas, both North and South. Mary chose Guadalupe as the site of her first apparition in the New World, and so it was proper protocol for Pope John Paul II to choose Guadalupe for the first pilgrimage of this pilgrim Pope.

She appeared as the Woman clothed with the Sun, standing on the Moon and her right foot crushed the serpent's head. She was pregnant. This was certainly the Woman of the Apocalypse: "Then the sanctuary of God in heaven opened and *ark of the covenant* could be seen inside it... Now a great sign appeared in heaven: a woman, adorned with the sun, standing on the moon, and with the twelve stars on her head for a crown. She was pregnant, and in labour, crying aloud in the pangs of childbirth." (Rev. 11:19; 12:1-2). That Woman of the Apocalypse is also the Woman of Genesis 3:15 and the *Ark of the Covenant*.

It was not until December 8, 1992, that I joined a group of American pilgrims and visited the shrine of *Our Lady of Guadalupe* at the invitation of Dr. Rosalie Turton of the 101 Foundation (see p. 198). There I saw the miraculous image of the Virgin and once more science bowed to religion. There I also saw the twisted iron Cross which tells me that God allowed the Cross to be bent just as He is prepared to bend and be merciful, but He will not tolerate any disrespect to His Mother. *The Ark* must be respected.

It is estimated that about two million people visited the shrine during that week. In fact, it is believed that the shrine is now visited by about 14 millon pilgrims annually, and so, as John Paul II once said, 97 percent of the Mexicans are Catholics, but 100 percent are Guadalupians!

The heart of the message of Mary in 1531 was "Yahweh is God, not Baal." It was a call to return to the one true God. It was the call of Carmel. As Francis Johnston said in the last chapter of his book *The Wonder of Guadalupe*, which was first published in 1981, 450 years after the apparitions: "There is a striking parallel between our age and that of the Aztec civilization immediately before the apparitions of 1531. Now, as then, society is dominated by godlessness, pagan excesses and immorality. Countless innocents are sacrificed on the altar of abortion, false deities abound everywhere, and Aztec polygamy and depravity are more than matched by today's universal moral collapse. A decisive collision seems inevitable and imminent, as it was in 1531. But all is not lost. The darkest hour will inevitably melt away in the radiant dawn of Our Lady's triumph over the serpent." As this twentieth century comes to an end, these words have become more and more relevant.

In the Aztec kingdom that was, the serpent god plucked the hearts out of the living victims who were given to him as sacrifice. Mary has since come to Guadalupe and to other parts of the world, asking us to give our hearts completely to her, who will place them within the Sacred Heart of her Son. This triumphant Queen, who will crush the head of the serpent, is *one of us*. As she said to Juan Diego: *"Am I not one of your kind?"* What greater privilege could God also bestow upon man! He made *one of us* Queen of the angels and Queen of heaven. In one masterly stroke, He also tested the humility of the angels. Satan and his followers failed the test.

Above: The original miraculous image of Our Lady of Guadalupe in the new basilica (see p. 192)

Below: A statue of Our Lady of Guadalupe erected at the site of the apparition (see p. 194)

Above: The new and the old basilicas (see p. 194)
Below: With Dr. Rosalie Turton and some pilgrims in Guadalupe (see p. 195)

## CHAPTER 29.

## *Betania: The Lourdes of the New World*

**"Six days before the Passover Jesus came to Bethany."**
John 12:1

To some, perhaps Spain's most important achievement was the promulgation of the Christian faith to the New World when, on October 12, 1492, Christopher Columbus landed in what was called Guanahani by the natives, and which was renamed San Salvador by Columbus, in honour of his Lord and Saviour.

It was while he was sailing around the shores of Trinidad that Columbus first caught sight of the American mainland. He then crossed the Gulf of Paria and five days later, in a small harbour on the Paria Peninsula, he and his men went ashore. It was the first recorded landing by Europeans on the American continent. The date was August 5, 1498.

Interestingly, although the feast of the Nativity of the Virgin is celebrated in the Roman Church on September 8, the apparition in Medjugorje is said to have told the visionaries that the actual date of her birth is August 5. If so, it may be said that Venezuela was a birthday gift from Columbus.

Collins Encyclopedia describes how the sight of the great volume of fresh water pouring out of the mouth of the Orinoco forced Columbus to record in his journal on August 15, 1498, the feast of the Assumption of the Blessed Virgin Mary: "I believe that this is a very great continent until today unknown." On a follow up voyage in 1499, Alonzo de Ojeda, accompanied by Amerigo Vespucci, followed the coast to Lake Maracaibo. Observing the Indians living in houses built on stilts on a shallow lake, reminded the Spaniards of Venice and so, the land was called Venezuela or little Venice.

From that time on, the country has witnessed several manifestations of the Virgin, and one of the most popular shrines in Venezuela is the shrine of *Our Lady of Coromoto*. On September 8, 1652, the feast celebrating the birthday of Mary, and 121 years after her apparitions in Guadalupe in Mexico, she appeared to the Indian chief of the Guanara tribe in his hut. She told him to go to the Spaniards who were evangelizing there, and be baptized. In anger, the chief threw things at her but she kept reappearing. He kept throwing and finally the Virgin took an object he threw at her and gave it back to him with her image on it. It was a tiny image of the Virgin with the Child Jesus. This image is still venerated in Guanara.

Sometime later, after being bitten by a poisonous snake, and seeing himself close to death, the chief eventually asked to be baptized, and also urged his tribe to be baptized and embrace the Christian faith. Catholicism grew rapidly in Venezuela from that time on, and remains today the chief religion of the country with over 90 per cent of the population being of that faith.

Four hundred and fifty years later, the Virgin appeared to the visionary Maria Esperanza de Bianchini in a finca or farm in an agricultural area located in the parish of *Our Lady of the Rosary* in the state of Miranda. The name of the parish should not go unnoticed. It is a fertile land surrounded by green hills and trees, and is home to a cascade of water which descends as a small waterfall close to a grotto. The farm is crossed by a small river called the river Tarma, and the name of the farm is Finca Betania (see pp. 207-9).

Betania is the Spanish word for Bethany (Greek *Bethania*), and according to popular etymology, it means the "house of the poor man" or "of Ananias." Interestingly, and obviously of significance, Ananias was the Christian Jew of Damascus who baptized the converted Saul (Acts 9:10-17: 22-12). And so, the name Betania is historically and religiously linked to the Sacrament of Baptism.

In the Gospel, Bethany was the place where Jesus frequently visited, rested and enjoyed the company of his friends, Martha, Mary and Lazarus. It was there, six days before the Passover and before His crucifixion, that He raised Lazarus from the dead, as told in John 11:17-44. However, the Gospel of John 19-28 also made reference to a Bethany across the Jordan where John the Baptizer was baptizing. In like manner, the Virgin has come to Venezuela in the spirit of John the Baptist, first to Coromoto, to influence the chief of the tribe to have his people *baptized* into the Catholic faith, then to Betania, the Bethany of the New World, where she has asked for *baptism*, conversion, Holy Communion and reconciliation.

The first apparition of the Virgin to Maria Esperanza in Finca Betania occurred at 8.30 a.m. on March 25, 1976, the feast of the Annunciation or the feast of the Incarnation. It was the occasion when Mary became the living *Ark of the new Covenant*. It was also the anniversary of the date in Lourdes when she said to Bernadette Soubirous in 1854: "*I am the Immaculate Conception.*"

Maria Esperanza describes the event in her own words: "She appeared to me through the branches of a huge tree in Betania. I saw a large cloud which came out of the interior and hovered over the top of the tree. *It was an immense cloud-like smoke.* I stared at the cloud and the cloud seemed to open and out came the Holy Virgin. I saw her all dressed in white with the most beautiful face... She appeared to be wearing a white mantle over her shoulders and on her head she had some kind of veil which became tangled in the trees.

"From her hands which were open and stretched out about waist level came rays in different directions. It was as if she was inviting me to approach her. I wanted to fly and be cradled in her breast."

Then Mary spoke to her for the first time: "Little daughter, you are beholding me with my hands outstretched with graces, wrapped in the splendour of light, to call all my children to *conversion*; this is the seed of glory that I offer as Virgin Mother and *Mother, Reconciler of People and Nations*, because I come to *reconcile* them... Little daughter, carry my messages to all. I shall keep you here in my heart from this day onward."

As Fr. Ken Roberts says in his book on Medjugorje *Up On The Mountain*: "Reconciliation results in the fulfillment of the first Great Commandment: Love the Lord your God with all your heart and mind and soul and being... But there is a second part of that Great Commandment: Love your neighbour as yourself. The reconciliation process is not complete, until man, reconciled with God, is also reconciled with his fellow man. Which means if you have 'ought against any,' there is still work to be done."

This title, *Mother, Reconciler of People and Nations*, is new to many. However, St. Ephrem of Syria, a Marian Doctor of the Church, who wrote many works in defense of Mary, and who was a poet and orator extraordinary, greeted her in one of his scholarly writings: "Hail, Reconciler of the whole world!" How long ago? St. Ephrem was born in 306 AD. He died in 373 AD.

As the days passed, on February 11, 1977, Maria Esperanza received word from the Virgin to make arrangements and preparation to take care of the spiritual needs of the people in the area of Betania. She asked for the Sacraments of Baptism and First Communion to be administered to them on that day. The Virgin's request was fulfilled, and February 11 was a most beautiful and memorable day in Betania.

According to Sr. Margaret Sims in her book *Apparitions in Betania*, what impressed Maria most was the *baptism* of the children in the grotto that day. February 11 is the feast of *Our Lady of Lourdes*. It is the date of the first of the eighteen apparitions of the Blessed Virgin Mary to the humble Bernadette in 1858. How well she chooses her dates! The statue in the grotto of Betania is a statue of *Our Lady of Lourdes* (see pp. 207-8).

On November 27, 1977, the Virgin appeared again to Maria Esperanza. She chose another special day. It was the feast of the Miraculous Medal, the anniversary of her apparition to St. Catherine Labouré in the Rue du Bac in Paris, when she asked for the distribution of the Miraculous Medal. On that occasion she told Maria that she would appear to her on March 25, 1978, once more on the feast of the Annunciation. She said that on that occasion, the group who would accompany Maria in Betania would also have the unusual opportunity to experience her presence and to see her, an unusual Marian privilege.

Indeed, as promised, on March 25, 1978, besides Maria Esperanza, fifteen other people saw the Blessed Virgin and witnessed a special phenomenon in the Sun which spun and seemed to hover over them. On that day the whole area appeared to be on fire. One of the pilgrims uttered a cry: "Everything is burning up!" Maria Esperanza then heard a soft tender voice within her saying: "Little daughter, this is not a dream: my presence among you is real. Obey and follow faithfully this Mother so that you may be happy for all eternity. Accept the arduous task of bringing my message of love and *reconciliation* to the people of all nations."

From then (1978) onwards only Maria saw the Virgin when she appeared in the grotto. Then, once more, on the feast of the Annunciation, March 25, 1984, the eighth anniversary of the first apparition, many people gathered for Mass. After Mass they were all enjoying a picnic lunch when suddenly a beautiful Lady appeared above the waterfall, clothed in light. She appeared under seven different Marian titles during three hours and fifteen minutes with intervals from five to ten minutes. She appeared as *Our Lady of Lourdes, Our Lady of Mt. Carmel, Our Lady of the Miraculous Medal...*, and at the end she appeared with the Child Jesus on her right arm.

These scenes lasted about thirty-five minutes and when they ended, once more, all the vegetation seemed to burn. One hundred and eight people have testified to this with their signatures. It was one of the most important events in Betania. It was the actual day of the collegial consecration of Russia and the world to the *Immaculate Heart of Mary* by Pope John Paul II in Rome. Like in Medjugorje, this was yet another symbol of Mary as the *burning bush*.

But there is yet another great symbol associated with Betania. Many pilgrims to Betania have had the joy and privilege of seeing a remarkable blue butterfly which often emerges from the Lourdes-type grotto, flying around the church to eventually disappear among the trees. It was the Virgin herself who said to Maria Esperanza that the blue butterfly would be a sign of her *presence*.

There are several interpretations of this phenomenon, but, to my thinking, it is a sign of the beauty of *conversion*. This symbolic interpretation will be found in St. Teresa of Avila's *The Interior Castle*. In 1577 she wrote this classic book, and in her chapter on *the Fifth Mansion*, this great daughter of Carmel talks about the butterfly. The change from the caterpillar to the butterfly is one of the most remarkable biologic events of nature, where instead of a large ugly worm coming out of the cocoon, out comes a lovely little butterfly.

Speaking to her fellow nuns, St. Teresa in 1577 said: "When the worm is full grown it begins to spin silk and build a house or cocoon in which it must die. My daughters, go on, speed ahead with your work, self will and detachment from earthly things; let us practice prayer, penance, obedience, dying to self, and all other good works that we know of. The silk worm must die. Now, let us see what becomes of this worm. As soon as the soul, by prayer and penance, becomes entirely dead to the world, out it flies like a lovely butterfly. Oh, how great God is! The difference is so great to the soul; it is as great as that ugly worm and the beautiful butterfly. The butterfly despises the work it did when it was worm. How could it be content to crawl around so slowly when it had wings to fly!"

It was in Bethany, the Betania of the Old World, that Mary Magdalen lived; she who was the convert of all converts. She was a caterpillar who changed into a beautiful butterfly and like her, the Virgin of Betania is calling us all to *conversion* in these apocalyptic times. She wants us all to throw off the old coat of the worm and to be as beautiful as butterflies. It is as if she is saying to us: "Come fly with me."

On the feast of the Annuciation, March 25, 1993, I suddenly saw a butterfly in the Betania grotto as it flew around the church and then quickly disappeared in the greenery. It was not blue. It was golden in colour. I wondered! In Medjugorje she always appears wearing a golden dress on her feast days!

As elsewhere, science has also been humbled in Betania and many miracles have been witnessed there. Each year Maria Esperanza receives the stigmata of Jesus from Good Friday to Easter Sunday and suffers the pains of His Passion (see p. 210). Several pilgrims have also seen a gold glitter that falls on them from the sky. I, too, have seen this phenomenon on one of my spiritual advisors, Fr. Neil Rodriguez, C.S.Sp. I have also personally interviewed a distinguished Venezuelan, Doctor Vinicio Arrieta, who was miraculously cured of disseminated cancer of the prostate which had metastasized to his bones. It was a fellow doctor giving his personal testimony and it was easy to recognize its authenticity.

However, the greatest of all the miracles of Betania was first witnessed by Fr. Otty Ossa Aristizabal, the chaplain of Betania. He was celebrating Mass at midnight on December 8, 1992, on the vigil of the feast of the Immaculate Conception, when, at the time of the consecration, several thousand people saw a bright light over the Host. Fr. Otty broke the Host in half, and then broke off a small particle to put into the chalice. It was then that the great miracle occurred. The remaining part of the Host began to bleed. Miraculously again, the blood on this wafer-thin Host did not seep through to the other side. The blood has been examined and it is human blood. As in Lanciano, Italy, the type was AB. Presumably, Mary's blood type is also AB. She was the sole human parent!

At present the miraculous Host is preserved in the Convent of Los Teques by the Recollect Augustinian Sisters and thousands, including myself, have had the great privilege of seeing this Host with the bright red stain in the centre of it, and of being allowed to hold the glass container with the Host and kiss it in adoration (see p. 210).

It was on one of those occasions when Fr. Rodriguez was holding the miraculous Host in its container for pilgrims to kiss and adore, that a young and most beautiful child, about five years old, with a most loving look and holy demeanour, mysteriously appeared at his side. A photograph was taken by a pilgrim from Trinidad. However, when I made a 35 mm. slide from it for projection onto a screen, a *pillar of cloud* appeared in front of the child, which was not on the colour print loaned to me.

Significantly, when, as recorded in a subsequent photograph, Fr. Cuthbert Alexander, a diocesan priest from Trinidad, was presented the Host to kiss, the child lovingly laid her hand on the shoulder of this priest. She subsequently disappeared from view. The question is still asked: "Who is this child?" (see p. 211).

Although I have been to Medjugorje seven times, I never had any call to go to neighbouring Betania until the feast of the Annunciation, March 25, 1993. I was the house guest of my friend, the Jamaican Ambassador to Venezuela, Dr. Matthew Beaubrun, and the name of the Ambassador's residence was *Don Bosco*. This too was of special significance as we shall see later on in this book.

As soon as I arrived in Caracas on March 24, he immediately took me to the back garden of his villa in which there was a small and beautiful grotto of *Our Lady of Lourdes*. I took a photograph of the grotto and to my surprise, when I developed the film a prominent *blue column* surmounted by a white *pillar of cloud* appeared to the left of the statue. It was the first time that I recorded on one photo both the *pillar of cloud* and a *blue column of smoke* linked together (see p. 208). By coincidence (or was it?), in Sr. Margaret Sims' book on Betania there is a photograph of Maria Esperanza in ecstatic prayer, and right next to her appeared the same image of a *pillar of cloud* and a *blue column*.

But there was yet another miraculous "imposition" on the film. A three-pronged sceptre, implanted into the ground, appeared to the left of the statue. The Ambassador has testified that no such object was present in his garden at that time nor to this day. *The sceptre was blue* (see p. 212).

Now, on October 12, 1984, the feast of El Pilar, the Argentinian visionary Gladys de Motta had a vision in San Nicolás in Argentina. She wrote: "I see an anchor and along its sides a fish and some bread. *The anchor is blue.*" Two days later the Blessed Virgin revealed: "It is I who am the anchor. I have anchored here." On November 16, 1983, the Virgin told Gladys: "I am the Patroness of this region. Assert my rights." (In 1900 she was proclaimed Patroness of the Americas, both North and South.) The trident in the photograph in Venezuela, therefore, seems to say: "I am Queen and Patroness of this land of Venezuela and I have come to assert my rights."

The following day, March 25, I was one of a huge crowd who gathered at the grotto in Betania for the great feast. At about 11:30 a.m. about thirty pilgrims were heard shouting with excitement, their hands pointing to the thick foliage to the right of the grotto some fifty yards away: "Mira, mira Maria!" I ran several yards across the field and arrived breathlessly just in time to see the apparition of the Madonna shortly before she disappeared in the greenery.

It was a stunning and moving experience which I will never forget, very brief as it was. I did not see her face from afar, but she wore a most beautiful chiffon-like long veil in light blue which floated majestically in the most gentle of breezes. There were those who saw her in some greater detail before I arrived and there were those who could not see her at all.

Very soon afterwards there followed a solar miracle when the Sun appeared to bud off smaller golden daughter-Suns which moved swiftly across the sky in various directions and then suddenly disappeared. Science again stood still and silent and bowed its head to the great Scientist who can change the laws of nature at His will.

In 1992 Maria Esperanza told a pilgrim, Wendy Benedict, that lasting signs will be left in all the places that the Virgin has appeared. She said that we will be able to see it and photograph it, but we will not be able to touch it. It is the prophecy of Garabandal! As I said before, could it be the *pillar of cloud* by day and the *pillar of fire* by night? Or could it be the *column of smoke* or the *burning bush*?

After three years of enquiry, Bishop Pio Bello Ricardo, a Jesuit who studied for his Master's degree in Theology in Burgos, Spain, obtained a Ph. D. with a thesis in Psychology, and is the Professor of Psychology in the Catholic University of Andres Bello in Caracas, published a pastoral letter on the apparitions in Betania on November, 1987. He said: "In consequence, after studying with determination the apparitions of Our Blessed Virgin Mary in Finca Betania, and after assiduously asking Our Lord for spiritual discernment, I declare that, to my judgment, these apparitions are authentic and have a supernatural character. I, therefore, officially approve that the site where the same have occurred be considered as sacred, the same be kept as a place for pilgrimages and as a place of prayer, meditation and worship and where liturgical acts can be celebrated."

207.

Above: The grotto in finca Betania with a statue of
Our Lady of Lourdes (see p. 200)
Below: Pillar of cloud and pillar of fire appear in front of the
statue in the grotto (Courtesy of Russell Gonzales)

208.

Above left: The pillar of cloud appears in a photograph in front of the "Ark" (see p. 205)
Above right: The pillar of fire in front of the "Ark" (see p. 205)
Below: Maria Esperanza in Betania "arched" by a pillar of cloud on her right and a column of smoke on her left (courtesy of Cindy Baylis) (see p. 205)

209.

Above: Maria Esperanza and her husband Geo, distributing Rosaries. Note the pillar of cloud.

Below: Pillar of fire in front of the statue of Our Lady, Reconciler of all Nations in Betania (Courtesy of Stasia Cabral)

210.

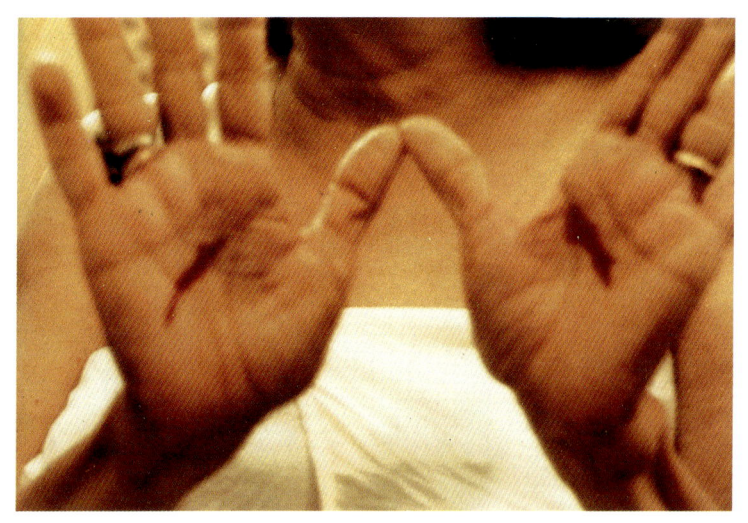

Above: The stigmata of Our Lord on the hands of Maria Esperanza (courtesy of Geo Bianchini Giani) (see p. 204)
Below: Host which bled miraculously in Betania (courtesy of Tulio Jiminez) (see p. 204)

Right: An unknown child appears during the adoration of the bleeding Host and places her hand on the shoulder of Fr. Cuthbert Alexander of Trinidad
(see p. 205)
(photo courtesy of Cindy Baylis)

Below: A pillar of cloud appears in front of the child on the photograph (see p. 205)

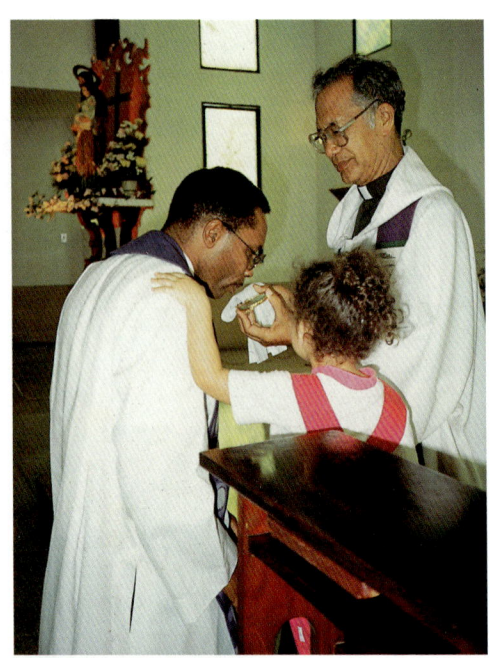

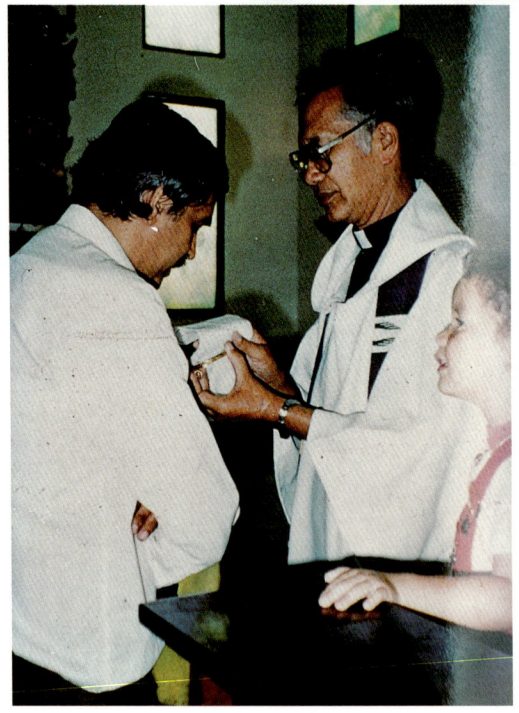

212.

Above: A small statue of Our Lady of Lourdes in the back garden of the Ambassador's residence (see p. 205)
Below: The pillar of cloud and a blue column of smoke appear on film. Note the blue trident on right (see arrow) (see p. 205)

## CHAPTER 30.

## *Mary's Messages in Betania*

"His mother said to the servants,
'Do whatever he tells you.'"

Luke 2: 5-6

These are but a few of the messages given by the Virgin to Maria Esperanza and, like Mary's messages from Medjugorje, they are in many ways more important than anything I have said in this book as they are from the Queen herself.

"My daughter, I am giving you a piece of heaven — Lourdes, the Betania of Venezuela. It is a place for everyone, not only Catholics. It is for everyone since there must not exist any distinction between races, nations and religions. This land will welcome all who wish to come here. This is your Mother who comes to you as she did in Lourdes, Fatima, the Pillar of Saragossa, Guanare and in so many other places where I will continue to appear. This will be a place of veneration, of prayer, of faith, of love and charity. I want to establish in this place a replica of my holiness. Lourdes is truth itself because I am there, and so I shall also be in Venezuela in this domain of Betania.

"This motherly water which I give you is the water of life. It is the water of salvation and of baptism. It is the beginning of the life in Christ. It will be the water of forgiveness which will wash away your sins and which will renew you, and while you magnify my name with the 'Ave,' that simple word, our union will be more alive and meaningful.

"My children, I am here amongst you, so that you can feel my presence and contemplate me among the branches of the trees in this little wood which I have chosen. I do this in order that you may find fulfillment, peace and love which this Mother wishes to give to you with her water, so that the love of our heavenly Father and of my divine Son and that of the Holy Spirit which sanctifies will burn eternally within you. Can you understand my message? Do you know what I am saying to you?

"I have called you to this place so that my union with you can be more intimate and significant, because the Holy Spirit will empower you to live your life of evangelization and apostleship more deeply. My children, I am your Mother, the *Refuge of sinners* and *Help of Christians*. For this reason, I am inviting you to come to me, to tell me what you feel — your preoccupations, your worries, your weaknesses, your hopes and anxieties, but especially I want you to consecrate your hearts to me, to give yourself unconditionally to me and put yourselves under my protection and my immaculate and steadfast gaze.

"We shall become united in that little house of Nazareth so that you will begin your apostolic preparation, and overcome all difficulties little by little, by being patient and carrying your cross, by receiving the Eucharist each day as food for your souls whereby you will be strengthened by my divine Son. My children, this is where you can free yourselves, break the bonds which bewilder and confuse you today when you begin to understand the call which my divine Son and this your Mother are making to your hearts. It is Our Father's wish to save all His children from the scorn and ridicule of the Pharisees of these apocalyptic times.

"*I come to rule with my sceptre,* all those who wish to submit themselves to my maternal heart. I also come here to alleviate the burdens of my sons, the priests, because in response to my call, they have made of this chosen place, a refuge in this time of calamity. Indeed, it is where my children shall take refuge to rebuild the walls of the new and triumphant Jerusalem where all will be saved by faith, love, truth and justice.

"Give yourselves to prayer, especially you, the faithful and my consecrated priests and missionary sisters. You must devote yourselves completely to prayer and to meditation which is much needed at this time in the history of the world. Actions, deeds and works are the foundation but without prayer, works are ruined.

"My children, as *Mary, Reconciler of all Peoples and Nations*, I have come in search of you to bestow faith on you, that faith which has been lost, *replaced by the clamour and noise of an atomic age which is about to explode.* Passion, power, material riches, greed have all made you cold, uncaring and selfish. This is the affliction of the great evil which is hovering over the earth with its shadow. Those who repent and are sorry for their sinfulness and tearfully approach this grotto where I appear, asking my forgiveness, shall receive many graces. All, all, all will be well received. Their souls will become as clean as on that day when they were purified by holy baptism. They will all come back to life with my Son.

"My children, today is the day which is of great importance to your souls. You must help me to build my house in this place, this refuge of a Mother known to you as *Mary, Reconciler of Peoples and Nations.* Pray, meditate and feed on the Eucharistic Bread which gives you supernatural life. I wish to be known as *Mary, Reconciler of Peoples and Nations,* because man needs to discover himself. Yes, my children, learn to value each person around you, wherever you are. Value their aspirations to a good life, even though they may seem to be negative influences, for they can be helped to fight the evil which surrounds them. They can be lifted out of it so that they can live in spiritual peace.

"My children, I have come to you in order to prepare you so that you can carry my message of reconciliation. *The great moment of truth is coming.* I want to take possession of your heart and give you the gift of knowledge through the Holy Spirit, so that you can understand the deep significance of my presence among you. I am offering you the opportunity of the great promise which my Son will reveal to you one day. It is so important in these times — the reconciliation of the Universe, man with God and man with man.

"That is why this Mother comes to you pleading as the lowliest of women — the least, the most humble but the most pure. She wishes to bring back to you purity of heart, simplicity, loyalty, obedience to service to one's brother, moderation in all things and above all, a constant zeal to work for the Church. Today one has to give witness with one's life and one's faith in God. My children, I am waiting for you. I am the Mother of God. I called you to Guanare and now I am calling you here to this place. I am the same Mother known to you by different titles, but I am Mary of Nazareth, the Woman of Calvary. No one was as courageous as I nor gave more proof of their love for God, our Father.

"My children, I am the *Mother of Good Counsel,* the mediator who endeavours to persuade you to listen to my call. It brings reconciliation to nations and peoples. It is the only thing which can save this century from the unmercifulness of war and eternal death. My children, the preservation of a world which pleads for justice is in your hands. If you do not change your ways and better your lives, you will perish in the fires of war and death. It is our wish to stop this evil which suffocates you, the evil of rebellion, so that you can be victorious over the darkness and oppression of the enemy. It is for this in this century that my divine Son is coming once more as the Shepherd of souls, so that you can follow His path and so that you can have the Covenant of peace between brothers.

"It is a difficult hour for all humanity and it is necessary to stop the misunderstanding between brothers. Nations must be united. My Jesus' love will be the door that will open hearts to give passage to a beautiful age which must resuscitate nations to the glorious teaching of unity. Take advantage of time because *the hour is coming when my Son will present Himself before all as Judge and Saviour. Do not believe this is far off. The great day on which my Son will come is approaching.* Pray very much so that the horrible chastisement that is coming can be delayed. Live together with my Son since He is the Saviour of the world. He wants to give you His Heart once again. How sweet is His Heart! Sons and daughters, look for the Heart of my divine Son which will make all difficult things easy."

## CHAPTER 31.

## *My Visit To San Nicolás in Argentina*

"I am the Patroness of this Region. Assert my rights!"
The Virgin Mary to Gladys

While Venezuela is at the northernmost point of South America, Argentina is at its most southern tip. In 1561 the Spanish navigator, Juan Díaz de Solís, explored the Argentine coast and discovered the great river, the Rio de la Plata. However, it was Sebastian Cabot in 1526, who was the first to ascend the Rio de la Plata and go north into the Paraná and Paraguay rivers. He then consecrated the River Paraná to Our Lady. In the next expedition from Spain, Pedro de Mendoza reached the site of what is now called Buenos Aires in February 1536, five years after the Virgin appeared in Guadalupe in Mexico.

Just as Betania is in the parish of *Our Lady of the Rosary* in the state of Miranda, San Nicolás "de los Arroyas" (St. Nicholas of the streams) is a small parish of the diocese of Rosario (meaning Rosary) about 230 kilometres from the capital, Buenos Aires. On April 14, 1748, Rafael de Aguiar built a chapel there dedicated to St. Nicholas of Bari, which was the foundation for the present day cathedral.

St. Nicholas was bishop of Myra in Asia Minor during the early 4th century. His appealing characteristics appear to have been his charity, kindness and generosity to the poor. He is regarded as the special patron of children and the legendary figure, Santa Claus, originated from the reputation of St. Nicholas. He has always been honoured with great veneration in the Latin and Greek Churches and, in fact, the Russian Church seems to honour him more than any other saint after the Apostles. His death occurred in Myra in the year 342. During the 11th century his relics were moved to

Italy and the Basilica of San Nicolás was built at Bari to receive them.

On December 6, 1821, San Nicolás of Bari was declared patron saint of the city of San Nicolás in Argentina, and on May 31, 1852, San Nicolás was the site of the "Accord of San Nicolás." It was a covenant signed by all the governors of the provinces who met there to draft the constitution of Argentina. It was the "covenant city."

Now, like the river Paraná, the parish of San Nicolás was also dedicated to *Our Lady of the Rosary* since its early history, and in 1884 the cathedral was opened. For the inauguration, Señora Carmen Acevedo de Insurcadic presented a gift of a statue of *Our Lady of the Rosary* to the cathedral. It came from Rome and was blessed by Pope Leo XIII. The Virgin was dressed in a pink gown with a blue mantle and a white mantilla on her head. She held the Christ Child on her left arm and from their hands fell a large Rosary. However, after an accident in which the right hand of the statue was broken, the statue was housed and disregarded for decades in the belfry of the church.

The Blessed Virgin first appeared on September 25, 1983, two years after the Medjugorje apparitions began in June 1981. Gladys Quiroga de Motta, a humble 46 year old mother of two children, was in her room praying the Rosary when the Virgin appeared to her with the Infant Jesus on her arm, with a gesture as if to give the visionary her Rosary. She then disappeared. Three days later, the Virgin appeared again and made the same gesture. On October 7, the feast of *Our Lady of the Rosary*, the first of a long series of conversations between Mary and Gladys Quiroga de Motta began (see p. 224).

On that day Gladys politely asked what she desired. Immediately, the image of Mary faded and the image of a large church appeared. The Virgin had spoken without speaking! It was a request frequently asked in many of her apparitions. Gladys memorized in detail the design of the church which she saw in the vision (see p. 222). This church is now being built. Six days later, October 13, the anniversary of her last apparition in Fatima in 1917, Mary spoke for the first time in San Nicolás: "You have been faithful. Do not be afraid. We will walk hand in hand and you will travel over a long road." Then she added a biblical reference. It was Ezekiel 2:4-10.

I wondered why she chose Ezekiel as her first reference since in her wisdom she always speaks with precision, purpose and prudence. Then I researched the Scriptures. The Introduction to the Book of Ezekiel in the Jerusalem Bible, states: "Ezekiel's teaching is centered on inner conversion, a new heart and a new spirit, which will be given by God."

Once more we see how the Virgin chooses her dates purposefully. In fact, I am sure that the dates of all her apparitions are meaningful but it would be difficult to research their relevance. One would need to know the history of the world over the thousands of years.

On November 15, the feast of Albert the Great, the patron saint of scientists, Jesus Himself spoke to Gladys for the first time: *"I am the sower. Gather the harvest. It will be great."* Brief and precise! On that same day, November 15, the Virgin appeared to Gladys again and said with great authority: "I am the Patroness of this region. Assert my rights!"

The following day, November 16, 1983, Mary said to Gladys: "I want to be near the river (Paraná). The water is a blessing." When asked on that day whether she wanted a chapel or a sanctuary, she replied to Gladys: "The Scripture says it." She then quoted Exodus 25:8: *"And they will make me a sanctuary and I will dwell in the midst of them."*

On November 26 she said to Gladys: "Bless you, your mission is great! You have no idea of the magnitude!" It was then that the visionary asked the Virgin whether she would like to be called *Our Lady of the Rosary of San Nicolás*. She replied: "It must be so. My wish is to be amongst you, to cover you with blessings, with peace, with joy, and bring you close to the Lord, our God. Read Colossians 3:15, 4:15 and 2 Corinthians 4." Never before in the history of her apparitions has she quoted Scripture so frequently. Undoubtedly, in so doing, she is calling us to read and to know the Bible.

It was on the following day, November 27, that the parish priest and spiritual director of Gladys, Fr. Carlos Perez, learned for the first time of the broken statue of *Our Lady of the Rosary* which was in the belfry of the church. Gladys then went with him to see it. To her utter astonishment, it had the same appearance as the apparition she was seeing. Then Mary suddenly appeared in front of the statue and said: "They had kept me in oblivion but I have reappeared. Put me up again because you see me just as I am." At that moment Gladys saw, in a vision, a stained glass window of the Holy Trinity behind the statue.

Soon afterwards, Father Perez had the statue repaired, and placed in its hands a new Rosary which belonged to Gladys. The repaired statue of *Our Lady of the Rosary of San Nicolás* moved to the church which is being built, as requested and designed by Our Lady.

I first visited San Nicolás on May 25, 1993, the 83rd anniversary of the independence of Argentina. I spent the day there and had the good fortune to meet the parish priest and rector of the church, Father Carlos Perez (see p. 224). He is a very intelligent, mature, prudent and spiritual person and his endorsement of the apparitions gives immense credibility to the authenticity of the events in San Nicolás. I also had a brief meeting with Monsignor Domingo Salvadore Castagna, Bishop of San Nicolás. The Bishop has long since informed the Episcopal Conference of Argentina of the events and, like him, many other bishops have expressed their support for and belief in the apparitions (see p. 224).

On the 25th of each month, in honour of the date of the Madonna's first apparition there, a monthly procession attracts tens of thousands of the faithful to San Nicolás. When I was there, I was witness to a most moving display of deep devotion to and veneration of Mary by about fifteen thousand devotees who turned out to pay tribute to her, waving their white handkerchiefs in fond greeting to her "image" as the revered statue of *Our Lady of the Rosary of San Nicolás* was paraded from the church through the city streets (see pp. 222-3).

My second visit to San Nicolás was on September 25, 1993. It was the great occasion of the tenth anniversary of the apparitions. This time there were 500,000 people on the banks of the Paraná. Everything was arranged for me by my Argentinian friends, Amalia Lopez Gaffney and Eloisa Almeyra, and I had a well-appointed seat for the ceremony. And what a ceremony it was! As usual, the days proceeding's ended with a Mass on the banks of the Paraná.

The last message was given on February 11, 1990. It was the feast day of *Our Lady of Lourdes*. Since then, the apparitions continue every day, as in Medjugorje, but without a message to the public. The messages are given to Gladys and, according to Fr. Rene Laurentin in his book *An Appeal from Mary in Argentina*, she does not render an account of them except to her spiritual director.

For my part, the authenticity of these apparitions has also been enhanced by the miracle which science has never explained. In his book on the apparition of San Nicolás, Fr. Laurentin records that on Friday, November 16, 1984, Gladys first experienced the terrible sufferings of the Passion of our Lord, and stigmata appeared on her wrists (see p. 224). At the request of the bishop, Dr. Eduardo Juan Telechea and Dr. Carlos Pelliciotta have carefully examined the phenomenon. The stigmata are given to Gladys during Advent and Lent, but blood only flows on Fridays in Lent. The doctors have also observed the stigmata on her feet. However, these occur only on Good Fridays, beginning a little after 3 o'clock in the afternoon. Gladys' left foot then comes to place itself upon the right foot, as if both feet were nailed with one single nail. The doctors tried to separate the feet, but when they took the left foot in their hands in order to raise it, the right foot below would follow as if both were one unit. On Good Fridays Gladys also experiences the agony of carrying the Cross, and her shoulder becomes marked with an extensive painful spot. At times a wound also opens up on her side, but without a flow of blood.

Gladys Quiroga de Motta is one of many souls chosen by God, not only to be a visionary and evangelist, but also to be a "victim soul." As John Haffert says in his book *The Meaning of Akita*: "The term 'victim soul' has a special meaning. It refers to souls offered entirely to God, ready to accept anything in self-immolation out of love for Him and the salvation of souls. In a lesser sense, we are all called to be 'victims' to offer up whatever God may send our way each day, in reparation for our sins and the sins of the whole world."

222.

Above: The artist's concept of the Basilica of Our Lady of the Rosary of San Nicolás (see p. 218)
Below: The statue of Our Lady of the Rosary of San Nicolás in procession as it leaves the basilica in construction (see p. 220)

223.

Above: On the 25 of each month thousands process at the shrine (see p. 220)
Below: Our Lady of the Rosary of San Nicolás (see p. 220)

224.

Left: In San Nicolás, Argentina, with the architect of the basilica, Amalia Lopez Gaffney and her son Matias (see p. 220)

Below right: Bishop Domingo Castagna, Bishop of San Nicolás (see p. 220).
Below left: Fr. Carlos Perez (see p. 220)

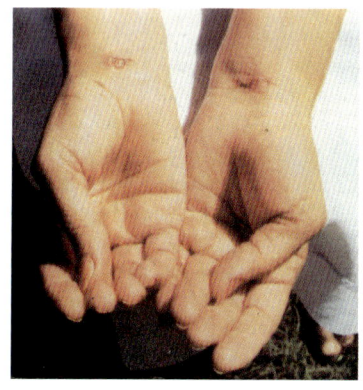

Above left: Gladys Quiroga de Motta (see p. 220)
Above right: The stigmata on the wrists of Gladys (see p. 220)

## CHAPTER 32.

# *Mary and Noah's Ark*

**"Then the Lord said to Noah: 'Go into the ark, you and your household, for you alone in this age have I found to be truly just.'"**

**Genesis 7:1**

I first became interested in San Nicolás particularly because of references to the *Ark of the Covenant* in the messages of our Lord and His Mother there. In Fr. Rene Laurentin's book *An Appeal From Mary in Argentina*, he states: "The central point (the point of convergence of more than 1800 messages given to Gladys from October 13,1983 to February 11, 1990) focuses on this: God wants to renew His covenant with his people through Mary, His *Ark of the Covenant*, for she is, according to Holy Scripture, the eschatological *Ark of the Covenant* — that is to say, the residence of God among men in the last times." I immediately made plans to visit San Nicholás.

Not only was the ancient *Ark of the Covenant* a herald of the Blessed Virgin, but so also was the *Ark of Noah*. And so, the two Arks are linked to Mary.

The first Covenant which God made with man followed the great flood when Noah and his family were saved in the Ark which God had instructed him to build: *"This is how you shall build it: the length of the ark shall be three hundred cubits, its width fifty cubits, and its height thirty cubits... Put an entrance at the side of the ark, which you shall make with bottom, second and third decks"* (Genesis 6:15-16). Note the three decks of the Ark.

This three storey aspect of the Ark is likened to Mary and her link with the Holy Trinity. Recall that on November 27, 1983, a vision of a stained glass window of the Holy Trinity appeared behind the statue of *Our Lady of the Rosary of San Nicholás*. Mary is not only the Mother of the Son, but she is the Daughter of the Father and the Bride of the Holy Spirit. As such she can become for Christians a locus of encounter with the three divine Persons. And as Noah received his children into the Ark and they were saved, so too, will all those who seek shelter in the living Ark, Mary.

Frank Duff, the great founder of the Legion of Mary, in his book *The Woman of Genesis*, referred to Mary and Noah's Ark: "I specify its dimensions: 525 feet long, 86 feet wide, 52 feet high. Strange to say, these proportions are stated by St. Augustine to be the same as those of the perfect human body. May we not see in this a pointing to the Ark as a symbol of Mary bearing the Life of the world within her?"

On October 12, 1984, the feast of *Mary, El Pilar*, and the anniversary of the discovery of the New World by Christopher Columbus, Gladys experienced this vision: "I see an anchor and on either side a fish and a loaf of bread. The anchor is blue." Two days later, on October 14, 1984, she had another vision: "I see a river. I think it is our river, and I see a great canoe. It looks like an ark. Then the Virgin said to me: 'I am the Anchor! I have anchored here. I am the Ark who wants to carry my children to the Lord.'"

On February 21, 1985, Gladys wrote in her diary: "Today I see Jesus, as always with His white tunic and the light around Him. With a soft and firm voice He says to me: 'I am not hiding. I want to save mankind. I am with my Ark, this time on land.'" Two months later, Mary said to Gladys: "Only a mean heart can doubt the presence of God in this place. Only a poor soul can fail to understand that the Ark is here and that there is room enough for those who wish to enter it. The Lord stopped me here so that from here I should call and receive my children."

On December 30, 1989, Jesus' last message to Gladys characterizes this central point of the messages of San Nicolás. He said to her: *"In the past, the world was saved by Noah's Ark. Today My Mother is the Ark. Through her, souls will be saved because she will lead them to Me. He who rejects My Mother rejects Me! Many are letting the grace of God pass by in these days. Go and evangelize."*

His statement: *"He who rejects My Mother rejects me"* — immediately reminded me of the *City of God* and the events before the ascension of Jesus, as revealed to the Venerable Mary of Agreda in a series of visions. In the chapter on The Transfixion she quotes some of the parting words of Jesus to His disciples: *"My children, I am about to ascend to*

**227.**

*My Father... Just as I told you that he who sees Me sees My Father, and he who knows Me, knows Him also; so I now tell you that he who knows My Mother, knows Me; he who hears her, hears Me; and who honours her, honours Me."*

Mary and the Child Jesus, Noah's ark, the dove and the rainbow

## CHAPTER 33.

## *The Messages of Jesus and Mary At San Nicolás*

**"I have a message from God for you."**
**Judges 3: 20**

There were sixty-eight messages from Jesus Himself from 1983 through 1989. The first was on November 15, 1983, the feast of St. Albert the Great, Patron of scientists, Bishop and Doctor of the Church. They were all short and precise. The following are a few abstracts from His messages. They are also powerful testimonies of His endorsement of His Mother.

*The Messages of Jesus to Gladys:*

"People always suffer from the same illness — Pride. It is evil in the eyes of God. Never deny God. Draw nearer and listen to His call. My Heart is big. It can receive every lamentation, every suffering. I am not deaf. I am not cold and my love goes as far as those who love me. My Heart wishes the salvation of all souls and loves them, even those who are in sin. Under the species of the Holy Eucharist, my Heart is introduced into all open hearts. It nourishes them; it satisfies them. He who loves the food which I give him must know that he is well-nourished. I am the food and drink of the soul which thirsts for God. My Heart is swelling with love, but there are hearts which are completely extinguished. They do not receive the love which I give to all souls.

"If this generation does not listen to My Mother, it will perish. I ask everyone to listen to her. She is the help that will make Christians come out of the darkness in order to lead them into the light. Invoke her name with an intense love. I warn the world, for the world is not aware, souls are in danger.

Many are lost. Few will find salvation unless they accept Me as their Saviour. My Mother must be accepted. My Mother must be heard in the totality of her messages. The world must discover the kindness which she brings to Christians. I have chosen the heart of My Mother so that what I ask will be achieved. Souls will come to me through her Immaculate Heart.

"My creatures should come to Me because it is only by being near to Me that they will live forever. My Mother will not allow them to go astray. She will lead them directly to Me. I, the heir of love of My Father, pour out this love in the world so that it may return to its point of origin, to My Most Holy Father."

The last message of Jesus to Gladys was on December 30, 1989: "Go and preach the Gospel. Little does it matter where you do it. Wherever you are, preach the Gospel to your brothers who do not know the Word of God. Preach the Gospel."

*Gladys received more than 1800 messages from Mary, and these are a few selections from her motherly discourses:*

### On the Holy Trinity

"I ask my children to live and to glorify the Most Holy Trinity. The Most Holy Trinity remains the secret of God. He knows it and it belongs to Him alone. Glory be to the Father, to the Son, and to the Holy Spirit. I ask my children to believe in the Holy Trinity, to love the Most Holy Trinity. Love the Father, Creator of heaven and earth; love the Son, Redeemer of mankind; love the Holy Trinity, Light of Hope."

On the feast of San Nicolás, December 6, 1988, Mary told Gladys: "My motherly heart cries out for the love of my children towards the Most Blessed Trinity: God the Father, Power and Love; God the Son, Love thirsting for love; God the Holy Spirit, Light and Love. The Blessed Trinity perfectly shows the love of God for souls. Most Holy Trinity, so often rejected and denied! Walk beneath its splendour which reflects so much love. Preach it."

### On the Eucharist

On June 1, 1986, the beginning of the month dedicated to the Eucharistic Heart of her Son, she extolled: "Jesus, the

Eucharist! It is His living and true Body. Adore It and love It. My dear children, it is in the Eucharist that you will be able to experience how much He gives Himself to you. It is in the Eucharist that He becomes Body and Blood once more, and it is through the Eucharist that He wants to save souls who are ready to receive Him." Gladys also received this advice from Mary: "The soul must unite itself to Jesus everyday and for that there is nothing better than Holy Communion, the Food of the soul for life, the Bread of Life."

*On Prayer*

"One cannot live without offering a daily prayer to our Father in heaven. He listens to all who pray with faith. Read James 1:2-12 (It reads: 'But when you pray, you must believe and not doubt at all. Whoever doubts is like a wave in the sea that is driven and blown about by the wind.') Pray and you will remain close to God. Recite the holy Rosary and let the Lord see that with its recitation comes your conversion. The holy Rosary is the weapon which the enemy fears. It is also the refuge of those who look for relief from their suffering and it is the door to enter my heart. You cannot imagine what the value of prayer is. Recite the holy Rosary while meditating on its Mysteries, and I assure you that your prayers will be elevated, like a true hymn of love to the Lord."

*On Reading the Bible*

"If I point out to you biblical readings at the same time as my messages, it is in order that the world may understand that they are authentic and that it may not create any doubt in you. Through these messages and Holy Scriptures the Lord will reveal to you what He expects of mankind."

*On Conversion and Consecration*

"My child, as the *'Help of Christians'* I want to redeem my children, asking them for conversion and their consecration to my Immaculate Heart as Mother. I will respond to your consecration with my protection. I want the conversion of the world. No longer must you disobey the Lord. My dear children, pray so that it may be so... It is good that my children should know that I ask them for consecration since when they are consecrated to my Heart, they belong to the Mother as well as to the Son.

On March 21, 1988, a very important scene was visualized by Gladys. She described her vision to Fr. Perez, the parish priest: "I see the earth divided into two parts; one part represents two thirds of the world and the other, one third. On it I see the Blessed Virgin with the Child Jesus and from her breast rays of light go towards the part which represents two-thirds of the earth." Immediately after this vision the Virgin appealed to Gladys, saying: "Gladys, you are seeing the world half-destroyed. These rays of light are sent from my heart which wants to save as many hearts as it can. My heart is all powerful, but it can do nothing if hearts are unwilling. The means to save souls are prayer and conversion."

## On the Youth

"My daughter, I see the youth adrift. Satan corners them and leads them to sin. Read Ecclesiastes 17: 25-26. (It reads: 'Return to the Lord and leave sin behind, plead before his face and lessen your offense. Come back to the Most High and turn away from iniquity, and hold in abhorrence all that is foul.') Parents, you are responsible for their steps. You must lead them to the Lord. Youth is sadly running to its perdition — the easy life and drugs. Such is the panorama which the evil one uses in confronting young people. Pray for the young people of the whole world. They need divine help, for a mortal danger is threatening them."

## On the Battle With Satan

"All of humanity is contaminated. It does not know what it wants and it is an opening for the evil one, but he will not triumph. Christ Jesus will win the great battle (for souls). The enemy is mercilessly challenging me; he is tempting my children openly. It is a struggle between light and darkness, a constant persecution of my beloved Church. Many times you will feel threatened, but do not be afraid. It is only that; only threats. Be prudent and he will not destroy you.

"Sin exceeds all measure. Satan wants complete dominion over the earth. He wants to destroy, but victory is in God. Read Apocalypse 21: 6-8." (It reads: 'I am the Alpha and Omega, the Beginning and the End. I will give water from the well of life free to anybody who is thirsty; it is the rightful inheritance of the one who proves victorious.')

"The prince of evil knows that his sad kingdom is coming to an end. And so, he sheds his venom with all his strength. There is only a little time left. He is astute, calculating and destructive but here it is he who will self-destruct. There is darkness everywhere. Evil continues to spread. It is the evil one in his apparent victory but the work of God will finish him. God's justice will save the just. *My daughter, the evil one is triumphant now, it is true, but it is a victory that will last briefly.* The Lord is only giving him time, the same time that He gives man to return to Him.

"Entrust yourselves to the Heart of Jesus, since it is by Him that you will be saved. Reinforce your faith from day to day. Allow the Holy Spirit to work in you. The enemy has already been attacked. His end is near. He is taking advantage of his last chance by capitalizing on human weakness — pride. *However, I am going to fight him and I have already begun. The world must know it. The Mother of Christ will triumph over Satan because near her will be found all the humble sons of her Son.*

"The coming of the Saviour is imminent. As the Gospel says, no one knows the date nor the hour, but the hour will come, and it is certain that the soul must be prepared for that hour. That is why, my daughter, the Mother wants to make known the Word of her Son. The hour of the Mother has arrived. I come from heaven to lead you to Christ. Make it known."

*On the Pope*

"All of you are a part of the Mystical Body, which is the Church and of which Christ is the Head. On earth the Vicar of my Son is responsible for the Body to continue. Therefore, follow his teaching which is ultimately the teaching of Christ. My sufferings are united with those of the Pope, for his sorrow is my sorrow. Offer this novena to the Lord, praying for the Pope, my most chosen son, given body and soul to the Lord and to Mary, Mother of Christ. John Paul II walks with his cross, taking Christ's peace and hope to all countries, conscious of the dangers to which he is exposed, and humbly continues to strengthen my Son's Church.

"My beloved children, the priests must follow the Pope, for to walk with him is to walk with Christ Himself. John Paul is faithful and consecrated to the Mother's heart, fears nothing, goes where the Mother calls him, overcoming every obstacle. He trusts the Mother and feels secure that in the most difficult of times, the Mother is with him. His heart, so often pierced by Christ's adversaries, continues to be strengthened by Christ. Daughter, he is a little child who has gradually grown and continues to grow in the Heart of Mary."

Above: John Haffert, co-founder of the Blue Army, with author near Fatima at the site of Our Lady's fourth apparition there (see p. 236)

## CHAPTER 34.

## *Mary And Fatima*
### The daughters of Joachim and of Mohammed

"In the end my Immaculate Heart will triumph."
                                    Mary in Fatima

On June 1, 1986, Mary said to Gladys in San Nicolás: "Jesus, the Eucharist! It is His living and true Body, adore It and love It." Devotion to the Eucharist was also the theme which ushered in the apparitions of Mary in Fatima in 1917. Indeed, the messages of Fatima are so important and apocalyptic that I have devoted much time in this book to them, and in chapter 37 the similarities of these messages to those of *Our Lady in Akita*, Japan, in 1973, will be discussed.

There is a great devotion to *Our Lady of Fatima* in my homeland Trinidad and Tobago, thanks to Count Finbar Ryan O.P., who was Archbishop of Port of Spain from 1940 to 1966. Born in Cork, Ireland, Count Finbar wrote the first book on Fatima in English in 1939. It was published by Browne and Nolan, Ltd., Dublin. (see p. 246).

This devotion to Mary has a long history in Trinidad and Tobago, and on March 24, 1816, the foundation stone of the Cathedral of the Immaculate Conception was laid. However, it was not until 1832 that the Cathedral, the largest in the English-speaking Caribbean, was finally completed. About 1875, a group of Portuguese immigrants to Trinidad founded a religious society to encourage Marian devotion and in 1878, Msgr. Gonin, O.P., the then Archbishop, received a 30 foot statue of Our Lady from France. It was erected on a hill called Laventille. Over the years the statue was badly damaged and in 1947 a new statue of Our Lady was erected on the top of the tower of a sturdy concrete church. From this lofty hill Our Lady watches over the city of Port of Spain (see p. 246).

On the feast of the Assumption, August 15, 1943, Count Finbar consecrated the Archdiocese of Port of Spain to the *Immaculate Heart of Mary*. On May 13, 1946, the anniversary day of the first apparition of Our Lady of Fatima in 1917, many pilgrims made their way to the Laventille Shrine for devotion to Our Lady. Archbishop Ryan was present and preached an impressive sermon. From then on, as is the custom in Fatima itself, devotions are held every thirteenth day of the month from May to October. However, it was not until August 1984 that I first visited Fatima with my daughter, Maria.

### Portugal 1646 - 1917

Portugal, since its very foundation, was called "La Terra de Santa Maria" and in 1646, two hundred years before she appeared in Lourdes, King Dom John IV and the entire nation swore fidelity to Mary under the title of *"the Immaculate Conception."* Since that year, the Mother of God has been proclaimed Queen and Patroness of Portugal. For that reason, the Portuguese monarchs never wore a crown. It has been reserved exclusively for the Immaculate Virgin.

However, in 1910, the monarchy was overthrown and a republic was proclaimed. A clique of Marxist-leaning anarchists and freemasons were in power and their avowal was to stamp out religion in that predominantly Catholic country. In 1911, Alfonso Costa, then Head of State, approved the law of total separation of Church and State in a drive to destroy the Catholic Church. The declaration ended with the words: "Thanks to this law, Portugal, within two generations, will have succeeded in completely eliminating Catholicism."

It was a prelude to Lenin's vow to eliminate God in Russia and the rest of the world. It was a time in Portugal when children were obliged to march through the streets with banners inscribed with slogans such as: "Neither God nor religion." Over a hundred churches were demolished in Lisbon alone. It is against this background that the apparitions of Mary, the Queen and Patroness of Portugal, took place in Fatima in 1917.

### A Village Called Fatima

Now, the history of the village called Fatima dates back to the time when the Mohammedans capitulated and left Spain and the Iberian peninsula. Their last holdings were in Portugal which they had occupied for centuries. Legend has it that among the last persons preparing to leave was a maiden named Fatima, the daughter of the last Moslem chief. She was in love with a Christian and was attracted to his faith. When her countrymen finally left Portugal, Fatima became a Christian, married, and to this day the village where the couple settled bears her name.

Fatima is also the name of the daughter of the Prophet Mohammed and after her death he wrote: "You shall be the most blessed woman in Paradise, after Mary." In a variant of the text, Fatima is made to say: "I surpass all the women, except Mary." In fact, the Koran has many passages on the Blessed Virgin and acknowledges her immaculate conception and also her virgin birth. However, Jesus is seen in the Koran as a Prophet, but not as great as Mohammed. Mohammed is seen as the ultimate and greatest Prophet of God, and the central doctrine of the Moslems is expressed in their frequent declaration: "There is no God but Allah, and Mohammed is His Prophet."

Islam denies the divinity of Jesus and also teaches that He was not put to death on the Cross. The Koran also condemns the dogma of the Trinity. It is, therefore, of more than passing interest that not only did Mary choose to appear in a village with the name of Fatima, but that her apparitions there were preceded by the proclamation of the divinity of Jesus and the adoration of the Holy Trinity by the "Angel of Peace."

In his book *Sign of Her Heart*, John M. Haffert, the co-founder of the Blue Army (see p. 233), records that in his address at the International Congress, preparatory to the closing of the Holy Year at Fatima in October 1951, the much revered Bishop Fulton Sheen asked the question: "Why should Our Lady be known by the same name as a descendant of Mohammed, albeit a convert?" The bishop, expressing his personal interpretation, answered his own question: "It is because Our Lady came for the conversion, not merely of the carriers of the hammer and sickle, but also of the carriers of the crescent and the star!"

Interestingly, just as Fatima bears the name of Mohammed's daughter, the town of Lourdes, where the Blessed Virgin said: "I am the Immaculate Conception," bears the name of a Moslem commander who could not be dislodged from a nearby fort during the anti-Moslem campaign of Charles Martell in 782 AD. This Moslem commander of a Fort in the Pyrenees, besieged by the Franks at the time of Charlemagne, refused to surrender *to any man*. According to Fr. Robert J. Fox in the Fatima Family Messenger (April-

June 1991) and John Bird in the audio tape *The Mantle and Shadow*, the Bishop of Le Puy was called upon to negotiate. He sent a message to the commander: "Safeguarding your honour and knowing you will not surrender *to any man*, will you consider surrendering to a Lady, the Sovereign Queen of Heaven — Settena Maryam (Holy Mary)." (The word Islam means "surrender"). This won the commander over. He surrendered and was later baptized, changing his name from Mirat to the Christian name Lorus, from which the town near the Fort got its present name, Lourdes.

It was barely one month before Mary appeared in Fatima that the history of the "hammer and sickle" began. This was on April 16, 1917, when, with the cooperation of the German government, Vladimir Lenin returned to Russia from exile in Switzerland to become leader of a group of political conspirators known as the Bolsheviks.

In the October Revolution of that year, the Bolshevik Party seized power in Russia, promising the great lie, as history has since shown, of "peace, land, and bread," and in March 1918 the Party changed its name to the Russian Communist Party. Its manifesto was that of Karl Marx. Marx had rejected the idea of a God, deciding that religion was merely the "opiate of the people," and his colleague Zinoviev also declared: "We shall vanquish God in His highest heaven!"

### The Angel of Peace

However, the divine drama in Portugal did not begin in 1917 when the Virgin first appeared in Fatima, but in the spring of 1916 while World War I was raging across Europe. It was in the Cova da Iria, about two miles from Fatima, that an angel, believed to be Michael the Archangel, appeared to three little children, Lucia, Jacinta and Francisco (see p. 247).

He said: "I am the Angel of Peace. Pray with me." Then, kneeling on the ground, he bowed until his head touched the ground and asked them to pray with him: "My God, I believe, I adore, I hope and I love you. I ask pardon for those who do not believe, do not adore, do not hope, do not love you." Then, raising his head, he said: "The Hearts of Jesus and Mary are attentive to the voice of your supplications." He then disappeared.

The second apparition of the angel took place two months later in the summer of 1916. Once more, he spoke of the Hearts: "Pray, pray, very much! The Hearts of Jesus and Mary have designs of mercy on you. Offer prayers and sacrifices constantly to the Most High."

In the autumn of the same year, the angel appeared for the third and final time. He was holding a chalice and a Sacred Host was suspended above it. Most significantly, and a confirmation of the transubstantiation as taught by the Orthodox and Catholic Churches, drops of blood fell into the chalice from the Host.

Leaving the chalice and the Host, both miraculously suspended in the air, he prostrated himself before the Sacred Presence and recited this prayer: "Most Holy Trinity, Father, Son and Holy Spirit, I adore you profoundly and I offer You the most precious Body, Blood, Soul and Divinity of Jesus Christ, present in all the tabernacles of the world, in reparation for the outrageous sacrileges and indifference with which He Himself is offended. Through the infinite merit of His Most Sacred Heart and the Immaculate Heart of Mary, I beg of you the conversion of poor sinners." He then gave the Host to Lucia and the chalice to Francisco and Jacinta from which to drink.

### Enter The Virgin Mary

On May 13, 1917, the Queen herself appeared for the first time to the three young children in the Cova da Iria. Significantly, it was eight days after Pope Benedict XI, at the height of World War I, urged the Catholic world to implore Our Lady to intercede with her divine Son for the gift of peace. May 13 was in those days the feast of *Our Lady of the Blessed Sacrament*, the Sacrament of the new and everlasting Covenant.

To quote Lucia's own words: "We beheld a Lady all dressed in white. She was more brilliant than the Sun and radiated a light more clear and intense than a crystal glass filled with sparkling water, the rays of the burning Sun shining through it." She wore a white mantle falling to her feet, edged in burnished gold. A prominent star shone from the hem of her robe, while from her hand hung an exquisite Rosary of white pearls (see p. 246). She said to the children: "I come from heaven. I want you to come here on the 13th of each month until October when I will tell you who I am and what I want."

She appeared again on June 13, and miraculously holding out her heart surrounded by thorns, which pierced it from all sides, she told Lucia: "God wishes you to remain in this world for some time because He wants you to establish in the world devotion to my Immaculate Heart, for the Heart of Jesus wants my Immaculate Heart to be venerated by His side. I promise salvation to those who embrace it and their souls will be loved by God as the flowers placed by myself adorn His throne." We note again the emphasis on the Hearts of Jesus and Mary, this time by the Queen herself. Lucia remained alive, as promised.

On July 13, she gave three revelations to Lucia which were not to be disclosed until a future date. In fact, it was not until 1927 that our Lord Himself appeared to Lucia and gave her permission to disclose the first two parts of the secrets. The first was a vision of hell, which was obviously meant to confirm that Satan did exist. The second revelation dealt with devotion to the Immaculate Heart, the five first Saturdays and prophecies concerning Russia.

### The Five First Saturdays

The Virgin said to Lucia: "You have seen hell where the souls of poor sinners go. In order to save them, God wishes to establish in the world devotion to my Immaculate Heart. If people do what I ask, many souls will be saved and there wil be peace. The war (World War I) is going to end soon, but if people will not stop offending God, another and more terrible war will begin during the reign of Pius XI... To prevent this, I shall come to ask for the consecration of Russia to my Immaculate Heart and a Communion of reparation on the five first Saturdays. If my requests are granted, Russia will be converted and there will be peace. If not, she will scatter her errors throughout the world, provoking wars and the persecution of the Church. The good will be martyred, the Holy Father will have much to suffer and various nations will be annihilated. In the end my Immaculate Heart will triumph, the Holy Father will consecrate Russia to me, Russia will be converted and a certain period of peace will be granted to the world."

This prophecy was made in July 1917 when Russia was still a very Christian country, and in November of that year, Vladimir Lenin started the reign of atheistic Communism in Russia. Indeed, the three little children did not know what Russia meant and thought that Russia was the name of a woman. As also prophesied, World War II began during the reign of Pope Pius XI (1932-1939).

Eight years later, on December 10, 1925, the Blessed Virgin appeared to Lucia again, this time with the Child Jesus. At that time she was in the Convent of the Sisters of St. Dorothy in Pontevedra, Spain. Once more she requested the five first Saturdays devotion in reparation for the sins committed against her Immaculate Heart. Among the sins committed against her Immaculate Heart are doubts cast against her Immaculate Conception, her virgin birth and her perpetual virginity, her intercessory and mediatory role with her Son, and disrespect for herself, her images and her psalter, the Rosary.

She showed Lucia her Heart encircled by thorns, and then the Child Jesus told her to have compassion on the Heart of His Mother. "This Heart," He said, "was pierced with thorns by ungrateful people and there was no one to make an act of reparation to remove them." The Virgin then said to Lucia: "You at least try to console me and say that I promise to assist at the hour of death, with the graces necessary for salvation, all those who, on the first Saturday of five consecutive months, shall confess, receive Holy Communion, recite five decades of the Rosary, and keep me company for fifteen minutes while meditating on the fifteen mysteries of the Rosary, with the intention of making reparation to me."

However, in her memoirs *Fatima in Lucia's Own Words*, Lucia has stated that Jesus lamented that whereas many begin the cycle of the five first Saturdays, few finish them, and those who did, did so merely to obtain their promised graces. It would please Him more, He said, if they said the five mysteries with fervour and with the intention of making reparation to the Heart of their heavenly Mother, than if they recited fifteen "in a tepid and indifferent manner."

## The Collegial Consecration

What is probably not known to many is that on June 13, 1929, the Virgin appeared privately to Lucia and said: "The time has come when God asks the Holy Father, in union with all the bishops of the world, to make the consecration of Russia to my Immaculate Heart, promising to save it by these means." And in one of her letters to her confessor, dated May 18, 1936, Lucia also confided that the Lord Himself said to her: "I want My whole Church to acknowledge that consecration as a triumph of the Immaculate Heart of Mary so that it may extend its cult later on, and put the devotion to the Immaculate Heart beside the devotion to My Sacred Heart."

However, it was not until fifty-five years later, on March 25, 1984, that this consecration was eventually made, specifically as the Virgin requested, in union with all the bishops of the world. It was made by Pope John Paul II in St. Peter's Square in front of the statue of *Our Lady of Fatima* which was flown from Fatima for this solemn and historic occasion. It was on the feast of the Annunciation (see p. 248).

One year after the consecration, almost on the same day, Mikhail Gorbachev rose to power in the Soviet Union in 1985, and immediately introduced *glasnost* (openness) and *perestroika* (restructuring) which heralded the collapse of the Communist system. On December 1, 1989, this leader of the Soviet Union, once the world's most militant atheistic State, met with Pope John Paul II at the Vatican, the first meeting ever between a General Secretary of the Communist Party of the Soviet Union and a Supreme Pontiff of the Roman Catholic Church (see p. 248).

### The Third Secret of Fatima

Whereas the first two secrets were revealed to the public in 1927, it was not until 1941 that Sister Lucia disclosed the existence of the controversial third secret of Fatima. She eventually requested it to be revealed to the Pope at her death or by 1960, whichever would come first, because, as she said: "it would become clearer at that time." This suggested to me that the contents of the secret pertained to the second half of the twentieth century. In fact, I vividly remember anxiously awaiting the revelation of the third secret of Fatima when I was a medical student in Dublin in 1960. It was not revealed, and so far four successive Popes have chosen not to reveal it.

The silence of the Vatican caused disappointment and confusion in the Catholic world but we did not know at that time that neither Lucia nor the Bishop of Fatima had ever said that the secret would be made public in 1960. All they said was that it was to be opened by the Pope in 1960. The present Pope, John Paul II, knows the secret.

Sandra Zimdars-Swartz, Associate Professor of Religious Studies at the University of Kansas, in her book *Encountering Mary* quotes an article which appeared in the German weekly *News Europa* on October 15, 1963, claiming that Lucia was told by the Blessed Virgin that in the second half of the twentieth century a great punishment would come to all humanity. Satan would succeed in planting confusion in the minds of those great scholars who invented weapons that could destroy mankind in a few minutes. He would bring the mighty ones under his power and make them manufacture armaments in great numbers.

Then God would punish people more severely than He did during the flood. Both the great and the powerful and the small and the weak would perish. A time of severe trials for the Church would come; cardinals opposing cardinals and bishops opposing bishops... There would be a "big, big war" in the second half of the twentieth century. The Virgin described fire and smoke falling from the sky, the oceans turning to steam, and the death of millions and millions of people. "The time of times is coming and the end of all ends, if people are not converted."

This was published in 1963 and it is so closely similar to the message of *Our Lady in Akita* ten years later in 1973 that it would be an uncanny coincidence if it were not true.

Another important public declaration concerning this third secret is found in an interview with Cardinal Ratzinger by the journalist Vittorio Messori in August 1984, as reported in the *Journal of Jesus*. Referring discreetly to the contents of the third secret, the Cardinal mentioned three important points: "The dangers threatening the faith, the importance of the 'last times' and the fact that the prophecies contained in this third secret correspond to what Scripture says."

With respect to this latter point, to someone who once questioned her on the contents of the third secret, Sister Lucia replied: "It is in the Gospel and in the Apocalypse. Read them." And on another occasion, she specified Chapters 8-13 of the Apocalypse. These chapters prophesy the destruction of one third of the earth, identify the number of the beast and refer to the *Ark of the Covenant* and the *Woman clothed with the Sun*.

### The Miracle of the Sun and the Column of Smoke

At her last apparition on October 13, 1917, the Blessed Virgin directed her hands streaming with light towards the Sun, and then the great miracle of the Sun took place. A crowd of 70,000 witnesses, including many skeptics, watched in awe as the Sun began to spin and change colours to green, red, violet and gold.

Among the crowd was Dr. Joseph Garrett, Professor of Natural Sciences at Coimbra University, who wrote the following testimony in December 1917: "The Sun had broken through the thick layer of clouds that hid it and shone clearly and intensely... It was a remarkable fact that one could fix one's eyes on the brazier of heat and light without any pain in the eyes or blinding of the retina... The Sun's disc did not remain immobile for it spun round on itself in a mad whirl, when suddenly a clamour was heard from all the people. The whirling Sun seemed to loosen itself from the firmament and advance threateningly upon the earth as if to crush us with its huge fiery weight. The sensation during these moments was terrible."

Dr. Garrett also testified to another great phenomenon on that historic day: "During the solar phenomenon there were changes of colour in the atmosphere... Soon after I heard a peasant who was near to me shout out in tones of astonishment: 'Look, that lady is all yellow!' In fact, everything, both near and far, had changed, becoming golden-yellow. People looked as if they were suffering from jaundice. My own hand was of the same yellow colour... All these phenomena which I have described were observed by me in a calm and serene state of mind and without any emotional disturbance."

However, another much less publicized phenomenon of especial significance preceded the solar miracle. According to Dr. Garrett: "A little after one o'clock the children arrived at the site. It must have been about half past one when there rose up on the precise spot where the children were, a *column of smoke*, a delicate and slender bluish column which went straight up above their heads and then evaporated. The phenomenon lasted for some seconds and was perfectly visible to the naked eye. It was repeated yet a second and a third time." This was her calling card, as it were. It was the Marian symbol — the *column of smoke* (Song of Songs 3:6;8:5).

But while the Sun was dancing to the utter amazement of the crowd, the visionaries viewed in the sky a tableau of scenes. St. Joseph had come as a member of the Holy Family and he blessed the crowd three times. Then Our Lady appeared as *Our Lady of Sorrows*, accompanied by her divine Son dressed in red, who also blessed the crowd. Finally, Lucia saw the Blessed Virgin Mary wearing the brown robe of *Our Lady of Mount Carmel*, holding the brown Scapular in her hand and her infant Son on her knee. It was during this last apparition that she announced to the visionaries: *"I am the Lady of the Rosary."* — but the Scapular was also in her hand!

Soon afterwards, a Masonic pamphlet was circulated to "all liberal Portuguese.": "Citizens! As if the pernicious propaganda of reactionaries were not enough, we now see a miracle trotted out in order further to degrade the people into fanaticism and superstition. There has been staged... a ridiculous spectacle in which the simple people have been ingeniously deceived by means of collective suggestion into a belief in a supposed apparition of the Mother of Jesus... As if, however, the declaration of these poor little dupes who affirm they have seen a 'Virgin' who, however, nobody else can see; and as if this were not sufficient, it is affirmed, or rather invented, that the Sun, at a certain hour on 13th October, 1917, and in the height of the 20th century, was seen to dance a fandango in the clouds."

The pamphlet went on to recommend that there should be "an intensive and tenacious propaganda, which will rouse the mentality of one's co-citizens to the realms of truth, reason and science, convincing them that nothing can alter the laws of nature... Let the professors in the schools and colleges educate their pupils in a rational manner, liberating them from religious preconceptions as from all others, and we shall have prepared a generation for the morrow, happier because more worthy of happiness."

History, of course, has shown that this 'propaganda' has not achieved its godless end and millions of people continue to journey to Fatima, some on their knees.

### The Thirteenth of the Month

In the light of the seriousness of the Fatima secrets, why did Mary choose the thirteenth day of the month for her six apparitions in Fatima? Abbé André Richard, D.D., one of the greatest experts on the Fatima message, was once asked: "What is the meaning of the star on Our Lady's robe when she appeared in Fatima?" He answered: "Read the Book of Esther."

The Book of Esther tells the story of the great and courageous Jewish Queen, Esther, one of the wives of King Ahasuerus of Persia, who was unaware of Esther's Jewish ethnicity. The Jews were in that land in exile from their homeland Israel after the Babylonians' victory over them. The treacherous anti-semitic Haman had persuaded the king to annihilate them. A date was chosen by lot for their destruction. It was the thirteenth of the month (Adar 13). It was then that the noble Mordecai, himself Jewish, entreated Queen Esther to intervene for the Jews: "I shall go to the king in spite of the law; and if I perish, I perish." The king acceded to Esther's plea and, through her courageous *intercession*, her people were saved from mass annihilation on the thirteenth day.

In Fatima this courageous Woman and "intercessor" appeared on May 13, wearing a star on the hem of her dress (see p. 246). She came to save her children and to warn us of the impending peril which the world was facing. Esther means "Star," and she came in the spirit of Esther to save us from mass annihilation.

She came calling for conversion and reparation for our souls' sake. She also came promoting adoration of the Holy

Trinity and the Holy Eucharist. She came proclaiming the divinity of her Son and calling for devotion to Their Sacred and Immaculate Hearts. She pleaded for the daily recitation of the Rosary, the wearing of the Scapular and the Communion of reparation on the five first Saturdays.

### The Rosary and the Scapular

On August 15, 1950, the feast of the Assumption of Our Lady, the only remaining survivor of the three children of Fatima, Lucia, now Sister Mary of the Immaculate Heart, in the Carmelite Cloister in Coimbra, Portugal, was asked why Our Lady held the Scapular in her hands in the final apparition in Fatima. She answered: "Because Our Lady wants everyone to wear the Scapular... The reason for this is that the Scapular is our sign of consecration to the Immaculate Heart of Mary." Asked if the Scapular is as necessary in the fulfillment of the requests of Our Lady of Fatima as is the Rosary, Lucia replied: "The Scapular and the Rosary are inseparable."

John Haffert once found the following account in the pages of an ancient history of the Carmelite Order written by a writer named Ventimiglia: "Three famous men of God met on a street corner in Rome. They were Friar Dominic, busy gathering recruits to a new Religious Order of Preachers; Brother Francis, the friend of the birds and beasts, and especially dear to the poor; and Angelus, who had been invited to Rome from Mount Carmel in Palestine because of his fame as a preacher. At their chance meeting, by the light of the Holy Spirit, each of the three men recognized each other and in the course of their conversation they made prophesies to each other. Saint Angelus foretold the stigmata of Saint Francis, and Saint Dominic said: "One day, Brother Angelus, to your Order of Carmel the Most Blessed Virgin Mary will give a devotion known as the Brown Scapular, and to my Order of Preachers she will give a devotion known as the Rosary. *And one day through the Rosary and the Scapular, she will save the world.*"

246.

Above left: Archbishop Finbar Ryan (see p. 234)
Above right: Note star on the hem of the dress of
Our Lady of Fatima (see pp. 238 & 244)
Below: The statue of Our Lady on the church steeple on
Laventille hill, Trinidad (see p. 234)

247.

Above: The three young visionaries, Jacinta, Francisco, and Lucia in 1917 (see p. 237)
Below: Pope John Paul II and Sister Lucia

248.

Above: Pope John Paul II consecrates the world to the Immaculate Heart of Mary in Rome in 1984 (see p. 240)
Below: Pope John Paul II and Mikhail Gorbachev in the Vatican (see p. 241)

## CHAPTER 35.

## *Garabandal: The Carmel of Spain*

"Before, the cup was filling up, now it is flowing over...
You are now receiving the last warnings."
                                    Mary to Conchita

Whereas in Fatima the number 13 was significant, in Garabandal it was the number 18. Between June 18, 1961, and June 18, 1965, four young children from Garabandal in Spain claimed to have seen apparitions of the Virgin Mary and Michael the Archangel. They were Conchita Gonzales, Marie Loli Mazon, Jacinta Gonzales and Marie Cruz Gonzales, all about twelve years old. Conchita and Jacinta are second cousins.

**Medical Testimonies**

With respect to the medical assessment of these young children, Dr. Celestino Ortiz Perez of Santander, a pediatrician specializing in child psychology, examined them when they were in a state of ecstasy during the apparitions. He concluded: "In this state of ecstasy, they gave proof that they are beyond the explanation of medical science and all natural laws. They showed no reaction to pain, pin pricks, et cetera. Once out of their trances however, they reacted immediately. The four little girls, from a pediatric and psychiatric point of view, have always been and continue to be normal. The trances in which we have observed these young girls do not fit into the framework of any psychic or any psychological pathology presently known. Our conceit falls apart when we are faced with this kind of dilemma which God bestows on us in order to point out our own medical limitations."

Dr. Ricardo Puncernai, a neuropsychiatrist and Director of neurological services at the University clinic in Barcelona, has also examined the visionaries during their ecstasies. He had this to say: "Even though we try to explain only part of these extraordinary phenomena, the truth is that we do not find any natural scientific explanation which could explain the whole affair."

## San Sebastian de Garabandal

San Sebastian de Garabandal is a tiny village in Spain. It is in the province of Santander in the heart of the Cantabrian mountains. In 1961 there were about 300 inhabitants in this poor little village of 70 stone houses (see p. 258). They were mostly farmers. Customarily, each year on July 18, the feast day of St. Sebastian, there would be a great celebration when the statue of the saint would be processed around the village.

The story of Garabandal opened on June 18, 1981, on a Sunday at 8:30 in the evening. June 18 was the feast of St. Aubert, Bishop of Avranches in France, to whom Michael the Archangel appeared in the year 706, requesting him to construct a sanctuary in his honor on Mount Tombé in Normandy. It was also on June 18, 1010, that the relics of St. Aubert were found. It does not appear to be a coincidence, therefore, that Michael first appeared to the children on June 18, 1961. It was a date of special significance to him.

## The Archangel Michael Appears

On that Sunday there was a sudden sound of thunder before the young girls saw a very bright and beautiful figure surrounded by a brilliant light. He looked liked a child about nine years of age, but at the same time appeared to be extremely powerful. He was wearing a long blue seamless robe and had wings which were large and pinkish. It was Michael, the same Michael who is the angel of the first and of the last decisive battles.

As the late Fr. Joseph Pelletier once said: "The fact that the angel of Garabandal was the Archangel Michael had a special meaning. It indicated the basic theme of what was happening in the little mountain village. Michael's very presence proclaimed a great spiritual drama that was unfolding on earth. It heralded a gigantic struggle in the world between the forces of good and the forces of evil, a renewal on earth of the supreme contest which had taken place in heaven between the faithful angels under the leadership of Michael and the rebellious spirits under the banner of Lucifer."

Nearly one week later on Saturday, June 24, 1961, the feast of John the Baptist, the angel appeared again. He held a sign on which were written Roman numerals which the children could not understand at that time. The following week, on Saturday, July 1, the angel spoke to them for the first time: "Do you know why I have come? It is to announce to you that tomorrow, Sunday, the Virgin Mary will appear to you as *Our Lady of Mount Carmel*." He talked to them for a while, then said: "I shall return tomorrow with the Blessed Virgin."

July 1 was the feast of the Most Precious Blood of Our Lord Jesus Christ, a feast instituted in 1849 by Pius IX, the same great Marian Pope who proclaimed the dogma of the Immaculate Conception one year later in 1850. The significance of this choice of date and feast for Michael to speak and to announce the arrival of the Virgin will unfold later on in this chapter.

### Our Lady of Mount Carmel

The next day, July 2, 1961, was the feast of the Visitation. It was the celebration of the occasion when, soon after the Incarnation when Mary became the *Ark of the Covenant*, she visited her cousin Elizabeth. As promised by the Archangel, it was on this day, July 2, that the Virgin "visited" the children for the first time. The site was Los Pinos, a plateau on a hill with nine beautiful tall pine trees (see pp. 258-9). Like the ancient *Ark of the Covenant*, she was surrounded by a brilliant light and on each side of her stood an angel, one of whom was recognized as Michael.

She wore a white robe and a blue mantle. She had dark long hair which fell down to her waist and was parted in the middle. Words, we are told, could not describe her beauty. On her head was a crown with twelve small golden stars and in her hand she held a large brown Scapular which had a mountain on one side and a cross on the other: "*I am the Lady of Mount Carmel,*" she said. Not equally known is the fact that she once appeared to Conchita alone, dressed as a Carmelite nun in the traditional brown dress of the Order, saying: "I am one and the same."

On the second day of her apparitions, July 3, she brought the Child Jesus with her. It was, as it were, first the "Visitation" then the "Nativity." On July 4, 1961, she told the children: "Do you know the meaning of the sign which was beneath the angel? It had a message that I am going to give to you in order that you may announce it publicly on the 18th of October." Then she said: "You must make many sacrifices, perform much penance and visit the Blessed Sacrament frequently, but first, you must lead good lives. If you do not, a chastisement will befall you. The cup is already filling up and if people do not change, a very great chastisement will come upon them."

### The Warning

Nearly four years later, on January 1, 1965, she told Conchita about a warning which would be given to the world. It was on the feast of the Mother of God. She said that the warning was to be followed by a great miracle and then a permanent sign would be left at the pines. If the warning and the miracle did not change people and turn them towards God, then a terrible and fiery chastisement will befall mankind. The year of the warning was revealed to Marie Loli; the date of the miracle only to Conchita.

It is said that the warning will be experienced by everyone in the world and will be felt interiorly. It will be like a personal judgment when everybody will see the consequences of his or her own sins. It will be like a purification in preparation for the grace of the great miracle to follow. We will, as it were, find ourselves all alone in the world no matter where we are at the time, alone with our conscience before God. It will be for the conversion of the world, and will be the expression of God's great mercy towards us. Reactions to this, some quite distressing, will vary from person to person.

### The Miracle

It is also said that the miracle will take place within twelve months of the warning and that it will be performed at the Pines. It will be so spectacular that all who see it will believe. Conchita will announce the date of the miracle eight days before it is due to occur. According to her, the miracle will coincide with a feast of a saint-martyr of the Eucharist. It will last about fifteen minutes and will take place at 8:30 on a Thursday evening. Notably, it was also at 8:30 p.m. that the first apparition of Michael had occurred.

Significantly, according to a few mystics who have been shown in visions the life of Jesus and His Mother, the institution of the Holy Eucharist at the Last Supper in the Cenacle on Maundy Thursday also took place at 8:30 p.m. This certainly leads us to conclude that the miracle will be Eucharistic. Conchita herself had always said that the

Eucharist is a key feature of Garabandal, and at various times Michael himself appeared to the girls and gave them Holy Communion. But on June 22, 1962, the Archangel told Conchita that not only would he give her Communion but that the Host would be visible to all.

Later, the Virgin told Conchita that the date for this miracle would be the 18th of July, and that she should announce it publicly fifteen days in advance. When Conchita did make the announcement, the news spread quickly throughout Spain and certain other parts of Europe and many people went to Garabandal to see the miracle which was to take place on that day. It was the feast day of San Sebastian.

However, after waiting all day many of the people went home disappointed because the miracle had not occurred. Eventually, after midnight Conchita left her home in ecstasy and several people immediately began to follow her. Interestingly, she had gone to Mass and Holy Communion on the morning of July 18, but Church law at that time did not permit one to receive Holy Communion more than once a day. Therein lies the explanation. Obviously, Michael complied with Church law and waited until after midnight to give Conchita the Sacred Host. Alejandro Damians, a businessman from Barcelona, caught the last seconds of the miracle with his camera (see p. 260). This was the evidence that so many people were looking for. The photograph circulated and more and more people then began to believe the girls.

### The Two Hearts

It was on November 17, 1988, that I first visited Garabandal. Curiously, I was the only pilgrim in the lonely village that day. Among many points of interest, I noted that in the little church in the village the beautiful main altar was flanked on both sides by two life-size statues, one of the Sacred Heart of Jesus and the other of the Immaculate Heart of Mary. Up to that time I could not recall ever having seen an altar so flanked, and it added another dimension to the apparitions in Garabandal. To me, it was also a call to devotion to the two Hearts.

According to Robert Francois in his book *O Children, Listen to Me*, Jacinta was also favoured with an apparition of the Sacred Heart, and of this event she remarked: "May the Blessed Virgin forgive me, but what I shall never forget is having seen the Sacred Heart! He was the most handsome of all men. He had a penetrating look that made me feel as though it would tear my soul right out of my body."

It is also not generally known that on July 20, 1963, Conchita had a long and memorable conversation with Jesus in the village church: "Will Russia be converted?" asked Conchita. "Yes, it will be converted and thus everybody will love Our Hearts," answered Jesus. "Shall I go to heaven?" "If you love much and pray to Our Hearts..." On November 13, 1965, the Virgin said to Conchita: "Conchita, I have not come for your sake alone. I have come for all my children, so that I may draw them closer to *Our Hearts*."

Relevant to this, June 18, the date of the first apparition in Garabandal, was not only the feast of San Sebastian de Garabandal and a date of significance for Michael the Archangel, but it was also the anniversary of the apparitions of the angel to St Catherine Labouré at the Rue du Bac in Paris in 1830. It was there that the Virgin showed this nun of the Visitation Order the design of the Miraculous Medal with two Hearts beneath a large `M' surmounted by a Cross. The message is clear.

As Fr. Phillip Bebie in his booklet *The Warning* wrote: "Somehow the miracle will show us how closely the Hearts of Jesus and Mary are united. Perhaps the two Hearts on the reverse side on the Miraculous Medal were a prophecy as well as a lesson foretelling an age ahead where all hearts will be reconciled as are the Hearts of Jesus and Mary. Reconciliation of hearts is what conversion is all about and it would seem that all the Marian apparitions concern themselves with it."

Just before he died, one of the last messages that Padre Pio gave to the world was to visit Marian shrines for "the world was on the threshold of its perdition." Interestingly, the Virgin had told Conchita that this saintly priest would see the miracle, and when he died on September 23, 1968, before the date of the miracle, Conchita was disturbed as she presumed that the prophecy was not fulfilled. However, to her joyous relief, she was told by a close associate of Padre Pio, Fr. Bernadino Cennamo, a monk at San Pascual monastery in Benevento, Italy, that he did indeed see the miracle before he died. Moreover, when asked by Garabandal devotee Joey Lomangino, whether the Virgin was appearing there, Padre Pio answered in the affirmative.

### The Permanent Sign

Following the miracle, a permanent sign will remain at the pines. One will be able to see it, photograph it, but not touch it. It will be miraculous and will stay in the Pines permanently. Interestingly, on November 18, 1961, a shepherd named Ramon Gonzales testified that he saw a column of smoke in the day and a fire at night, close to the nine pines. They were also seen from the village for two or three months in the autumn of 1962 and on November 25, 1965, by four reliable French witnesses.

### The Message of October 18

The message given by the Virgin to the visionaries on July 3, 1961, was, as instructed, revealed to the world on October 18, 1961. It called for sacrifices, penance, frequent visits to the Blessed Sacrament and conversion. Then on June 18, 1965, nearly four years later, Michael delivered this message on behalf of the Virgin:

"As my message of October 18 has not been complied with and has not been made known to the world, I am advising you that this is the last one. Before, the cup was filling up, now it is flowing over. Many cardinals, bishops and many priests are on the road to perdition and are taking many souls with them. Less and less importance has been given to the Eucharist. You should turn the wrath of God away from yourselves by your efforts. If you ask His forgiveness with sincere hearts He will pardon you. I, your Mother, through the intercession of St. Michael the Archangel, ask you to mend your lives. You are now receiving the last warnings. I love you very much and do not wish your condemnation. Pray to us in sincerity and we will grant your request. You should make more sacrifices. Think about the Passion of Jesus."

In her last apparition to the children on November 13, 1965, Mary's closing remarks to Conchita were: "Conchita, why do you not go more often to visit my Son in the Tabernacle? He waits for you there, day and night." Then she said: "Remember what I told you. When you present yourself before God, your hands must be filled with good works done for your brothers and for the glory of God. But at the present time, your hands are empty."

It was only after reading this that I came to understand why Conchita inscribed these words in Spanish on the front page of a book on Garabandal which she gave to me as a gift when I was a dinner guest at her home on August 29, 1989 (see p. 260): "With love it is my wish that the Blessed Virgin would be your Light to lead you to eternal happiness, and that on the way you will bring many souls to her. Pray for me. Conchita."

The 1917 prophecy of Mary, concerning the conversion of Russia is coming to pass with the sudden collapse of Communism. However, Russia is not fully converted as yet, and it is interesting that on July 20, 1963, Jesus told Conchita that Russia will be converted as a consequence of the miracle to come in Garabandal.

## The Last Pope

In 1962 the Virgin also told Conchita that after Pope John XXIII, who was Pope at that time and who died the following year, there will only be three more Popes, and then it will be "the end of time." However, when Conchita asked the Madonna if this meant the "the end of the world," she replied: "No, the end of the times." According to some, a more satisfactory translation from the Spanish is "the end of this epoch or era" or "the end of the present period." Since Pope John XXIII (1958-1963), there have been Pope Paul VI (1963-1978) and Pope John Paul I (1978). The third Pope is John Paul II (1978-).

## The Apocalyptic Photograph

But the most apocalyptic sign I received in Garabandal occurred when I was leaving the Pines, after spending an hour on that "holy ground." As I reached the foot of the hill leading up to the Pines, I saw a large ceramic plaque with the traditional painting of the fallen angel Satan vanquished at the feet of the victorious Archangel Michael. His wings extended up to Michael's knees. Below the plaque was the following inscription: "On Sunday, June 18, 1961, the Archangel Michael appeared for the first time to the children."

It was a bright sunny November day and I took two photographs of the plaque fifteen seconds apart, one closer up than the other. When the films were developed, the first print showed the plaque as described above, but the *Shekinah*, in the form of a cloudy shaft of light, appeared on the second photograph, completely obliterating the image of Satan, including his wings which reached up to Michael's knees (see p. 261). To many, it was a dramatic and symbolic depiction of the prophesy of Genesis 3:15: *"I will put enmity between you and the woman, and between your seed and her seed; (s)he will crush your head..."* It was a depiction of the forthcoming decisive victory of the Woman over the ancient serpent; the victory of Light over darkness.

Our Lady identified herself in Garabandal, saying: *"I am the Lady of Mount Carmel."* Carmel is the mountain where the Israelites renewed the Covenant with Yahweh after the victory of Elijah over the pagan prophets of Baal. *Our Lady of Mount Carmel* and the *Ark of the Covenant* are but one.

Above: Our Lady of Mt. Carmel as described by the children of Garabandal

258.

Above: Garabandal between the mountains (see p. 250)
Below: The 9 pine trees in Garabandal (Los Pinos) (see p. 251)

Above: A plaque of Our Lady of Garabandal on the pine tree in front of which she first appeared (see p. 251)

Below right: Clouds appear on a photograph of the tree taken a few seconds later (see p. 251)

260.

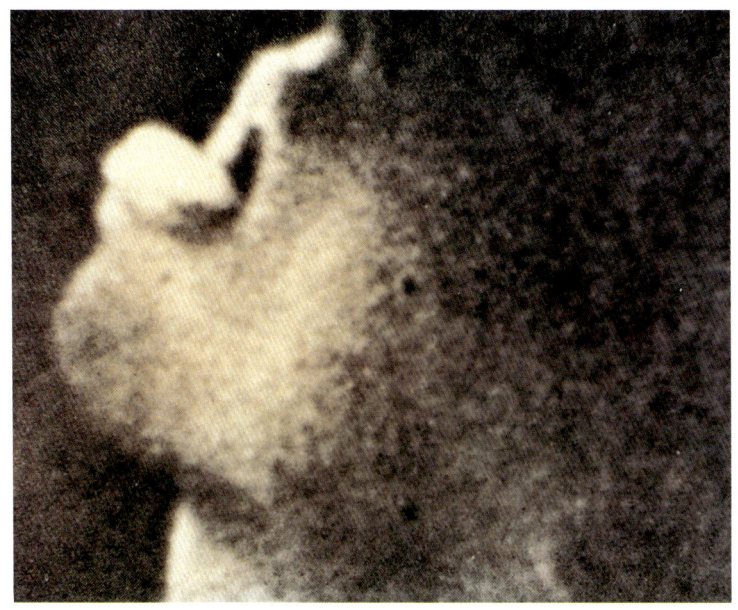

Above: The Host miraculously appears on Conchita's tongue on July 18, 1962 (see pp. 252-253)

Below: Photograph in 1989 with Conchita, Dr. and Mrs. Jeronimo Dominguez, and friends in New York (see p. 255)

261.

Right: The ceramic plaque erected at the foot of the hill leading to the pines (see p. 256)

Below: The cloud obliterates the image of Satan (see p. 256)

## CHAPTER 36.

# *Why is Mary Crying?*

"A voice was heard in Ramah, wailing and loud lamentation. Rachel weeping for her children."
                                                    Matthew 2:18

The Christian Church, particularly the Roman Catholic and Orthodox Churches, has long been accused of worshipping images and statues in defiance of the Second Commandment, and in spite of the rebuttal of these false criticisms over the centuries, even today, there are those who remain ignorant of the facts and parrot these accusations with relentless regularity.

The Second Commandment says: *"You shall not make for yourself an idol whether in the form of anything that is in the heaven above, or that is on the earth beneath, or that is in the water under the earth. You shall not bow down to them or worship them. For I, the Lord, your God, am a jealous God"* (Exodus 20: 1-5). However, in the same Book of Exodus, God Himself ordered Moses to make two cherubim of beaten gold with their faces looking toward the propitiatory or mercy-seat on top of the Ark of the Covenant (Exodus 25: 17-22).

God, therefore, does not forbid the making of images per se, but He forbids the making of idols in order to worship them. The word Icon stems from the Greek (Eikon), meaning image, and in the liturgy of the Eastern Churches, icons play a part similar to that of statues in the Roman Church. Because icons are only symbols, Orthodox do not worship them, but reverence and venerate them. Indeed, the chief champion of the icon in the seventh century AD was St. John of Damascus

(675-749). He carefully distinguished between relative honour or veneration shown to material symbols, and worship due to God alone.

Like the Orthodox Church in the case of their icons, Roman Catholics do not worship images or paintings. They use these physical objects to remind them of Christ, His Mother and His saints, just as photographs are used to remind us of loved ones, and just as statues are commonly sculptured and erected to pay homage to national heroes and exemplars.

There have been a number of Marian apparitions and weepings of sacred images over the centuries in both the Eastern and Roman Churches, but never in the history of our world have there been so many apparitions and weepings as in the past few decades. The first recorded weeping of the Virgin occurred in France nearly a century and a half ago in 1846. It was also the year when Giovanni Ferretti succeeded Gregory XVI as Pope and took the name of Pius IX. He approved the apparition six years later, on August 24, 1852. France at that time was in turmoil, and religion was under persecution and severe pseudo-intellectual attack. Fewer and fewer went to Sunday Mass, the Sacraments were neglected, and Christian attitudes and observances capitulated to self-indulgence, greed and worldliness.

It was on a French alpine mountain about three miles distant from the little village of La Salette that the Blessed Virgin appeared as the Lady of Tears to 14 year old Melanie Calvat and 11 year old Maximin Giraud. It was around 3 o'clock in the afternoon on Saturday, September 19, 1846, twelve years before the apparitions in Lourdes. Suddenly the two young children saw a glowing circle of light. As the children continued to watch the glow it became even more dazzling, then, incredibly so, it began to open as if it were a wondrous shell, and revealed Our Lady (see p. 269).

She was seated on a large rock bent forward, with her face buried in her hands and her elbows rested on her knees. Just as her Son wept over Jerusalem (Luke 19:41), she was weeping as though she had suffered the greatest loss of her life. The strikingly beautiful woman then stood up and tears were still streaming down her face. She prophesied the great famine of Europe and the decline of religion and morals in the world. She also predicted that a great war would follow (World War I). It was a long litany of woe and the Virgin cried throughout the whole apparition.

The following extracts of the Virgin are taken from an the exact text written down in 1878 by Melanie Calvat: "The sight of the holy Virgin was itself a perfect paradise. She was all beauty and all love; the sight of her overwhelmed me. In her finery as in her person, everything radiated the majesty, the splendor, the magnificence of a Queen beyond compare. The word LOVE seemed to slip from her pure and silvery lips. She appeared to me like a good Mother, full of kindness, amiability, of love for us, of compassion and mercy.

"She had a beautiful crucifix hanging from her neck (the brightness in which she was enveloped seemed to come from the crucifix). At times the Christ appeared to be dead. At other times, He appeared to be alive, His head erect, His eyes open. He seemed to be on the Cross of His own accord. At times, too, He appeared to speak and seemed to show that He was on the Cross for our sake, out of love for us, to draw us to His love.

"The holy Virgin was crying nearly the whole time she was speaking to me. Her tears flowed gently, one by one, down to her knees, then, like sparks of light, they disappeared. They were glittering and full of love. She seemed to be saying to me: 'There are so many who do not know me!' But these tears of our sweet Mother, far from lessening her air of majesty, of a Queen, seemed, on the contrary, to embellish her, to make her more beautiful, more powerful, more filled with love, more maternal, more ravishing.

"The eyes of our Mother cannot be described in human language. To speak of them, you would need a seraph. You would need more than that. You would need the language of God Himself, of the God who formed the Immaculate Virgin, the masterpiece of His omnipotence. They appeared thousands of times more beautiful than the rarest diamonds and precious stones. In her eyes, you could see paradise. They drew you to her. The more I looked, the more I wanted to see her; the more I saw, the more I loved her and I loved her with all my might.

"She began to speak with these words: 'If my people do not wish to submit themselves, I am forced to let go of the hand of my Son. It is so heavy and weighs me down so much I can no longer keep hold of it. I have suffered all the time for the rest of you. If I do not wish my Son to abandon you, I must take it upon myself to pray incessantly.'"

She criticized the depravity and the laxity of the world, including many of the clergy and added: "Woe to the inhabitants of the earth! God will exhaust His wrath upon them... The leaders of the people of God have neglected prayer and penance, and the devil has bedimmed their intelligence. They have become wondering stars which the old serpent will drag along with his tail to make them perish... For now is the time of all times, the end of all ends. The Church will be in eclipse, the world in dismay. There will be bloody wars and famines, plagues and infectious diseases. There will be thunderstorms which will shake cities; earthquakes which will swallow countries. Voices will be heard in the air. The fire of heaven will fall and consume three cities.

"In the year 1864, Lucifer together with a large number of demons will be unloosed from hell; they will put an end to faith little by little, even in those dedicated to God. They will blind them in such a way that, unless they are blessed with a special grace, these people will take on the spirit of these angels of hell. Several religious institutions will lose all faith and will lose many souls. Evil books will be abundant on earth and the spirit of darkness will spread everywhere a universal slackening in all that concerns the service of God.

"The true faith of the Lord having been forgotten, they will abolish civil rights as well as ecclesiastical; all order and all justice will be trampled underfoot, and only homicides, hate, jealously, lies and dissension would be seen without love for country or family. All the civil governments will have one and the same plan, which will be to abolish and do away with every religious principle, to make way for materialism, atheism, spiritualism and vice of all kinds.

"The earth will be struck by calamities of all kinds. There will be a series of wars until the last war, which will then be fought by the ten kings of the anti-Christ, all of whom will have one and the same plan. Before this comes to pass, there will be a time of false peace in the world. People will think of nothing but amusement. The wicked will give themselves to all kinds of sins... And so, my children, make this known to all my people."

About a week later a spring gushed out beside the rock upon which the Virgin sat. This had been a water source, but only after heavy rains or when the snows were melting. Now, with neither having occurred, the spring flowed steadily and copiously and has done so ever since. Numerous miraculous cures have been attributed to the water. In 1879 a basilica built on the mountain was completed at last and La Salette has been attracting thousands of pilgrims every year to this "second mount" where Mary cried copiously.

Among the many recent weepings of statues and icons of the Virgin is that of the official and original 1947 International Pilgrim Virgin Fatima statue to North America, which wept in New Orleans on July 17 and 18, 1972. The same statue wept again three days later in Atlanta on July 21, and in a small town in New York State on August 5, 1972 (see p. 270). A second International Fatima statue was also blessed in 1947 to tour Europe. This special statue has wept at least thirty times over the years.

Another miraculous weeping occurred in an Orthodox church which serves the Albanian community in Chicago. It was reported in the *Washington Post* of December 18, 1986. The event happened in St. Nicholas church which was built in 1961 on the northwest side of Chicago. The parish priest was Father Phillip Kuofos and he had held the post for two years.

St. Nicholas is very popular in the Eastern Church and his feast is celebrated with great solemnity. On the eve of his feast, December 5, Father Kuofos was saying vespers during which both he and the people in the congregation noticed something strange on the icon of the Virgin and Child in front of the iconostasis. It seemed to be moisture, and on looking closely, they could trail a trace of it from each of the eyes of the Virgin.

On the following day, Father Dali who had built the church, joined Father Kuofus to celebrate Mass on the feast day, during which occasion the icon wept copiously. "How we got through the liturgy I will never know. Both of us were leading each other through it. At one point Father Dali leaned over me and said: 'I am going to cry.' It was very emotional for us," said Father Kuofos in an interview.

Not long afterwards, long queues began to file past the icon, and television and newspaper men joined in to spread the word further as the moisture continued to ooze from the painting daily. I read about this weeping in Chicago in the 1987 Epiphany issue of the *MIRecorder*, a bulletin of the Medjugorje Information Service of Sussex, England, and I immediately became curious.

Coincidentally, about one month later, I was invited to a medical conference in Chicago and accepted the invitation, mainly because I also saw this as an opportunity to visit the Church of St. Nicholas. Soon after arriving in Chicago on May 7, 1987, I telephoned Father Kuofus to be told that, happily, the icon which had stopped weeping for the past month, had resumed weeping the day before.

I immediately took a taxi and eventually found this small church in the northwestern area of Chicago. There, in front of the iconostasis, I saw the icon of the Theotokos (Mother of God) with light tears slowly oozing down from her eyes. I stayed for one hour in the front pew of the church observing this wondrous phenomenon. The following day I returned to the church and witnessed the weeping again. I then had a long conversation with Father Kuofos who was convinced that the phenomenon was a sign of the apocalyptic times in which we are now living (see p. 271).

This privilege of witnessing the miraculous weeping in the Orthodox Church of St. Nicholas was my first such experience, but it was not the last. On Sunday, April 25, 1993, I was invited by my friends Leticia Villar and Patricia Ruppell to visit the home of Roy and Nita Soliven and their family in Staten Island, New York. That day I had given a talk in Asbury, New Jersey, on the *Ark of the Covenant* at the home of Dr. Rosalie Turton, the foundress of the 101 Foundation, named after the 101 times that the statue of Our Lady of Akita had wept in Japan.

It was around midnight while I was on my way to a New York Airport hotel, that I was welcomed by the Solivens, a family with a deep devotion to Our Lord and His Mother and the Infant Jesus of Prague. Indeed, since February 25, 1993, five statues of the Infant Jesus were exuding oil in their home, and I personally witnessed this miracle that night. But, another outstanding phenomenon occurred that night. I drew to their attention that a small statue of *Our Lady of Fatima* was also weeping. It was the first time that this statue was seen to weep in their home. I have no scientific explanation for this. I testify only to what I saw that night (see p. 271).

It was on the feast of the Annunciation that the apparitions in Betania, Venezuela, began in 1976, and I was there for the eighteenth anniversary as the guest of Dr. Rosalie Turton who brought with her close to 200 pilgrims from the United States of America. On the following day we visited the home (now a chapel) of Mrs. Odette Loudonadje in Turmero, about two hours by car from Caracas, where an icon of *Our Lady of Perpetual Succour* has been oozing copious amounts of oil since January 27, 1986. Once more, I was witness to another weeping.

But why is the Virgin weeping, particularly in this twentieth century? Father Stefano Gobbi held a cenacle of his Marian Movement of Priests in Akita, Japan, on September 15, 1987. It was the feast of *Our Lady of Sorrows* and the sixth anniversary of the last weeping of the statue of Our Lady of Akita, which wept 101 times during the period 1973-1981. She said to Fr. Gobbi:

"I am weeping because humanity is not accepting my motherly invitation to conversion and to its return to the Lord..., the Lord openly denied, outraged and blasphemed.

Your heavenly mother is publicly despised and held up for ridicule. My extraordinary requests are not being accepted; the signs of my immense sorrow which I am giving are not believed in.

"Your neighbour is not loved: everyday attacks are made on his life and his goods. Man is becoming ever more corrupt, godless, wicked and cruel. A chastisement worse than the flood is about to come upon this poor and perverted humanity. **Fire will descend from heaven**, and this will be the sign that God in His justice has as of now fixed the hour of His great manifestation.

"I am weeping because the Church is continuing along the road of division, of loss of the true faith, of apostasy and of errors which are being spread more and more without any offering opposition to them... And so, even for the Church the moment of its great trial has come, because the man of iniquity will establish himself within it and the abomination of desolation will enter into the holy temple of God.

"I am weeping because, in great numbers, the souls of my children are being lost and going to hell.

"I am weeping because too few are those who accede to my request to pray, to make reparation, to suffer and to offer.

"I am weeping because I have spoken to you and I have not been listened to; I have given you miraculous signs and I have not been believed; I have manifested myself to you in a strong and continuous way but you have not opened the doors of your hearts to me.

"At least you, my beloved ones and children consecrated to my Immaculate Heart, little remnant which Jesus is guarding jealously in the secure enclosure of His divine love, harken to and accept this sorrowful request of mine which, from this place, I address again today to all the nations of the earth. Prepare yourselves to receive Christ in the splendour of His glory, because the great day of the Lord has even now arrived."

269.

Above: Shrine of Our Lady of La Salette in the French alpine mountains (see p. 263)
Below: Our Lady of La Salette weeps copiously

The International Pilgrim Virgin weeps (see p. 265)

Above: The icon which shed tears in the Church in St. Nicholas in Chicago (see pp. 266-267)
Below: Nita Soliven shines a light on a weeping statue of Our Lady of Fatima (see p. 268)

## CHAPTER 37.

## *Mary in Akita, Japan*

**"There is a season for everything ... a time for tears ..."**
                                        **Ecclesiastes 3: 1-4**

On October 9-12, 1991, I participated in a conference on retroviruses and leukemia in Kumamoto, Japan, and at the end of the meeting I flew to Akita, where a statue of the Virgin Mary wept in the convent of the Institute of The Handmaids of the Eucharist. It first happened eighteen years previously on Friday, June 29, 1973. It was the feast of the Sacred Heart.

Sister Agnes Sasagawa was praying in the convent chapel, when she suddenly saw a brilliant light shining from the tabernacle, and then several angels appeared chanting: "Holy, Holy, Holy," as they faced the Blessed Sacrament. Suddenly, she heard an angelic voice to the right of her, praying the daily prayer of the Handmaids of the Eucharist, which was composed for them by the former Bishop of Niigata, Bishop John Shojiro Ito:

"Most Sacred Heart of Jesus, present in the Holy Eucharist, I consecrate my body and soul to be entirely one with your Heart, being sacrificed at every instant on all the altars of the world and giving praise to the Father, pleading for the coming of His Kingdom.

"Please receive this humble offering of myself. Use me as you will for the glory of the Father and the salvation of souls. Most Holy Mother of God, never let me be separated from your divine Son. Please defend and protect me as your special child. Amen."

The feast of the Sacred Heart was therefore a most appropriate day for this event. The vision disappeared when the prayer was over, and on the following day, June 30, Sr. Agnes felt a severe pain in the palm of her left hand, then a wound, about 2 cm. wide and 3 cm. long, appeared in the centre of her hand. It was as though a cross had been engraved in her skin. On Thursday, July 5, a little hole then appeared in the centre of the two branches of the cross from which blood then flowed.

In the early morning of Friday, July 6, Sr. Agnes saw an angel who smiled at her and identified herself: "I am the one who is with you and watches over you." The angel then beckoned her towards the chapel. In a place of honour in the chapel was a wooden statue of the Blessed Virgin, sculptured by a famous Japanese sculptor, Saburo Wakasa, and fashioned after the image of the *Lady of All Nations*, which the Virgin Mary called herself when she appeared to the visionary Ida Peerdeman in Amsterdam in 1945 (shown in chapter 6).

As Sr. Agnes entered the chapel, she felt that the statue of the Virgin, now bathed in a brilliant light, had come to life and was about to speak to her. The voice was indescribably beautiful: "My daughter... do you say well the prayer of the Handmaids of the Eucharist? Then let us pray it together."

As Our Lady began the prayer, the angel also joined in. Sr. Agnes started to pray together with them: "Most Sacred Heart of Jesus, present in the Holy Eucharist..." At this point, the Virgin suddenly interrupted her, saying: "Truly present. From now on you will add TRULY." From that day on, the prayer has been changed to "Most Sacred Heart of Jesus, TRULY present in the Holy Eucharist, I consecrate my body and soul..."

When the prayer was finished, the angel disappeared and the statue resumed its normal appearance. That same day the other nuns in the convent noticed the appearance of an identical wound and blood flowing from the right hand of the statue of the Blessed Virgin. Three months later, on September 29, 1973, the wound in the statue disappeared. It was the feast of Michael the Archangel.

One day when Sr. Agnes was speaking to a stranger who visited the convent, she described the beautiful voice as "a voice which certainly could not have come from this world." The visitor then asked: "Was it comparable to that of the angel?" Whereupon she replied: "The two voices are beautiful, but the voice of Mary is something more divine. One can say that the voice of the angel resembles a song and that of Mary, a prayer!"

However, it was on October 13, 1973, that *Our Lady of Akita* made this apocalyptic warning and prophecy: "My dear daughter, listen well to what I have to say to you. You will inform your superior. As I told you, if men do not repent and better themselves, the Father will inflict a terrible punishment on all humanity. It will be a punishment greater than the flood, such as one will never have seen before. **Fire will fall from the sky** and will wipe out a great part of humanity, the good as well as the bad, sparing neither priests nor faithful.

"The survivors will find themselves so desperate that they will envy the dead. The only arms which will remain for you will be the Rosary and the Sign left by my Son. Each day recite the prayers of the Rosary. With the Rosary, pray for the Pope, the bishops and the priests.

"The work of the devil will infiltrate even into the Church in such a way that one will see cardinals opposing cardinals, bishops against other bishops. The priests who venerate me will be scorned and opposed by their confreres... churches and altars sacked; the Church will be full of those who accept compromise and the demon will press many priests and consecrated souls to leave the service of the Lord. The thought of the loss of so many souls is the cause of my sorrow. If sins increase in number and gravity, there will no longer be pardon for them."

This message is extremely similar to the messages given to Lucia in Fatima, to the children in Garabandal, and the article in the German weekly News *Europa*.

The date the Virgin chose to give this apocalyptic message to Sr. Agnes was October 13. It was the anniversary date of her last apparition in Fatima, 56 years earlier in 1917, when the great atomic reactor, the Sun, came hurling down to Earth. Its significance is clear. According to the Catholic magazine *Voice of the Sacred Hearts*: "Bishop Ito was of the opinion that the Akita message does make known the previously unrevealed third secret of Fatima. He asked Cardinal Ratzinger (who has read the Fatima secret) if this was true. The Cardinal indicated that it was indeed true." It seems, therefore, that she may have discretely disclosed her Fatima message of July 13, 1917, in a less publicized shrine in Japan. Japan was also the first victim of an atomic explosion in 1945!

Howard Dee, former Ambassador of the Philippines to the Holy See (see p. 279), in his recent book *Mankind's Final Destiny* also reports that he asked Cardinal Ratzinger about the correlation of the Fatima and Akita messages. He said: "I knew it was a delicate question as his answer might reveal indirectly the third secret of Fatima. To my surprise, he confirmed that these two messages were essentially the same."

Ambassador Dee also quotes a German periodical *Stimme des Glaubens*, which reported the reply of Pope John Paul II to a question from a small group of pilgrims in Germany as to why the third secret of Fatima was never published. The Pope is reported as saying: "Given the gravity of the contents... my predecessors in the office of Peter have diplomatically decided to subdue its publication... Many want to know out of curiosity. They forget that to know demands a responsibility." He then took out his Rosary and said: "Behold! Here is the remedy against the evil. And do not ask for anything else. Confide everything to the Mother of God."

It is also reported that someone in the group then asked the Pope: "What will happen to the Church?" He replied: "We must be prepared to undergo before long great trials which will demand of us a disposition to lay down our lives, a total dedication to Christ and for Christ. With our prayers it is possible to mitigate this tribulation; it is no longer possible to turn it back. Only in this way can the Church be effectively purified. How many times has blood brought forth the renewal of the Church! It shall not be any different this time."

On January 4, 1975, the feast of St Elizabeth Ann Seton (1774-1821), who converted from the Episcopal Church to Catholicism, the statue in Akita wept for the first time. This phenomenon of tears was observed on 101 separate days over a period of six years before the weeping stopped on September 15, 1981, the feast of Our Lady of Sorrows. Bishop Ito was himself a witness of the weepings on four occasions and he had the tear liquids examined on two occasions. Scientific investigations by Professor Sagisaka of Japan, an expert in forensic medicine, proved that the liquid was identical with human tears. The weepings have also been seen on television by many millions of Japanese, yet many still do not believe or have chosen to forget the event (see p. 277).

The Akita phenomenon was so obviously supernatural, yet there were those "scientists" who attempted to explain away the miracle by the ridiculous hypothesis that Sr. Sasagawa had certain paranormal powers, permitting her to transfer her own tears and blood to the statue, the so-called "ectoplasm" hypothesis. In fact, true science can only remain silent in the face of a miracle which it cannot explain, and it is nothing but "bad science" to attempt to explain an extraordinary event of nature by an absurd hypothesis which is even more unscientific than the miracle itself.

On September 28, 1981, Sr. Agnes suddenly felt the presence of the angel at her side during adoration of the Blessed Sacrament. It was the eve of the feast of Michael the

Archangel. She did not actually see the angel in person, but a Bible appeared open before her eyes and she was invited to read Genesis 3:15: *"I will bring enmity between you and the woman; and between your seed and her seed; (s)he will crush your head..."* Then the angel explained that this passage in Scripture was relevant to the tears of Mary: "There is a meaning of the figure 101. This signifies that sin came into the world by a woman and it is also by a woman that salvation came to the world. The zero between the two signifies the Eternal God who is from all eternity until eternity. The first one represents Eve and the last the Virgin Mary."

Eve spelt in reverse is still Eve. Similarly, 101 reversed is still 101. The zero reminds me of the great saint and Doctor of the Church, Catherine of Siena (1347-1380) to whom God said in Dialogue 10: "Think of the soul as a tree made for love, living only on love. The circle in which this tree's root, the soul's love, must grow in true knowledge of herself; knowledge that is joined to Me, who like the circle has neither beginning nor end."

On October 13, 1989, I was the guest of the Handmaids of the Holy Eucharist for two days in the convent in Akita, and there I witnessed devotion to and adoration of the Blessed Sacrament as I have never seen before. It was also my privilege to meet Sr. Agnes Sasagawa whose hands were covered with gloves to hide the stigmata. She gave me a gift of a blue bag in crochet which she made herself, and which was meant to be the "ark" for my Rosary.

That same morning I met another visitor to the convent. She was a young Japanese lawyer who had come with her mother to give thanks on the anniversary of her miraculous cure by *Our Lady of Akita* of an illness called Takayasu's syndrome, a disease of unknown etiology, involving major arteries and usually fatal after about five years. She was a most intelligent witness of the disease and of her instant cure. I believed her.

That afternoon the novice mistress of the Congregation, with quiet authority, calmly instructed me: "Go and spend a long time in the chapel with *Our Lady of Akita*. She is there waiting for you." The weepings had stopped since 1981 and so I did not see the famous statue weep when I was in the chapel, but it is of significance that, as recorded by Fr. Teiji Yasuda, the most copious weeping occurred on March 25, 1979: "There were true streams of tears which covered her face. We never saw them so abundant as at that time." It was on the feast of the Annunciation, the celebration of that day when

Mary became the Ark of the Lord. It was the *Ark of the Covenant*, in the spirit of Rachel, weeping for her children.

Above: The tears of Our Lady of Akita (see p. 275)
Below: The wooden statue of Our Lady of Akita
(photo courtesy of Larry Galloway)

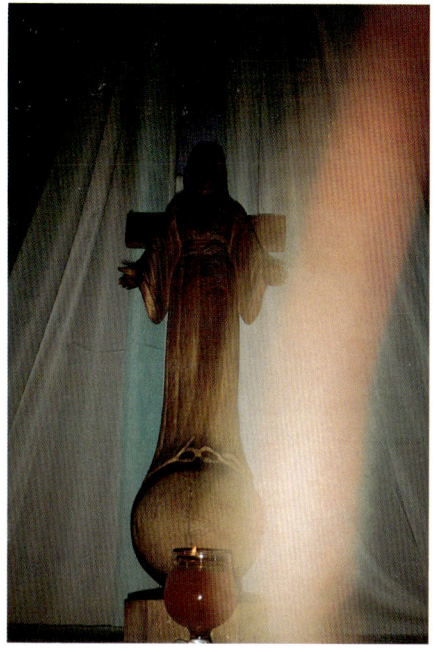

Above: The pillar of fire in front of the statue of
Our Lady of Akita (photo courtesy of Maria Hurley)
Below: Fr. Teiji Yasuda in Akita stands behind the statue.
To his left is current Bishop Francisco Keiicji Sato
(photo courtesy of M. Francis Fukushima)

Handmaids of the Eucharist in adoration in Akita (see p. 272)

Sister Agnes Sasagawa greets the 101 pilgrim group in Akita

Ambassador Howard Dee and Pope John Paul II (see pp. 274-5)

## CHAPTER 38.

## *Mother of Mercy*

### "Hail, Holy Queen, Mother of Mercy!"

To understand the significance of and justification for referring to Mary as *Mother of Mercy* we will have to journey back to the Sinai trek. On the top of the ancient *Ark of the Covenant* was the *"mercy seat"* or seat of propitiation (reparation). There between the golden wings of the Cherubim rested the *Shekinah* who spoke to Moses, Joshua, the Judges, Samuel, Nathan, David, Solomon and all the prophets, and gave mankind the Old Testament (Exodus 25: 200-22).

The word "mercy" comes from the Latin *misericordia*, meaning to give one's heart to a person who is *in misery*. Indeed, the Covenant God of Israel was always known as a God, not only of justice but of mercy: "The Lord, a merciful and gracious God" (Exodus 34:6); "His mercy endureth forever" (Psalm 118); *"Be merciful as your father also is merciful"* (Luke 6:36). Moreover, the Book of Sirach 35:24 says "Welcome is his mercy in time of distress as rain clouds in time of drought."

It appears to me quite likely that this latter quote is probably the source of Portia's speech in Shakespeare's *The Merchant of Venice*, after she concluded that Shylock should be merciful: "On what compulsion must I? Tell me that," asked Shylock. To which Portia replies: "The quality of mercy is not strain'd. It droppeth as the gentle rain from heaven upon the place beneath; it is twice bless'd: it blesseth him that gives and him that takes... It is an attribute to God Himself, and earthly power doth then show likest God's, when mercy seasons justice. Therefore, Jew, though justice be thy plea, consider this — that in the course of justice none of us should see salvation; we do pray for mercy, and that same prayer doth teach us all to render the deeds of mercy..." In similar vein, Matthew records Jesus' sermon on the Mount of the Beatitudes: "Blessed are the merciful for they shall obtain mercy" (Matthew 5:7).

In 1984, while I was working with a stained glass artist in Dublin on designs for windows for the Church of St. Francis in Trinidad, I saw a leaflet on the work-bench with a strikingly beautiful image of Christ. It was the portrait of the *Divine Mercy*, and it was the first time that I had heard of the devotion of the Divine Mercy and of Sister Faustina Kowalska. I was so attracted to the portrait that I discarded the rough sketch of Christ which I had initially presented to the artist, and insisted that he reproduce the portrait on stained glass. This he faithfully did, and this image of the Divine Mercy in stained glass is the only one that I know of in the world. It was executed by Mr. William Earley of Dublin (see p. 286).

Helena Kowalska, the "secretary," as Our Lord called her, of this devotion to His Divine Mercy, was born on August 25, 1905, in the village of Glogowiec in Poland. On August 1, 1925, she entered the Congregation of the Sisters of Our Lady of Mercy. She was then sent to the Novitiate House in Crakow where, at her profession, she was given the name Sister Mary Faustina to which she added "of the Most Blessed Sacrament." She took her perpetual vows on May 1, 1933, and died seven years later on October 5, 1938 (see p. 286).

The diary of Sister Faustina is a seven hundred page record of her life's experience. She records that on February 22, 1931, Jesus appeared to her, bringing with Him a wonderful message of mercy to all mankind: "In the evening when I was in my cell I became aware of the Lord clothed in a white garment. One hand was raised in blessing, the other was touching His garment at the breast. From an opening in the garment at the breast there came forth two large rays, one red and the other pale. In silence, I gazed intently at the Lord: my soul was overwhelmed with fear but also with great joy. After a while, Jesus said to me: *'Paint an image according to the pattern you see with the inscription: Jesus, I trust in You... I desire that this picture be venerated first in your chapel and then throughout the whole world'*" (see p. 286).

This apparition of Jesus repeated itself several times until her confessor advised her to ask for an explanation of the red and white rays. She did so and was told: *"The rays represent the blood and water which gushed forth from the depths of My mercy when My agonizing Heart was opened on the Cross.*

*The pale rays symbolize the water which makes souls righteous; the red rays stand for the blood which is the life of the soul. These rays shield the soul before the wrath of My Father. Fortunate is he who lives in their shelter for the just hand of God shall not lay hold of him. Proclaim that mercy which is the greatest attribute of God."*

Jesus also called for a feast of the Divine Mercy to be celebrated throughout the Church: *"I desire that it be celebrated with great solemnity on the first Sunday after Easter. From that day the depths of My Mercy will be open to all. Whoever will go to confession and Holy Communion on that day will receive complete forgiveness of sin and punishment... Let no soul fear to draw near to me, even though its sins be as scarlet."*

It is not by coincidence, therefore, that the Gospel of the "first Sunday after Easter" relates to the institution of the Sacrament of Reconciliation: *"Receive the Holy Spirit, for those whose sins you forgive, they are forgiven: for those whose sins you retain, they are retained"* (John 20:23). On February 10, 1938, Sister Faustina quoted the Lord as saying: *"When you approach the confessional, know this, that I Myself am waiting there for you. I am only hidden by the priests, but I Myself act in your soul. Here the misery of the soul meets the God of Mercy."*

Jesus' request for a feast of the Divine Mercy reminds me of the history of the most important holy day in Israel. I refer to the feast of Yom Kippur. In ancient Israel it was the only occasion when the High Priest was allowed to enter the Holy of Holies in the Temple containing the *Ark of the Covenant.* This was an annual day for atonement, fasting and erasing of sin, and many offerings were sacrificed.

This annual event remains a high holy feast for Jews up to this day. On this "Day of Atonement," Israel virtually comes to a standstill and many of the populace attend all-day services in the synagogues. A constant refrain throughout the day is the prayer: "Father, we have sinned before Thee." The worshippers then recount a catalogue of sins that cover the wide gamut of human misbehaviour. It brings to mind the traditional opening prayer of Catholics before their confession: "Bless me Father for I have sinned."

As Rabbi Morris Kertzer says in his book *What is a Jew?*: "Solemn as the day may be, there is still an element of joy in Yom Kippur — a joy that comes with the thought of forgiveness, for the pious Jew *trusts* implicitly in God's *mercy* and *forgiveness.*" In a way, therefore I see a link between this proposed Christian feast of the Divine Mercy requested by Our Lord through Sister Faustina and the great Jewish feast of Yom Kippur.

Sr. Faustina further revealed that the Lord also requested that this feast of the Divine Mercy be preceded by a novena which would begin on Good Friday and end on the eve of the feast. He gave her an intention to pray for each day of the novena.

Notably, the intention for the last day was for souls who had become lukewarm: "*These souls caused Me more suffering than any others; the sight of these caused My soul untold grief and anguish in the Garden of Olives. It was on their account that I said: 'Father, if it is possible, let this cup pass away from me.' The last hope of salvation for them is to seek refuge in My Mercy. These are the souls who thwart my effort; souls without love or devotion, souls full of egoism and selfishness, proud and arrogant. They have hardly enough warmth to keep themselves alive. I cannot bear them because they are neither good nor bad.*"

This anguish caused by lukewarm and indifferent souls is also voiced in Revelation 3:15: "*I know all about you, how you are neither cold nor hot. I wish you were one or the other but since you are neither, but only lukewarm, I will spit you out of my mouth.*"

Moreover, let us not forget that as far back as four centuries ago, the Venerable Louis of Granada (1504-1588) once gave this warning: "Besides those who defer their conversion to the hour of death, there are others who persevere in sin, trusting in the mercy of God and the merits of His Passion. We must now disabuse them of this illusion... You say God's mercy is great, but if you presume upon it, you show that you have never studied the greatness of His justice, for as St. Bernard said: 'God has two feet, one of justice and the other of mercy.' You must embrace both, lest justice separated from mercy should cause us to despair, and mercy without justice should excite us into presumption" (In Cantica, serma. 80).

### Mother of Mercy

In his Encyclical *Dives in Misericordia* (On God's Mercy), Pope John Paul II stated that, "Mary is also the one who bestowed mercy in a particular and exceptional way, as no other person has... She is the one who has the deepest knowledge of the mystery of God's mercy. She knows its price. She knows how great it is. In this sense we call her the *Mother of Mercy*. The whole work of Redemption was an act of divine mercy, and God's mercy — made flesh, was incarnated in her."

That great Franciscan of modern times, St. Maximilian Kolbe, once wrote: "So often in the family a father is pleased when the mother's intercession stays his punishing hand over the child. In that case, justice is given satisfaction yet mercy is shown. Similarly, in order not to punish us God gives us the spiritual Mother whose intercession He never refuses." He is saying that she is our Advocate. She is the Queen Mother.

At 3 o'clock on Good Friday we commemorate the hour of utmost Mercy, and Rev. F. Boyce, in his book *Mary, Mother of Mercy*, had this to say: "We come to the hour of utmost Mercy: the greatest bestowal and manifestation of the compassionate love of the Heart of Our God. Since the Blessed Virgin closely and actively cooperated in this supremely redemptive hour of her Son on Calvary, it is here that she becomes in the fullest sense the *Mother of Divine Mercy*." This was long appreciated and expressed in the eleventh century canticle: "Hail Holy Queen, Mother of Mercy... Turn then, most gracious Advocate, your eyes of mercy toward us."

But it was in Guadalupe in Mexico on the morning of September 9, 1531, which was then the feast of the Immaculate Conception, that the Virgin herself revealed to Juan Diego: "I am your merciful Mother, the Mother of all who live united in this land, and of all mankind."

In Vilnius there is the Shrine of *Our Lady of Mercy*. The image of *Our Lady of Mercy* is painted in a brilliant gold colour just as the ancient *Ark of the Covenant* was covered inside and outside with the purest gold (see p. 285). On top of the ancient Ark was the mercy seat or propitiatory. And so, we can now understand why the living *Ark of the New Covenant* is also the *Mother of Mercy*. It was at the Shrine of *Our Lady of Mercy* in the city of Vilnius, now within the boundaries of Lithuania, that the image of Jesus, the *Divine Mercy*, painted by Eugene Kazimierowski, was first seen in public in 1935. The newest image was painted in 1982 by Robert O. Stempt.

In his classic book *The Admirable Heart Of Mary* written in 1680, St. John Eudes wrote on the *Ark of the Covenant*. Referring to the mercy seat, he said: "What could be more symbolic of Our Lady's holy companionship with the angels than the golden cherubim designed to guard the propitiatory?" Then he added: "The propitiatory is regarded as another figure symbolic of the glorious Virgin because by her intercession the flame of God's wrath was extinguished, His Divine Majesty was turned to look upon mankind with favour and His infinite mercy moved Him to compassion for our infirmities."

It is recorded that Sister Faustina had a special apparition of the Blessed Virgin Mary on March 25, 1936. On that day, the feast of the Annunciation, she recorded: "In the morning, during meditation, God's presence enveloped me in a special way, as I saw His immeasurable greatness and at the same time His condescension to His creatures. Then I saw the Mother of God who said to me: "I gave the Saviour to the world. As for you, you have to speak to the world about His great mercy and to prepare the world for the Second Coming of Him who will come, not as the merciful Saviour but as a just Judge. Oh, how terrible is that day! The angels tremble before it. Speak to souls about this great mercy while there is still time for granting mercy."

On Sunday, April 18, 1993, Pope John Paul II beatified Sr. Faustina Kowalska of Poland. Thus, the Holy See has recognized the authenticity of the apparitions to Sr. Faustina and the urgency of the message of Divine Mercy. That Sunday, April 18, was the second Sunday of Easter. It was the day which Jesus had requested for the feast of Divine Mercy!

The merciful Saviour died at the age of thirty-three. So did his "secretary," Sr. Mary Faustina Kowalska of the Most Blessed Sacrament (1905-1938). She was the perfect secretary. She was her Master's voice.

Painting of Our Lady of Mercy in Vilnius (see p. 284)

286.

Above: Our Lady of the Rosary and the Divine Mercy on stained glass window in St. Francis Church, Trinidad (see p. 281)
Below left: Sister Helen Kowalska (see p. 281)
Below right: "I am your Jesus of Mercy" (see p. 281)

## CHAPTER 39.

## *Don Bosco and Mary, Help of Christians*

**"Do not ever forget these three things; Devotion to the Blessed Sacrament, devotion to Mary, Help of Christians, and devotion to the Holy Father!"**

**Don Bosco**

Constantinople had fallen in 1453 and the whole of the East was under Moslem rule when the Virgin appeared in Guadalupe in 1531. In the year 1571, a huge Turkish armada set sail to capture the Eternal City and an insignificant combined Christian fleet of Spain, Venice and the papacy assembled in defiance at Lepanto near Greece. It was a spectacle that no survivor of that great sea battle would ever forget. Two great galleys, one flying the pennant of the crucified Christ, the other, a huge flag with verses from the Koran, will be rowing directly at each other, gathering speed all the time as the galley masters whipped their slaves to even greater efforts.

In *La Real*, the Spanish flagship, Don John of Austria drew his sword and braced himself for the inevitable head-on clash as Ali Pasha, the Turkish commander, ordered his men on the *Sultana* to prepare to board. The Cross was meeting the Crescent in what many at that time believed to be the last great encounter between galley fleets. The date was October 7, 1571.

Now, in 1570, Archbishop Montufor, the second archbishop of Mexico, had a small reproduction of the holy image of *Our Lady of Guadalupe* made, touched it to the original and sent it to King Philip II of Spain. It was then given by the king to Admiral Giovanni Doria and it was in the Admiral's cabin during that great naval battle of Lepanto. He is said to have prayed for Mary's intercession to save his fleet from what looked like certain destruction. That 1570 copy, about half the size of the original, is now in the Church of San Stefano d'Aveto in Italy.

### Help of Christians

From the human point of view the outcome was inevitable. The Pope of the day, Pope Pius V, called upon every Catholic in Europe to evoke the aid of the Mother of God under her title *Help of Christians*, and to storm heaven unceasingly with Rosaries. The faithful responded and the battle got on the way. At a critical moment when it seemed that the Christian forces would lose, greatly outnumbered as they were, a tremendous wind came up and blew the Turkish navy into total disarray. It would be many days afterwards before word reached Rome of the outcome of the struggle, but the Pope was mysteriously informed of the outcome because, at the very moment when the victory was gained, he suddenly broke off a conversation and said: "Let us give thanks to God; the victory is won." The Turks lost 230 galleys; the Christians, 16.

The Pope's words were taken down and sealed, and a fortnight later a messenger arrived in Rome announcing the glad tidings of the victory which took place exactly at the moment when the Pope announced the outcome of the battle. Forthwith he proclaimed that day of the victory, October 7, 1571, a new feast in honour of *Our Lady of Victories*. The following year it was renamed the feast of *Our Lady of the Rosary*. And so, the title *Mary, Help of Christians* became linked to *Our Lady of Victories* and then to *Our Lady of the Rosary*, a trinity of titles referring to the same event and the same Woman. In 1815, the invocation Help of Christians was added to the litany of the Blessed Virgin in Loreto.

### St. John Bosco

In the same year that the title *Mary, Help of Christians* was honoured in the litany of Loreto, John (Giovanni) Bosco was born in Turin, Italy. He entered the seminary in 1835 when he was twenty years old, and was ordained a diocesan priest on June 5, 1841. Among the resolutions he made was: "The charity and gentleness of St. Francis de Sales shall be the guide in all I do." He was the founder of the Society of St. Francis de Sales, which eventually was officially approved by the Holy See on April 3, 1874. From then on Don Bosco's followers would be called "Salesians" after the gentle seventeenth century bishop.

Don Bosco was himself a man of wonders. God gave him the gift of miracles. Numerous people were cured of deadly diseases by his blessing, and after his prayers on their behalf, the deaf heard, the lame walked, and once a dead boy was raised to life. He also had the gift of prophecy. He could read souls and his dreams were really visions. All these gifts were so common that Pope Pius XI once observed: "In Don Bosco the extraordinary becomes ordinary" (see p. 295).

It was in 1844 that the Virgin Mary appeared to Don Bosco and requested him to build a church under the title *Mary, Help of Christians*, providing him with precise instructions down to the last detail of its construction, just as she has recently done in San Nicholás, Argentina. This great Basilica of *Mary, Help of Christians* in Turin, Italy, was consecrated in 1868 (see p. 296).

There was an Argentinean connection with Don Bosco. In 1875 he sent abroad his first missionaries and when his Salesians left Genoa for Argentina, they received a brief personal note from him: "Do what you can; God will do what you cannot. Trust everything to Our Lord in the Blessed Sacrament and to *Mary, Help of Christians*, and you will see what miracles are" (see p. 296).

Five years later in 1880 Pope Leo XIII called Don Bosco to Rome and invited him to undertake the seemingly impossible task of building the Sacred Heart Church in Rome, the financial burden of which Italy was unable to accommodate. It was a mammoth task, but Don Bosco accepted the challenge. He decided to go to France: "France has always been generous. They have always helped me."

He left Turin on January 31, 1881. He was at that time 66 years old. France knew all about him and as the newspapers said: "Paris threw herself at his feet." In the Church of the Archconfraternity for the conversion of sinners, known as the Church of *Our Lady of Victories*, when he was preparing to say Mass, the crowds overflowed outside. "What ever is going on?" asked a casual visitor. A woman answered her: "It is a Mass for the conversion of sinners and it is being said by a saint!"

In 1886 he returned to France and the reception was no less enthusiastic. Then in May 1887 he travelled to Battersea in London and discussed the proposed opening of Salesian work in England. Later that same year he sent his first Salesians to Battersea. The year of 1887 was also the year of his last visit to Rome. Feeble as he was, he demanded to be present at the opening of the Sacred Heart Church.  After nearly seven years of unrelenting labour in building it, he said his first and only Mass in the new church.

Tired and ailing, he took to his bed in Turin in December 1887, and just before his death on January 31, 1888, he summoned some of his Salesians and said: "Do not ever forget these three things; Devotion to the Blessed Sacrament, devotion to *Mary, Help of Christians*, and devotion to the Holy Father!" It is also noteworthy that several years after Don Bosco had died, whereas his body was found to be corrupt, his Scapular was miraculously intact.

### Our Lady of Victories

On June 14, 1993, I visited the Church of *Our Lady of Victories (Notre Dame des Victoires)* in Paris.  The church was built in 1629 and since 1836 it has been a place of pilgrimage and devotion to Mary.  It was founded in 1629 by Louis XIII, in thanksgiving for his victories and according to a vow which he had made.  It is a place of intercession and thanksgiving, as the numerous plaques in the church testify.  St. Thérèse of the Infant Jesus, St. John Bosco and many other saints all prayed there (see p. 296).

In 1832, two years after the apparition of Our Lady to Catherine Labouré in Paris, Fr. Charles des Gennettes was the parish priest of the Church of *Our Lady of Victories*.  For a century and a half, the parishioners were known for their devotion to the Blessed Virgin.  However, with the anti-clerical French Revolution, the church fell upon evil days, and eventually there were only a few parishioners left.  Fr. des Gennettes found that scarcely anyone came to Mass or received the sacraments.  At length, he became discouraged.

On Sunday, December 3, 1836, he began to say Mass in an almost empty church, when he was seized by a distressing distraction, the conviction that he must resign.  He could scarcely keep his mind on the Mass.  At that moment he heard a soft distinct voice say very solemnly: "Consecrate your parish to the *Most Holy and Immaculate Heart of Mary.*"  Convincing himself that it had been his imagination, he knelt to say his prayers.  Again, he heard the words: "Consecrate your parish to the *Most Holy and Immaculate Heart of Mary.*"

Taking up a pen, he then composed the rules for a Confraternity of Our Lady.  The Bishop approved the rules that same week.  The following Sunday, Fr. des Gennettes told the ten people at Mass about his project. He said that there would be vespers of Our Lady that evening and that he would give them the full details of the Confraternity. When he entered the church that evening, he found it full for the first time in years. More than four hundred people were there.

The parish continued to flourish from then on. People began to come to *Our Lady of Victories* from all parts of Paris, and then from all of France, and soon the fame of the shrine was world-wide. In 1838 Pope Gregory XVI made the Confraternity the "Archconfraternity of the *Holy and Immaculate Heart of Mary* for the Conversion of Sinners." Today, thousands of plaques in thanksgiving for cures line the walls of the church.

On June 14, 1993, when I visited this Church of *Our Lady of Victories*, I observed a marble plaque with the face of Don Bosco engraved on it, and with the following inscription: "On Saturday 28th April 1883 St. John Bosco celebrated Mass at this altar." I took a photograph of the plaque and when the film was developed, a distinct *pillar of cloud* appeared obliquely across the photograph (see p. 295). I knew then that I had to go to Turin.

### The Basilica of Our Lady, Help of Christians

I arrived in Turin on the evening of August 10, 1993, and the following morning, with the help of one of the Salesian priests there, I toured the great Basilica of *Our Lady, Help of Christians*, including the chapel dedicated to St. Francis de Sales (see p. 296). Poised on top of the large cupola of the church is a beautiful golden statue of *Mary, Help of Christians*, and on the facade of the basilica are two lateral cupolas, on each of which stands an angel holding a banner. Don Bosco, subsequent to having received a vision, had one banner inscribed with the date 1571 (the date of the battle of Lepanto) and the second banner with the incomplete date, 19 _ _. This is said to indicate that in the latter part of this twentieth century, *Mary, Help of Christians* will again be called upon to rescue Christendom from a seemingly all-powerful enemy.

### The Dream of the Two Columns

Timothy Cardinal Manning, former Archbishop of Los Angeles, said of Don Bosco: "There is a wonder world of dreams. Favoured people in the history of salvation, such as Joseph of the Old Testament and Joseph of the New, were visited from on high through the medium of dreams. St. John Bosco is very much of that context and his dream visitations are an integral part of his life and sanctity."

He had his first prophetic vision when he was only nine years old and many years later when he became a priest, Pope Pius IX instructed him to write down his dreams for the encouragement of his Congregation and the rest of the world. In the book *Dreams, Visions and Prophecies of Don Bosco* is found the *Dream of the two columns*. It was narrated on May 30, 1862, by Don Bosco. Here are exerpts from the actual text:

"A few minutes ago I had a dream... The vast expanse of water is covered with a formidable double array of ships in battle formation... All are heavily armed with cannons, incendiary bombs and fire-arms of all sorts, even books, and are heading towards one stately ship, mightier than them all. As they closed in, they tried to ram it, set it on fire and cripple it as much as possible. This stately vessel is shielded by a flotilla escort... In the midst of this endless sea, two solid columns, a short distance apart, soar high into the sky: one is surmounted by a statue of the Immaculate Virgin at whose feet a large inscription reads: Help of Christians; the other, far lofty and sturdier, supports a Host of proportionate size and bears beneath it the inscription: Salvation of Believers.

"The flagship commander the Roman Pontiff, seeing the enemies' fury and his auxiliary ships' very great predicament, summons his captains to a conference. However, as they discuss this strategy, a furious storm breaks out and they must return to their ships... Standing at the helm, the Pope strained every muscle to steer his ship between the two columns, from whose summits hung many anchors and strong hooks linked to chains.

"The entire enemy fleet closes in to intercept and sink the flagship at all costs. They bombarded it with everything they have: books and pamphlets, incendiary bombs, firearms, cannons. Beaked prows rammed the flagship again and again, but to no avail, as unscathed and undaunted, it keeps on its course. At times, a formidable ram splinters a gaping hole into its hull, but, immediately, a breeze from the two columns instantly seals the gash.

"Meanwhile, enemy cannons blow up, firearms and beaks fall to pieces, ships crack up and sink to the bottom. In blind fury the enemy takes to hand to hand combat, cursing and blaspheming. Suddenly, the Pope falls, seriously wounded. He is instantly helped up but, struck down a second time, dies. A shout of victory rises from the enemy and wild rejoicing sweeps their ships. But no sooner is the Pope dead than another takes his place. The captains of the auxiliary ships elected him so quickly, that the news of the Pope's death coincides with that of his successor's election. The enemies' self assurance wanes.

"Breaking through all resistance, the new Pope steers his ships safely between the two columns and moors it to the columns; first, to the one surmounted by the Host and then to the other, topped by the statue of the Virgin. At this point something unexpected happens. The enemy ships panic and disburse, colliding with and scuttling each other... A great calm now covers the sea" (see p. 294).

Don Bosco then explained: "The enemy ships symbolize persecutions. Very grave trials await the Church. What we suffered so far is almost nothing to compare to what is going to happen. The enemies of the Church are symbolized by the ships which strive their utmost to sink the flagship. Only two things can save us in such a great hour: *Devotion to Mary and to the Blessed Sacrament*. Let us do our very best to use these two means and have others use them everywhere."

This was in 1862. But in 33 AD Jesus had already made this solemn promise to the first Pope: *"You are Peter and upon this rock I will build my church; and the gates of hell shall not prevail against it"* (Matt. 16:18).

It is not for me to interpret who are the two Popes in the dream. However, one thing is certain, and it is that, as prophesied by Don Bosco, a great victory of Mary will take place before the twentieth century is over, and that victory will be attained by devotion to the *Blessed Sacrament and to the Blessed Virgin*. It will be a devotion to the *Eucharist* — the *Sacrament of the New Covenant* and to the *Ark of the Covenant*.

294.

The dream of Don Bosco (see pp. 291—293)

295.

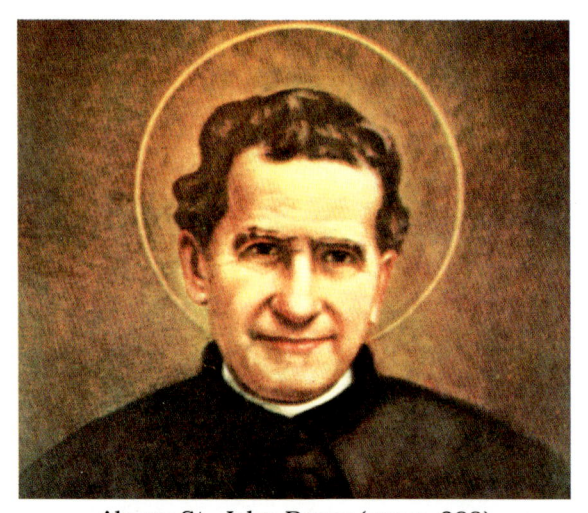

Above: St. John Bosco (see p. 288)
Below: Shekinah appears across a marble plaque of Don Bosco in the Church of Our Lady of Victories in Paris (see p. 291)

296.

Above left: The Basilica of Our Lady Help of Christians in Turin (see pp. 289 & 291)
Above right: Our Lady Help of Christians
Below left: Our Lady of Victories in Paris (see p. 290)
Below right: Our Lady of Victories in St. Peter's Church, Trinidad

## CHAPTER 40.

## *The Messenger of Mary's Royalty*

"The miracles she performs along the way are such that we can scarcely believe our eyes."

**Pope Pius XII**

On May 13, 1920, José Thedim, the famous Portuguese sculptor, carved a cedar statue of *Our Lady of the Rosary of Fatima*, and it was installed in a place of honour in the shrine in Fatima. Today, this first image of Thedim still stands in the Chapel of the Apparitions, built on the spot where Mary appeared to the three little shepherds in 1917.

On May 13, 1942, the twenty fifth anniversary of the 1917 apparitions, the statue of *Our Lady of the Rosary of Fatima* was taken to Lisbon for a Catholic Youth Congress, and such was the upsurge of faith and conversions that a second journey was made to the city in 1943. On that occasion three white doves let loose by someone in the crowd, fluttered down and rested at the feet of the statue, remaining there for days without food or drink. It is recorded that after the pilgrimage to Lisbon, the doves settled in the Cova da Iria behind the Chapel of the Apparitions and stayed there until they died.

On May 13, 1946, World War II having ended, Pope Pius XII sent Cardinal Masella as his legate to Fatima to crown the statue of the Virgin as the *Queen of the World*. The crown which weighed 1200 grams was a gift from the women of Portugal, who contributed their jewels in thanksgiving for Portugal's preservation from both the Spanish Civil War (1936-1939) and the Second World War (1939-1945).

## The International Pilgrim Virgin

One year later, on May 13, 1947, José Thedim's second statue of *Our Lady of the Rosary of Fatima*, known as the International Pilgrim Virgin statue, was blessed in the Cova da Iria and sent on a world-wide mission "to spread the message of Fatima." The International Pilgrim Virgin statue is world famous and was sculptured by Thedim according to the specifications of Sister Lucia. Sister Lucia has said that the expression on the face of that Pilgrim Virgin statue is similar to that of Our Lady during her last apparition in Fatima on October 13, 1917. The statue has travelled all around the world and is sometimes known as the "Weeping Madonna." Indeed, its miraculous shedding of tears has been documented more than thirty times (see pp. 270, 310, 312, & 315).

As far back as 787 AD, the Second Council of Nicea in Asia Minor, referring to the question of statues, declared: "The honour of the image passes to the original." Relevant to this, in 1984, Mary is reported to have said to Fr. Stefano Gobbi when a Marian Cenacle of Priests had recited the Rosary around her statue: "Beloved children, I welcome this Rosary you are reciting together with such great love and fervour. As a Mother I want to tell you that I am here with you, represented by the statue you have here.

"Each of my statues is a sign of a presence of mine and reminds you of your heavenly Mother. Therefore, it must be honoured and put in places of greater veneration. Just as you look with love at a photograph of a cherished person because it transmits to you a reminder and a likeness, so too, you should look with love at every image of your heavenly Mother, because it transmits to you a reminder of her, and still more, it becomes a particular sign of her presence among you."

On October 11, 1954, Pope Pius XII issued an encyclical *Ad Caeli Reginam* in which he saluted the Pilgrim Virgin statue as "The *Messenger of Mary's Royalty*," and stated that "in the doctrine of the Queenship of Mary lies the world's greatest hope for peace." It was then that he decreed that the feast of the *Queenship of Mary* should be celebrated on the 22nd day of August.

The signs and wonders that accompanied the Pilgrim Virgin as she journeyed from country to country also caused the Pope to exclaim: "I crowned her *Queen of the World* at Fatima in 1946 and the following year, through the Pilgrim Virgin, as she set forth as though to claim her dominions, the miracles she performs along the way are such that we can scarcely believe our eyes..."

## The Victorious Queen Peace Flight

It was on Sunday, June 21, 1992, that Dr. Rosalie Turton, President of the 101 Foundation, invited me to accompany the International Pilgrim Virgin and nine hundred and thirty nine peace pilgrims on the Victorious Queen Peace Flight to Lourdes, Lisieux, Paris, Fatima, Prague, Moscow, Leningrad (St. Petersburg), Warsaw and Rome. However, we soon realized during the journey that whereas Rosalie Turton, John Haffert, the co-founder of the Blue Army, Fr. Edgardo Arellano and Leonila Santos of the Philippines were the organizers of this great pilgrimage, it was Mary, represented by her Ambassador, the International Pilgrim Virgin, who was in charge!

It was to be one of the most historic journeys in Marian and Church history and for me it was the most romantic experience in my life. It was a journey of love with the Queen of heaven and earth. Eight video tapes have been produced by Faith Films Inc., Beltsville, Maryland, U.S.A., recording the highlights of the whole pilgrimage. They are narrated by Fr. Ken Roberts and are frequently shown on Mother Angelica's Eternal Word Television Network (EWTN).

Two 747 jumbo jets with the insignia of Mary carrying the Rosary in one hand and the Scapular in the other, the insignia of the Blue Army, flew from New York to Europe with the nine hundred and forty peace pilgrims, wearing the blue jackets of the 101 Foundation (see p. 310). We carried six tons of religious articles (Bibles, Rosaries and religious leaflets) for the people of Russia. The flight numbers chosen and assigned to the planes were 101 and 333, the first being the number of the Foundation and the other signifying the Trinity. I thought it was most appropriate that the charter planes were from Tower Air. In the litany of Loreto the Blessed Virgin is called Tower — Tower of David!

## The Miracle of the Doves

The peace pilgrims eventually arrived in Fatima from Lourdes on October 13, just in time for the start of the procession in the huge esplanade of the shrine. It was the seventy fifth anniversary of the apparitions in Fatima and there were about three quarters of a million people there for that grand occasion. The original statue of *Our Lady of the Rosary of Fatima* stood on a bed of hundreds of flowers and was carried in procession by several bearers, while the peace pilgrims paraded with two large icons of Christ the King of All Nations and *Our Lady of Guadalupe*. The icons were clearly seen by all as they towered above the heads of the crowd.

It was during the procession that the marvel of marvels occurred, bringing copious tears of joy to the thousands of pilgrims. Three doves were let loose and appeared resplendent against the blue sky. They circled around several times over the huge crowd and eventually one of them landed at the feet of the original statue of *Our Lady of the Rosary of Fatima*, and another slowly fluttered down to perch gently on the top of the icon of Christ the King of All Nations. It was about 1:00 p.m., the exact time of the miracle of the Sun in Fatima seventy-five years ago on October 13, 1917 (see p. 311 & 312).

The dove, the symbol of peace, which perched on the top of the icon of Christ the King of All Nations, looked to the right and left at the crowds of pilgrims in the esplanade, and then turned around for a moment to face the 940 blue-jacketed members of the 101 Foundation, nodding its head repeatedly, as if acknowledging the peace pilgrims accompanying the International Pilgrim Virgin on their way to Russia. It stayed on top of the icon for several minutes while the thousands of pilgrims cheered and waved their handkerchiefs in appreciation of that most glorious event. It was a stunning display of the blessing of the Holy Spirit on "the image of His Bride" and of her Son, the King. It was all recorded on video.

### Respect For The Ark

Two days later, on October 15, the twenty coaches carrying the peace pilgrims assembled before driving along the coast line of Portugal to the airport on our way to Prague, Czechoslovakia. At about 3:30 in the morning, as the pilgrims were boarding coach number nine which carried the International Pilgrim Virgin statue, accompanied by her custodian Richard Fasanello, to the surprise of all, the new Portuguese driver refused to accept the statue into the coach.

He adamantly insisted that she be placed in the luggage compartment or, pointing to the spot with his right hand, on the floor of the aisle of the coach and not on the passenger seat where, covered with a blue bunting bag, she is always placed and securely strapped. He was most abusive and disrespectful, but the pilgrims stood their ground and eventually he had to accept the fact that the coach would not be allowed to leave without the "Messenger of her Royalty" in her proper seat.

The coach then started on its way to the airport, but one hour later it suddenly came to a slow halt. The disrespectful driver suddenly suffered a stroke, slumped on the wheel and then fell on the floor, at the very spot on the aisle where he wished to place the Pilgrim Virgin statue. He was completely paralyzed on the right side and lost his speech. He was disrespectful to the *Ark of the Covenant*. The same right hand which he used to point to the floor was stricken.

By a miraculous coincidence, the coach happened to stop exactly opposite a coach station with but one empty coach, which had the same number of seats. Within twenty minutes the fifty peace pilgrims were transferred to that vehicle. The paralyzed driver was then sent to hospital by car.

In the days of the ancient *Ark of the Covenant*, those who disrespected that holy and sacred object were stricken with disease or died on the spot. Indeed, in modern times there has been a well-known American television evangelist who repeatedly insulted the name of Mary. One of his frequent quips was: "When Jesus comes again, He will not be saying, 'Hail Mary!'" He too "fell" some time ago — in total disgrace.

Pope Pius XII, one of the great Marian Popes, expressed this warning in his famous encyclical of 1954, *Ad Caeli Reginam*: "The name of Mary, more delicious than nectar, more precious than any gem, is to be held in the highest honour. Let no one dare to utter abuse — surely the mark of a mind that is vile — against this name so beautiful in its dignity, so honourable in its divinely privileged motherhood; let no one dare to utter anything lacking due reverence."

### The Pilgrim Virgin in Prague

We arrived in Prague on October 15. It was the feast of Saint Teresa of Avila and it was an extra special occasion for those of us who, like John Haffert and Rosalie Turton, were Third Order Carmelites. Our first stop was the Cathedral in Prague which was bursting at its seams with Czechs in excited expectation of the famous Pilgrim Virgin. After seventy-five years of Communist oppression and the closure of the churches there, the "Messenger of her Royalty" was carried into the Cathedral by four priests, just as the Levites used to carry the ancient Ark during the Sinai trek. It was an evening I will never forget. Prague was exuberant with joy.

That evening there was a bit of confusion with respect to my room in the appointed hotel as my name could not be found among the guest list. The Duke of Braganza, who will be king of Portugal if the monarchy is reestablished, was scheduled to be among the pilgrims, but at the last moment he was unable to join us. Observing my plight, Rosalie Turton calmly said to me: "Just tell them you are the Duke of Braganza!" "Duke of who?" I exclaimed in surprise! In jest and with tongue in cheek, I then told the receptionist that I was the Duke of Braganza. To my amazement, I immediately received the keys to a room. Now, there are not many countries in the world where I could pass for the Duke of Braganza!

Two years later, on the eve of the 77th anniversary of the apparitions of Our Lady in Portugal, I was the dinner guest of John Haffert in Fatima and, to my surprise, Don Duarte, the Duke of Braganza, was his other guest. I told them the story of Prague. The Duke was not lacking in a sense of humour when John Haffert quipped: "Well, you do look alike. You both have moustaches!"

**To Russia With Love**

To return to the Victorious Queen Peace flight, the following morning the Pilgrim Virgin, accompanied by her nine hundred and forty escorts, was en route to Moscow. It was a two hour flight and we did not know what sort of reception we were going to receive in Russia. We did know that there was opposition in certain quarters, and before we landed I well remember Fr. Ken Roberts using the microphone system and praying with us the prayer of Saint Michael for protection. By then, many of the pilgrims were ill and exhausted. In fact, one died on the trip and another broke her pelvis. Some of the physicians on the pilgrimage were kept very busy.

As we approached Moscow airport, I heard an apparently well-known hymn for the first time, the plaintive refrain of which I will never forget. All the peace pilgrims on the flight seemed to know it, except me: *"On this day, O beautiful Mother: On this day we give thee our love ..."* There was a quiet apprehension on board the planes, but we were all consoled because we were receiving reassuring messages daily from "the Queen" through five respected visionaries who accompanied us on the tour with their spiritual directors.

On October 10, while we were in France, our first stop, Estela Ruiz, a visionary from South Phoenix, Arizona, received this message from Our Lady (private revelation worthy of belief without any obligation to believe): "I wish to speak to you, my little ones, who are embarked on this mission of great importance. Many still do not understand that you are living in the reign of my Immaculate Heart, and that this journey is part of my plan to bring many souls to God. Many have understood that this mission that you are on is of historic importance, but even the most learned of all of you cannot begin to understand the impact it will have on the world.

"In a very appropriate and significant way, you are travelling and making the necessary stops, and strengthening yourselves through prayer, as you, my warriors, accompany me to embrace and welcome my lost child into my arms and my love. My heart rejoices as you, my instruments of peace, come with me to greet with love and compassion, your sister Russia into our fold. I have used many of my devoted instruments to bring this about, and you may never understand my deep gratitude for your work.

"This journey to Russia has dealt the evil one a great blow and this is indeed a glorious victory. Even now he continues to attempt to stop us, but we will not fail. Believe and understand that I am with you every moment, every step of the way. Michael the Archangel is in the forefront leading this mission of love... On this day, I your Mother, your Lady of the Americas, ask all my beloved children in America to support your brothers and sisters with great prayer and sacrifice. You are the important part of this plan that welcomes your sister Russia into the fold of the faithful... I want all the faithful to know that my Son, in His Most Sacred Heart and united with my Immaculate Heart, is pouring forth tremendous graces upon you and this great event of love."

On the following day, October 11, there was this message from Our Lord, received by Janie Garza during adoration, and authenticated by her spiritual director, Fr. Henry Bordeaux:

"*This is a* very important event in your lives. Know that you will never understand the special event that is about to unfold. You, my dear ones, are making history that will resound around the world from nation to nation. You are proclaiming God's kingdom on earth by joining together My Most Sacred Heart and the Most Immaculate Heart of My Mother. Through this gathering you are living witnesses that I am the King of All Nations, together with the reign of My Most Holy Mother. This event will join together your separated and long lost sister, Russia.

"You are the soldiers who have been picked and blessed by the Queen of Peace herself. Go and sing loudly as you approach your sister Russia, singing 'Onward Christian Soldiers.' Go marching with the Cross of Jesus, King of All Nations, and the Queen of heaven who is guiding this faith journey. Go and make peace. The heavens rejoice! The heavens rejoice!"

At 4:00 p.m. on October 16, the two jumbo jets flew over the Kremlin and landed at Moscow airport. It was a most unforgettable moment. Four priests disembarked first, carrying the *Ark of the Covenant* on their shoulders with two poles, followed by five bishops, twenty priests and then the lay pilgrims (see p. 312). As we entered the large Immigration room in the airport, I waited anxiously to see whether there would be any problems with the Immigration Officers. The pilgrims all sang the Ave Maria as the four priests approached the serious-faced Immigration Officer. They presented their passports to him, while still carrying the two poles and the platform bearing the Pilgrim Virgin.

After what seemed to be an unduly long time, they were eventually allowed through with the *"Messenger of her Royalty."* There was great relief and loud applause from all of us as we saw the beautiful image of the Queen moving into Moscow. Who would have believed it! John Haffert, who has been closely associated with the Fatima message and the International Pilgrim Virgin statue since 1942, waited fifty years to see that day. As for me, I wondered whether they had stamped her Jewish passport!

It took us about two hours to be cleared by the Immigration and Customs authorities and then we journeyed, tired as we were, to our various hotels in Moscow. It was October 16 when we flew over the Kremlin and landed in Moscow. Once again, it was the feast of St. Margaret Mary Alacoque, that privileged nun to whom Jesus appeared in 1673 in Paray le Monial, France, showing His Sacred Heart. It was also a personal coincidence for me in that it was on that same feast day that I was asked to speak in St. James Church in Medjugorje, and that I arrived in Saragossa in Spain to visit the Basilica of El Pilar.

And so, the Pilgrim Virgin statue of *Our Lady of the Rosary of Fatima,* which is also the symbol of devotion to the Immaculate Heart of Mary, arrived in Moscow on the feast day of that great saint who promoted the devotion to the Sacred Heart of her Son. Moreover, the theme of the pilgrimage was The Alliance of the Two Hearts, and printed on the left breast of our blue jackets was the outline of a Rosary in the shape of a heart which, in turn, enclosed two hearts linked together. Above it was written *Unus in Sui Amore* (One in Their love).

But that arrival day was not associated with only one "coincidence." Indeed, it was a trinity of coincidences. October 16 was the anniversary of the election of the great Marian Pope John Paul II in 1978. Thirdly, that date was the fulfillment of a prophecy which St. Maximilian Kolbe made in October 16, 1917, three days after the miracle of the Sun in Fatima: "One day the cavaliers of Our Lady will carry her statue over the heights of the Kremlin and into the heart of Moscow." We did just that!

The following day, Saturday, October 17, three hundred youths from all over the world joined us for a Youth Congress which was held in the huge auditorium of the Cosmos hotel in Moscow. The theme of the Congress was The Alliance of the Two Hearts. None of us will ever forget the emotion of the moment when the Pilgrim Virgin statue entered the sloping steps of the great auditorium in the heart of Moscow.

### Red Square

That night we all went to bed to prepare for the great event of the morrow when we planned to process with the Pilgrim Virgin in Red Square. As far as I know, we had no official permission to parade through Red Square for it is forbidden by the Russian authorities, even to their citizens. When we arrived there were several guards in the large and empty Red Square. It was Sunday, October 18, and as on the day of the miracle of the Sun in Fatima on October 13, 1917, it was raining fairly heavily. It was the only rainy day of the pilgrimage (see p. 313).

As we waited with our umbrellas for all twenty coaches to arrive, a Russian Orthodox priest quietly placed a replica of Russian Orthodoxy's most venerated icon of *Our Lady of Kazan* in a make-shift wooden hut adjoining Red Square, where the great Cathedral of *Our Lady of Kazan* is to be rebuilt. This famous Cathedral was totally demolished in 1917 by the Communists. The priest discreetly left immediately afterwards but by his action, he seemed to be saying: "We, the Orthodox, are with you on this day."

Soon afterwards we were allowed to pass the barriers and march into Red Square — a miracle in itself! It seemed as though the guards were totally mesmerized by the discipline, determination and devotion of the crowd. They then entreated us to keep an orderly file to one side of the Square. This we did. We marched with the two large icons of Christ the King of All Nations and Our Lady of Guadalupe and one of our pilgrims had a very small 18 inch replica of the Pilgrim Virgin statue of Fatima.

As Our Lord had requested in His message to Janie Garza on October 11 in Paris, we led the procession with the Cross which was carried by Judge Daniel Lynch, and the two icons stood out prominently as we marched singing "Onward Christian Soldiers." We then reached the raised dais from which the decrees of the Czars were proclaimed in the pre-Communist days. Owing to the unexpected late arrival of the International Pilgrim Virgin, which was in the coach with the bishops, Fr. John Hoke held up the small statue of the Pilgrim Virgin of Fatima, and John Haffert, that great lay apostle of Mary, was asked to crown the statue there (see p. 314).

The crown was taken from a small statue of the Infant Jesus of Prague which another one of the pilgrims carried with her. And so, as it were, Christ Himself crowned His Mother Queen in Moscow's Red Square. It was a moment of tumultuous applause and tearful expressions of joy. It was good to be there.

In retrospect, we believe that this was the way that the Queen willed it. You see, in Russia, icons are used by the Orthodox Church and not statues, and so it was proper protocol that icons should be carried during our daylight march through Red Square, and that the small statue of *Our Lady of Fatima* should take the place of the larger and more visible International Pilgrim Virgin statue.

Precisely at the moment when the small image of *Our Lady of Fatima* was being crowned, Janie Garza was privileged with a vision of *Our Lady of Fatima* over Red Square, wearing a crown. She saw light streaming from Mary's heart. It flooded the Square and then bounced back upwards and outwards in all directions. Fr. Henry Bordeaux, O.C.D., her spiritual director, later signed a statement that, based on the humility, holiness and his personal knowledge of the said person, it is credible that her witness is true and that Our Lady did appear in Red Square in the manner described.

But there was yet another Marian coincidence. That Sunday, October 18, 1992, when we marched through Red Square, was the feast of St. Luke in the Roman Church, but in the Russian Orthodox Church it was the feast of the *Intercession* of the Blessed Virgin Mary. This great Russian feast commemorates one of the greatest victories in Russian history over the Tartars in 1552, believed to have been accomplished through prayers to the Virgin. It was the most appropriate feast day for the crowning of *Our Lady of Fatima*. When she appeared in Fatima in 1917, she wore a star on the hem of her dress. She was Esther (meaning "Star") *interceding* for her children.

That night a second crowning took place. This time the three hundred members of the World Youth Congress accompanied us into Red Square. It was still raining heavily and in the dark of night we carried the International Pilgrim Virgin statue to the Square. Once more the guards allowed us in. It was agreed that the crown would pass from hand to hand, from one delegate of the Congress to the next, so that each and every member of the Congress would physically participate.

It was midnight when the miraculous Pilgrim Virgin statue was crowned by a sixteen year old Russian girl who was baptized only two weeks before. Coincident with the crowning, there was the ceremony of the midnight changing of the guards in Red Square! The rain which was pouring all day stopped immediately after the crowning (see p. 314). Heaven had exhausted its tears of joy.

Bishop Paolo Hnilica, who flew from Rome for the great event that night, spoke to the peace pilgrims at the end of that glorious ceremony. His voice choking with emotion, he said: "From today on Russia belongs to Our Blessed Mother. Today is your hour, the hour of the apostles of *Our Lady of Fatima*, who have been prepared for years for these times, the times of the triumph of the Immaculate Heart of Mary. The essential part of Fatima's message is centered on the conversion of Russia. It was given to prevent a great catastrophic militant atheism and to announce the deepest and greatest grace of this century of ours — the triumph of the Immaculate Heart of Mary, the triumph of God's infinite mercy on Russia and upon the world through the tenderness of His Mother's Heart.

"Divine Providence has chosen the Holy Father, John Paul II, to fulfill the heavenly request made at Fatima. The attempt made on his life on May 13, 1981, and the Act of Consecration made on March 25, 1984, are all fundamental signs of his pontificate to help us recognize that he is the shepherd chosen to accomplish the promised triumph. It is, in fact, under his pontificate *'Totus Tuus,'* that the triumph of the Immaculate Heart of Mary must be realized..."

After we left Moscow on Monday, October 19, we flew to St. Petersburg for a day and then to Poland, first to Warsaw, and then to Niepokalanow, the home of Maximilian Kolbe, and finally to the shrine of *Our Lady of Czestochowa*. Words cannot describe the reception we received in Poland.

### Rome — The End of the Journey

The last leg of the month long pilgrimage was Rome (see p. 315). As we drove into Rome on the morning of Sunday, October 25, we saw a most beautiful rainbow across the sky. It was the sign of the Covenant and a fitting farewell greeting from the *Ark of the Covenant*.

We alighted at St. Peter's Square as we had special invitations to attend the beatification of a hundred and twenty-two martyrs of the Spanish Civil War, fifty-one of whom belonged to the same seminary in Barbastro, a city of Aragon in Spain. They were Claretians from the Congregation of the Missionary Sons of the Immaculate Heart of Mary. Nine were priests and forty-two were seminarians.

The outbreak of the Spanish Civil War in 1936 marked the start of a merciless persecution of Catholic clergy and laity, and during the short period of the war 6,832 bishops, priests and religious were shot to death. The number of lay martyrs has not been calculated. The Claretians defied their Communist oppressors and chose martyrdom rather than deny Christ and His Blessed Mother as they shouted: "Long live the Immaculate Heart of Mary" and "Long live Christ the King."

These martyrs of Barbastro walked in the steps of their founder St. Anthony Mary Claret, who voiced the same desire to shed his blood for the love of Jesus and Mary: "For you, my Queen, to give my blood." Such a lover of the Virgin he was that his statue has been given a special place of honour at the right side of the sanctuary of the High Altar in the Basilica of Fatima. The Pilgrim Virgin of Fatima, the Messenger of her Royalty, had good reason to be there in Rome that day to pay tribute to her martyrs, the Missionary Sons of the Immaculate Heart of Mary. It was a fitting way to end this historic pilgrimage. Only heaven could have arranged this.

### A Message From the Queen

The day before the beatification, October 24, 1992, was the feast of Saint Anthony Mary Claret, and the visionary Estela Ruiz, from Phoenix, Arizona, testified that she received this message from the Virgin for the peace pilgrims in Rome:

"My dearest ones, I come to be with you today in a very special way, to thank you and to tell you of my love for you. At this moment I speak to the peace pilgrims, whom I commissioned to take my love to my daughter Russia, that she may know of my love for her through you... On this mission, I chose to bring some of those who had been committed to my work, who know what I ask of those who love me... My beloved little ones, you must begin to understand the significance of the event in which you have been involved. This event is the spark that ignited the fire that will become a blaze throughout the world of the love of my Immaculate Heart.

"It is through Russia's conversion that the world will know that these times are truly the reign of my Heart and that my love for God and my earthly children will triumph over evil, so that all nations will know and acknowledge that my Son, Our Lord Jesus, is the King of the world and the hope and salvation of all... My peace pilgrims, it is only fitting that this event finalizes in Rome, where my beloved son, John Paul, the Vicar of my Son, resides. He knows of this event, and in his heart has blessed it. United in love, my Son's Most Sacred Heart and my Immaculate Heart have also blessed it. I love you and thank you for listening to my words."

310.

Left: The International Pilgrim Virgin of Fatima (see p. 298)

Below center: With Judge Daniel Lynch and Fr. Ken Roberts

Below: The Tower Air jumbo jet with an insignia of Our Lady (see p. 299)

311.

Above: The dove appears above the crowd in Fatima (see p. 300)
Below: The dove slowly descends towards the crowd (see p. 300)

312.

Above: The dove alights and perches on the icon of Christ, King of all Nations (see p. 300)

Below: The priests and John Haffert carrying the Ark of the Covenant into Russia (see p. 304)

Above: The Peace pilgrims lined up to "invade" Red Square
Below: Pilgrims entering Red Square (see p. 305)

314.

Left: John Haffert crowns the small statue of Our Lady of Fatima (see p. 307)

Right: Fr. John Hoke raises the crowned statue for all to see

Below: The statue is crowned by a young Russian girl (see p. 307)

315.

Above: The International Pilgrim Virgin leads the peace pilgrims into St. Peter's Square (see p. 308)
Below: Pope John Paul greets the peace pilgrims

## Chapter 41.

## *Our Lady of China*

**"China will turn to the Mother Church... after much conflict."**

**Our Lady of All Nations, Amsterdam**

Gianna Talone Sullivan is one of the visionaries from Scottsdale, Arizona. She has since moved to Emmitsburg, Maryland, where the Virgin continues to appear to her everyday. I have had several personal and spiritual experiences with Gianna which have absolutely convinced me that she is an authentic visionary. Fr. René Laurentin has written about her in his book *Our Lord and Our Lady In Scottsdale* and Fr. Robert Faricy and Sr. Lucy Rooney in their book *Our Lady Comes to Scottsdale*. The Riehle Foundation has also published three volumes entitled *I Am Your Jesus of Mercy*, which have recorded the Scottsdale messages chronologically.

On October 19, 1994, Gianna, her husband Dr. Michael Sullivan and myself flew from Baltimore to Manila in the Philippines to join 425 blue-jacketed Triumphant Queen Peace Flight pilgrims of the 101 Foundation. They were escorting the International Pilgrim Virgin statue of *Our Lady of Fatima*, this time to her shrine in Portugal, the Holy Land in Israel, Manila in the Philippines, Shanghai and Beijing in China and finally Akita, Japan. The pilgrims had already visited Fatima and the Holy Land in their chartered 747 jumbo jet from Tower Air before we joined them (see p. 322.)

We arrived in Manila in time for the International Family Conference on October 22-23, 1994. From Manila we flew to Shanghai where our first commitment was to visit

She-Shen, the Shrine of *Our Lady Help of Christians*, the national Marian Shrine in China.

It has been said that what Lourdes is to France, Fatima to Portugal, Guadalupe to Mexico and Czestochowa to Poland, the Shrine of She-Shen is to China. The basilica which commands a panoramic view of the city is called the Jewel of China. As *Voice Magazine* of January-February, 1994, stated in its advertisement of the pilgrimage: "*Our Lady of Fatima* goes to visit her 'jewel,' bearing the triumph of the changes in Russia and the promise of the triumph of her Immaculate Heart."

It was the seventh centenary year of the founding of Christianity in China, and also the centenary of the death of Saint Maximilian Kolbe, a great missionary to China.

Interestingly, it was twenty years previously, almost to the day, that I accompanied the Prime Minister of Trinidad and Tobago to China. However, this time I was but one of 425 peace pilgrims accompanying another Head of State, "*the Messenger of her Royalty,*" the International Pilgrim Virgin statue of Fatima, representing the Queen of heaven and earth. It was the largest charter flight ever to enter China from America.

However, in China there is disunity among the Catholics. There is the Chinese Catholic Patriotic Church which is approved by the Chinese government, elects its own bishops and does not accept Vatican authority over its activities, and the so-called Underground Church loyal to the Pope, and who in their fidelity to the magisterium of the Pope have often suffered persecution, sometimes heroically.

In Shanghai, as we entered the basilica and its huge grounds, we were most impressed by the devotion of the priests and seminarians of the Catholic Patriotic Church who lived nearby (see pp. 322 & 323). We were told that there were nine priests in residence who celebrate Mass partly in Chinese and partly in Latin, as was required by the Vatican during the 1950s.

On the left side of the inside of the basilica was a most beautiful wooden statue of *Our Lady of China.* She held a *scepter* in her right hand and the Child Jesus on her left. It was, in fact, a Chinese statue of *Our Lady Help of Christians.* We all crowded around the statue to take photographs of this beautiful carving and in my third photograph a large white cloud enveloped the whole statue, leaving only the head surrounded by a crown of twelve stars in view. It was the only one of seventy-two photographs that I had taken during the pilgrimage in which a cloud appeared on a print! (see p. 324). Its significance was clear to me. The high point of the pilgrimage was China.

But it was two days later when we were in Beijing that the Virgin herself appeared to Gianna in the Church of the Immaculate Conception. Behind the main altar was a large painting of *Our Lady of All Graces* with streams of bright rays flowing down from her outstretched hands (see p. 325).

This is how Gianna described the event: "She was surrounded by hundreds of angels who enveloped her in a cloud. There were beautiful colours of lavender around her and a bright light emerged from her hands. She wore a crown on her head and was very beautiful. She said that she was *Our Lady of All Graces*.

She revealed that her Immaculate Heart will reign but not as we think it will. She added that *the purpose of our trip to China was for the unity of the Church there*. She also said that there were many priests in the Patriotic Church who desired to be loyal to Rome but could not because of government pressure and that they had a great love for her Immaculate Heart.

The importance and significance of the Virgin appearing in a Catholic Patriotic church in China can hardly be over-emphasized. By appearing there she has visibly confirmed that she wished this unity, just as she and her Son desire that **unity** between the Orthodox and the Catholic Church be re-established.

That she chose the *Cathedral of the Immaculate Conception*, that she appeared as *Our Lady of All Graces*, and that the painting behind the altar was that of *Our Lady of All Graces*, were no haphazard choices of the Virgin.

She appeared as *Our Lady of All Graces*... in other words, as the *Mediatrix of All Graces*. We need, therefore, to recall that, as already stated in chapter 6, on April 4, 1954, she said to the visionary Ida in Amsterdam: "Satan is still the prince of this world. That is why the *Lady of All Nations* had to come now, into these times, for she is the Immaculate Conception and, therefore, also the *Co-Redemptrix, Mediatrix* and *Advocate*. These three are but one. Is that clearly understood, theologians?"

I am no theologian, but I believe that I have "clearly understood" what she was saying by appearing in Beijing as *Our Lady of All Graces*. In that image, she represents all three. I also believe that *the Immaculate Conception* showered many graces on the Church in China that day through the prayers and sacrifices of the peace pilgrims who accompanied the "Messenger of her Royalty," the

International Pilgrim Virgin statue of Fatima.

It was therefore not altogether surprising to read a *Reuter* report from Beijing exactly two months later on December 25, 1994: "Hundreds of police turned out to control thousands of Chinese who packed churches in Beijing on Sunday for Christmas midnight Mass. Church officials had to bar the doors of the Church of Our Saviour after more that 2000 people jammed the most important Catholic church in Beijing for midnight Mass, leaving hundreds outside in the freezing cold hoping for a chance to get in for the next service.

"'More than 40,000 people have attended services today,' one church official said as Christmas Eve gave way to Christmas Day. 'The order has been a little chaotic.' Inside the blue and white Gothic church built by a French bishop in 1887, the faithful jostled with crowds of curious sightseers for space to pray. The church, closed in the 1966-76 Cultural Revolution, reopened in 1985 and held three Masses on Christmas Eve and four on Christmas day."

Following this, one week later, *The Washington Post* of December 30, 1994, reported: "The Communist Party in China, which for much of its history dismissed religion as 'feudal superstition,' has taken a relatively lenient posture toward religion during the past 15 years. It subsidized the restoration of 14 Catholic churches and seven Protestant churches in Beijing and permitted the formation of new seminaries. On a typical Sunday, those churches are packed with the faithful. Many churches have overflow rooms where people watch or listen to the services on closed-circuit televisions or on speakers.

"Religious experts close to the government estimate that there are about 12 million Christians in China today: some church groups say the number can be as high as 50 million... A young physics and computer student said that as he learned about the Universe at a Beijing university he realized that science could not explain everything... 'In the past, we thought it was possible to eliminate religious belief overnight,' said a scholar on religion at a government think tank. 'Now we realize that religious values will not be eliminated by administrative force.'"

The magazine *30 DAYS* also reported that a mysterious thing happened at the Catholic rally in Manila and the focal point of it was the Chinese delegation to the tenth World Youth Day on Sunday, January 15, 1995, when Pope John Paul II visited the Philippines.

The magazine commented that at the beginning, news

of developments in the Philippines had heightened the general euphoria at the presence in Manila of 24 lay people, priests and sisters from Communist China, for they were attending with the approval of the Catholic Patriotic Association and of the Chinese government. Even the more cautious observers saw this as significant. It was the first time in decades that members of this community, led by bishops of the Patriotic Church, who were ordered by the regime to break off relations with the See of Peter and so with the universal Church, had ever participated in a meeting in the presence of the Bishop of Rome.

The press immediately headlined the "fall of the wall" and "the thaw" between the Vatican and Beijing. Priests from the Chinese delegation concelebrated the Mass with the Pope, having already met the conditions which the Vatican had set down — the profession of faith, including an oath of fidelity to Peter's successor. This is the oath taken by every Catholic priest serving the Church.

Indeed, Our Lady's statement to Gianna in October 1994 that "there are many priests in the Patriotic church who desired to be loyal to Rome, but could not because of government pressure," was verified three months later by an article in the magazine *Inside the Vatican*, February 1995. Under the headline "I am still loyal to you," the article stated: "Vatican sources have told us privately that at least 38 of the c. 100 bishops nominated by the Patriotic Association have written personally to the Pope to affirm their allegiances."

Bishop Aloysius Jin Luxian, Patriotic Bishop of Shanghai, is 79 years old, but he is still considered to be the most clear-thinking exponent of that part of the Chinese Church which agreed to collaborate with the government and submit to the control of Patriotic bodies. He was imprisoned in 1955 and sentenced to 18 years and a further nine years of banishment to the frontier, so for 27 years he was unable to celebrate Mass. Then in 1982, he agreed to go back and run the Shanghai seminary and in 1985, the Patriotic Association named him bishop of the diocese, but he had no apostolic mandate, no Pontifical approval.

He was recently interviewed by Gianni Valente of *30 DAYS*, who asked him his opinion of this historic occasion, whereby a delegation of Chinese Catholics was allowed to participate in a Mass with the Pope in Manila. He replied: "There is no doubt that all of us who pray for the normalization of relations between China and the Holy See see this as a great sign. It is important because it has come from both sides. It was the Cardinal Archbishop of Manila Jaime Sin who, with the Holy See's permission, invited Chinese Catholics to the Philippines. And I thank God — and Cardinal Sin — for this."

When asked to comment on this signing of the oath of fidelity to the Pope and whether Beijing might see this as some kind of provocation, he replied: "I don't think it presents any problem. It was restricted to the faith, not politics... In any case, our divisions do not concern the faith. In the field of the faith and liturgy, we are as faithful as the Underground Church... Our faith is the same. We are all faithful to the Pope and it was a source of joy for the priests who went to Manila that they had the opportunity of signing this profession of faith.

"Fidelity to the Pope is certainly not exclusive to underground Catholics. We also recognize the Petrine Primacy in all its aspects. The only point on which we cannot follow the Holy See is a political one. The Holy See maintains diplomatic relations with Taiwan and Taiwan considers the Beijing government a usurper, illegitimate. But we on the mainland cannot say that our government is illegitimate."

This participation in the concelebration of the Mass with the Pope by 24 young Chinese Catholics of the Patriotic Association founded in 1957, is the first such occasion in more than four decades since 1951, the year in which the People's Republic of China severed relations with the Holy See. Since then, on June 4, 1995, Pope John Paul II concelebrated a beatification in Belgium for Fr. Damien de Veruster of the Congregation of the Sacred Hearts of Jesus and Mary, with three priests from mainland China, after they made a profession of faith.

In Chapter 6 of this book it is recorded that on December 31, 1951, the Virgin appeared in Amsterdam as the *Lady of All Nations* and said: "China will turn to the Mother Church... after much conflict." And so, during this prayerful and historic pilgrimage, Her Majesty appeared to Gianna Talone Sullivan in the Church of the Immaculate Conception in Beijing on October 28, 1994, and said: "The mission (of the pilgrimage) was for the unity of the Church in China." The Virgin was referring to the unity of the Patriotic and Underground Churches of China!

Above: Author with Gianna Talone Sullivan on the
Far East pilgrimage (see p. 316)
Below: The Shrine of Our Lady Help of Christians in Shanghai
(Courtesy of Larry Galloway) (see p. 317)

Above: The Peace Pilgrims visit a seminary in Shanghai
(see p. 317)
Below: The seminarians talking to Dr. Antoine Mansour

324.

Above: The wooden statue of Our Lady of China (Our Lady Help of Christians) (see pp. 317 & 318)
Below: The Shekinah appears in front of the statue (see p. 318)

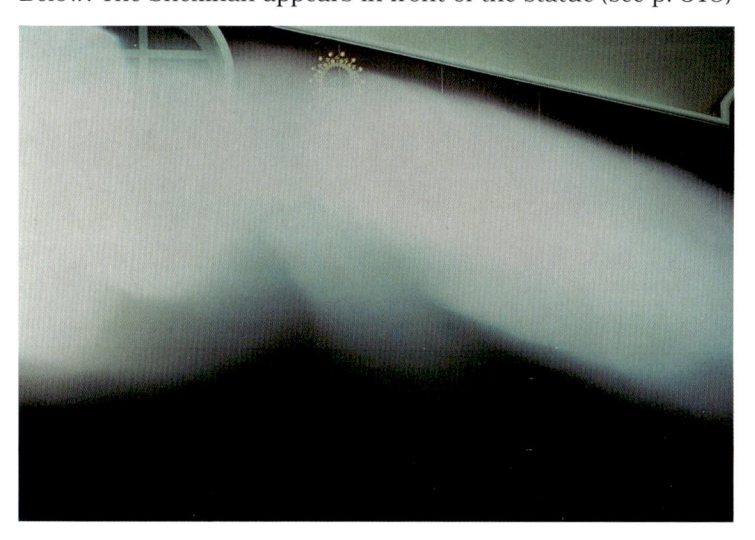

325.

Above: The peace pilgrims in Tiananmen Square in Beijing
Below: The painting of Our Lady of All Graces behind the main altar in the Cathedral of the Immaculate Conception in Beijing, China (see p. 318)

## Chapter 42.

## *The Triumph of the Immaculate Heart of Mary*

**"In the end, my Immaculate Heart will triumph"**
                                        Our Lady of Fatima

Since her first major apparition in 1531 in Guadalupe, the Virgin has accelerated her earthly visits to such an extent that some chosen visionaries are receiving daily apparitions, an extravagance of visitations which can have only one interpretation.

She first identified herself in Guadalupe as "the perfect and perpetual Virgin Mary, the Holy Mother of God," and assured us of her protective role: "Listen, and be sure, my dear son, that I will protect you." It was on the feast of *the Immaculate Conception*. It was the year of Halley's comet.

In 1917, Europe was engulfed in the appalling horrors of World War I, the first major war of this fateful 20th century. After all his diplomatic efforts to bring about peace and an end to the war bore no fruit, Pope Benedict XV sent out a stirring pastoral letter to the Catholic world on May 5, 1917. He urged the Church to join him in a fervent appeal for protection and peace to the Mother of God and of Mercy.

On May 13, the eighth day after Benedict XV's appeal to Our Lady, and the date on which the Church formerly celebrated the feast of *Our Lady of the Most Blessed Sacrament*, the Most Holy Virgin appeared to the three little shepherds at Fatima. In her first apparition, she gave a direct response to the Pope's appeal in her parting words to the children: "Pray the Rosary every day, in order to obtain peace for the world and the end of the war." She later prophesied: "The war is going to end soon but if people will not stop offending God, another and more terrible war will begin during the reign of Pius XI." This was in 1917. The events leading to World War II started in 1939 during the reign of Pius XI (1922-39).

In the wake of the war, the end of 1932 and the beginning of 1933 was a time of widespread unemployment, of bread lines, of hunger, and throughout the western world unemployment had soared. More than two million Britons were out of work and food riots were common. In America, some 14 million were jobless and in Germany, five million unemployed looked to Adolf Hitler's Nazi party to solve their problems.

It was against this background that the Virgin chose a day in November 1932 to appear to five children and repeated her Guadalupean identity: "I am the Mother of God... I am the Immaculate Virgin." In August 1994, I spent two days in Beauraing in Belgium. There the visionaries saw a heart of gold surrounded by glittering rays of light on the Virgin's breast. It was the Immaculate Heart of Mary, for she literally and figuratively has a heart of gold, a pure heart. The date was November 29. It was the anniversary date of her apparition to Catherine Labouré in the Rue du Bac in Paris in 1830.

Scarcely had the apparitions come to an end when she appeared again in Belgium in January 1933. It was in a village called Banneux. This time she identified herself as *The Virgin of the Poor*. In appearing as *The Virgin of the Poor* she was also simply confirming her Son's warning: *"No one can be the slave of two masters... You cannot be the slave both of God and of money"* (Matthew 6:24).

According to Abbé Omer Englebert in his book *Catherine Labouré and the Modern Apparitions of Our Lady*: "Her message in Banneux was that wealth was not a sign of true distinction, that poverty is in no way shameful, and that money should remain in the place assigned for it in the Gospel, namely, at the lowest rung in the scale of human values.

"The difficulty," he continued, "is due, of course, to the fact that we can scarcely amass wealth without being guilty of injustice, in that zeal for amassing a fortune leaves little time for contemplating the soul... that, in fine, riches make man so self-sufficient that he does not feel the need to throw himself into the arms of the Heavenly Father or recite the *Pater Noster*, for why should a man who has enough ask God for his daily bread!"

Since then, she has been appearing frequently on all five continents. Many have seen the Virgin come from heaven to earth in the twinkling of an eye, to pass through walls, and to walk above tree tops. As described by those who have seen her, she is always elegantly dressed, her gown always reaching to her feet. Her voice, her smile, her walk, her gestures are all beautiful and queenly. Reserved and modest, she attracts attention and respect but while so feminine and seemingly all fragile, she is decisive and strong.

She has usually appeared to simple, humble and unlearned young people. They had no university degrees any more than had St. Joseph or many other saints in heaven. Her chosen ones remind us of her Son's prayer. *"I bless you Father, Lord of heaven and of earth, for hiding these things from the wise and the clever and revealing them to mere children"* (Matthew 11:25).

### The Signs of the Times

Never in the history of the world has there ever been a "generation" wherein man has within his power the mechanism to self-destruct and to annihilate nations upon nations. It is only the blind who will not see the *signs of the times*. Indeed, on August 25, 1993, the Virgin said in Medjugorje: "Read Sacred Scripture, live it, and pray to understand the *signs of the times*."

Luke, physician and saint, wrote on the signs of the end of the age, as revealed by Jesus: " *When you see a cloud rising in the West, you say immediately that rain is coming — and so it does. When the wind blows from the South, you say it is going to be hot — and so it is. You hypocrites! If you can interpret the portents of earth and sky, why can you not interpret the present time" (Luke 12:54-56)?* "*Nation will rise against nation, and kingdom against kingdom; there will be great earthquakes, and in various places famines and plagues; and there will be dreadful portents and great signs from heaven*" (Luke 21: 10-11).

Matthew quotes more of Jesus' words:"*Immediately after the suffering of those days the sun will be darkened, and the moon will not give its light; the stars will fall from heaven, and the powers of heaven will be shaken*" (Matthew 24: 29).

Paul also writes in 2 Timothy 3:1-5: "You must understand this, that in the last days distressing times will come. For people will be lovers of themselves, lovers of money, boasters, arrogant, abusive, disobedient to their parents, ungrateful, unholy, inhuman, implacable, slanderers, profligates, brutes, haters of good, treacherous, wreckless, swollen with conceit, lovers of pleasure rather than lovers of God, holding to the outward form of godliness but denying its power. Avoid them."

Never in history have we witnessed such a decline of civilization with worldwide violence among men and widespread displays of man's inhumanity towards man as in this twentieth century. It is the century which gave us two World Wars and threatens us with a third.

In fact, the Virgin has recently said in one of her shrines that the sins of our times are greater than those at the time of Noah. One of the characteristics of the human race before the great flood in the days of Noah was uncontrolled violence: *"Now the earth was corrupt in God's sight, and the earth was filled with violence"* (Genesis 6:11). As never before, today we are witnessing a worldwide spate of violence.

The Centers for Disease Control (CDC) in Atlanta, Georgia, first labelled violence as an epidemic in 1990 and it is now a public health threat as bad as cancer and heart disease. In fact, homicide is now the highest cause of death among young men, and violence as entertainment has been so glamorized that it has escalated tenfold in the last decade, conditioning societies to accept this behavioral pattern as inevitable and even justifiable.

Jesus, in His discourse on the Mount of Olives three days before He died, also said that the days before His Second Coming would be like the days of Noah: *"For as the days of Noah were, so will be the coming of the Son of Man"* (Matthew 24:37).

Already the birth pangs have begun — earthquakes, more frequent than ever before, floods and bizarre weather throughout the world, especially in America; famine, pestilence and plagues. Bubonic plague killed a full quarter of Europe's population during the 13th and 14th centuries, and whereas World War I claimed about ten million lives, the influenza virus of 1918-19, which caused the so-called "Spanish flu" epidemic, exceeded that figure in a short period of time.

After more than a decade since its discovery, a cure for the AIDS virus, the human immunodeficiency virus (HIV), still eludes the world's best scientific minds. By the year 2000, the global number of HIV infections could reach 40 million, and yet mankind has not heeded the message of this virus — the message of chastity and fidelity. In the meantime no one knows whether its ongoing mutations will result in a more virulent strain with a shorter incubation period.

We are witnessing violence, corruption in high places, drug addiction destroying minds and families, whole societies reverting to primitive behaviour, internecine warfare, murders on a scale never witnessed before, scandals, calumnies and pornography, the latter being brought into the privacy of the home through television. Surely, it is Satan's hour.

We are obviously in the throes of a spiritual warfare of warfares and the battle is for our immortal souls. Paul, once of the Jewish faith, then turned Christian, who fought the good fight and kept the faith (2 Timothy 4:7), has also advised us: "Put on the armour of God that you may be able to stand against the wiles of the devil. For our wrestling is not against flesh and blood but against principalities and powers, against the spiritual forces of wickedness on high" (Ephesians 6: 10-12).

As the saintly and beloved Padre Pio said before he died in 1968: "The world is on the threshold of its perdition. My advice to you is to pray and to get others to pray... Visit Marian shrines." Indeed, they are the Mother's oases in this desert in which we live. I have written this book because, like millions of people, I too believe that we are experiencing the beginning of the chastisement and that, as the *Lady of All Nations* said in Amsterdam, "time is short."

### Science and Religion

On July 16, 1945, in the deep privacy of a New Mexico desert, an event occurred which was one of the most important happenings of the twentieth century. No one was more instrumental than Robert Oppenheimer, director of the Los Alamos project. A chain reaction of scientific discoveries which began at the University of Chicago and centered at "Site Y" at Los Alamos was culminated in the successful detonation of the first atomic bomb. Of curious apocalyptic significance, it was on the feast of *Our Lady of Mount Carmel!*

As he watched the mushroom cloud rising high over the desert floor there was awe tinged with fear. "I remember," Oppenheimer said, "a line from the Bhaganad Gita: 'I am become death, the destroyer of worlds' and I suppose we all thought that.'"

Forty-nine years later, in July 1994, chunks of inter-stellar debris, the size of a huge mountain, smashed into the largest planet in the solar system. According to *Time Magazine*, it was one of the most violent encounters that humanity has ever witnessed. The agent of destruction, a comet, long held captive by Jupiter's gravity, broke up into a fleet of twenty-one megabombs. Prior to that, the largest hydrogen bomb ever detonated in Earth's atmosphere was the Soviet Union's 58 megaton blast in 1961.

Compared to that blast, the combined energy of the twenty-one impacts on Jupiter reached about 20 million megatons. This cosmic crash occurred on July 16, 1994. Once more, it was on the feast of *Our Lady of Mount Carmel!* Notably, it was also in 1961 that the Virgin Mary chose to appear in Garabandal with an apocalyptic message. She came as *Our Lady of Mount Carmel!*

It was on Mount Carmel that the Prophet Elijah called upon Yahweh in his battle against the worshippers of the pagan god Baal. In 1 Kings 18:38-39, the event is recorded: "Then the **fire** of the Lord fell and consumed the burnt offering, the wood, the stones, and the dust, and even licked up the water that was in the trench. When all the people saw it, they fell on their faces and said, 'The Lord is God; the Lord is God!'" It was only after that manifestation of fire that the Israelites returned to the true worship and renewed their Covenant with God.

Previous collisions have left their telltale marks on the Universe, and the Moon and Earth itself are pocked with craters which were almost certainly caused by incoming comets and asteroids. Is Jupiter's plight on July 16, 1994, a herald of things to come? Will it take another "fire to fall" before mankind renews the Covenant once more?

In Akita, Japan, the Virgin said to Sr. Sasagawa on October 13, 1973: "...Fire will fall from the sky and will wipe out a great part of humanity, the good as well as the bad, sparing neither priest nor faithful. The survivors will find themselves so desolate that they will envy the dead. The only arms which will remain for you will be the Rosary and the Sign left by My Son."

Why was Japan chosen for this announcement? We do know that at precisely at 8:15 a.m. on August 6, 1945, fifty years ago, a nuclear chain reaction in a bomb created a fire ball of 300,000 degrees Celcius. Hiroshima was the target, resulting in 100,000 deaths in less than one second. Survivors spoke of a noiseless flash and a light brighter than a thousand Suns.

"A bright light filled the place," wrote Lt. Col. Paul Tibbits, the pilot of the Enola Gay, the B-29 that dropped the first atomic bomb. "We turned back to look at Hiroshima. The city was hidden by that awful cloud... boiling up, mushrooming." For a moment, no one spoke. Then everyone was talking. "Look at that! Look at that!" exclaimed the co-pilot, Robert Lewis. Then he turned away to write in his journal. "My God, what have we done?" The second bomb dropped three days later on August 9 on Nagasaki convinced Japan to surrender. Is this the last nuclear assault on mankind or are we to expect another?

I recall the last line of one of Baldwin's books: "God gave Noah the rainbow sign. No more water, **the fire next time**." It was an echo of the prophecy of Peter (2 Peter 3: 1-18). It will be a time of great suffering,

### The Co-Sufferer

Six centuries ago, on May 8-9, 1373, Lady Julian of Norwich recorded certain *Revelations of Divine Love* in her book by this title which records her visions. She says of Mary: "I saw part of the love and suffering of Our Lady Saint Mary, for she and Christ were so joined in love that the greatness of His love caused the greatness of her grief. And so in this, I saw the instinctive love that all Creation had for Him. This natural love was shown most of all by His dear Mother and surpassed all others, for as she loved Him more than all the rest, by so much was her pain beyond all theirs. For the higher, the greater and the sweeter the love is, so the greater grief it is to those who love, to see their loved one suffer."

This topic and problem of suffering is certainly not a scientific one, although science has enlightened us on the mechanism of pain. Suffering in some cases is mediated through neural elements and there are endorphins even in earthworms. This indicates that they suffer pain, although it is believed that pain becomes less intense as we go down the phylogenetic spectrum, and is often not as acute in the non-human as in the human family.

As Holmes Rolston reminds us, it is false to think that chronologically suffering entered the world after sin and on account of it. There was suffering in the biological world for long epochs before humans came. What happens to humans has happened to every living thing. Every life is chastened and christened, straitened and baptized in struggle. Everywhere there is vicarious suffering, and all world progress and history is ultimately brought under the shadow of a cross.

The story, therefore, was a passion play long before it reached Christ and since the beginning of time, myriads of creatures have been giving up their lives as a ransom for many. The ram which was sacrificed in place of Isaac, and the many lambs immolated in the Temple are but some of the many examples in relatively recent times. In that sense, Jesus is not the exception to the natural order, but the chief and highest exemplification of it. It was the martyrdom of the God-Man. Creation has known of no greater anguish, no greater suffering, physical, emotional or spiritual.

As narrated in both Testaments, to be chosen by God is not to be protected from suffering. Indeed, it is to travel the road from Gethsemane to Calvary. It is often a call to suffer and to be delivered as one passes through it. It is the iron which passes through the fire of life in order to become steel. This is what unbelievers like Nietzsche (1844-1900) neither fathomed not sought the grace to understand. And so, he who once said that "God is dead," also said: "What really raises one's indignation against suffering is not suffering intrinsically, but the senselessness of suffering." This was the logic of that Professor of classical philology at the University of Basel, Switzerland!

Dr. Tagashi Nagai, MD, pioneer professor of radiology at the University of Nagasaki, Japan, died of atomic disease six years after the second atomic bomb fell on his hometown on August 9, 1945. His was a spiritual pilgrimage from his native Shintoism to Christianity and a very special Marian devotion. His book *The Bells of Nagasaki* was an immediate success.

How this scientist suffered! He, too, had once been troubled by the age-old problem: How can there be a loving omnipotent God when there is so much evil and pain in the world? Eventually he expressed his conviction: "Unless you have suffered and wept you really do not understand what compassion is, nor can you give comfort to someone who is suffering. If you have not cried you cannot dry another's eyes. Unless you have walked in darkness you cannot help wonderers find the way. Unless you have looked into the eyes of menacing death you cannot help another rise from the dead and taste anew the joy of being alive.."

The Apostle Paul was also enlightened. In his letter to the Hebrews he said: "As it was his purpose to bring a great many of his sons to glory, it was appropriate that God, for whom everything exists and through whom everything exists, should make perfect, *through suffering*, the leader who would take them to their salvation" (Hebrews 2:10). He was talking about the Redeemer. But co-suffering with Him beneath His Cross was the Mother. O God, how she suffered!

She is appearing all over the world in these apocalyptic times, pleading for her children's conversion and is asking us to *stop sitting on the fence and to "take a side"* in this battle foretold by God in Genesis 3:15: *"I will put enmity between you and the woman, and between your seed and her seed; (s)he will crush your head..."* And so, we have been promised the outcome of that battle, but not without losses.

Fr. Phillip Pavich, a Franciscan priest in Medjugorje, said in his homily on the feast of the Assumption of Mary in St. James Church several years ago: "God is not content with half of Genesis 3:15; He is not content with cutting things in half. He is not content with half representation of the Gospel. He is not content with spotty evangelization. Who would dare evangelize and not bring that blessed Woman into it? What is that Gospel? That is not the Gospel of the Scripture. It is clear what is the Gospel of the Scripture. It is the "Woman and her seed," the Woman and her Son. It is Mary and Jesus. That is the Gospel!"

She is *Our Lady of Victories* and she will usher in the reign of the Sacred Heart of her Son. In fact, the signs of the times are such that many of us believe that ours is the generation which will witness the victory of the Woman and her seed over the ancient serpent and his seed, and that this is the final hour of that battle.

Who is this Woman? She is the humble handmaid of the Lord (Luke 1:48). She is God's masterpiece, His most beautiful creation. She is the Woman who became the Mother of her own Creator. Indeed, God so loved His creation, man, that He made one of us His Bride. It was the marriage between heaven and earth, between God and humankind, between God and His Church.

Mother of the Prince of Peace, she is the Queen of Peace (See p. 338). As Bishop Paolo Hnilica once said: "This peace, 'shalom,' is the perfect harmony between the creature and the Creator, between the creature and creation, and among the creatures themselves." Queen of heaven and earth. Her Majesty is also the Co-Redemptrix and must be recognized as such. The time has come. This is her hour.

The front cover of *Time* magazine of December 30, 1991, featured Mary as portrayed in the painting of Raphael's *Madonna del Granduca*. The caption was *The Search For Mary*. It was a most unusual coverage for this secular magazine. The five-page cover story began this way: "When her womb was touched by eternity two thousand years ago, the Virgin Mary of Nazareth uttered a prediction: 'All generations will call me blessed.' Among all the women who have ever lived, the Mother of Jesus Christ is the most celebrated, the most venerated, the most portrayed, the most honored in the naming of girl babies and churches. Even the Koran praises her chastity and faith. Among Roman Catholics, the Madonna is recognized not only as the Mother of God but also, according to modern Popes, as the Queen of the Universe and Queen of heaven... A grass roots revival of faith in the Virgin is taking place world-wide. Millions are flocking to her shrines, many of them young people. Even more remarkable are the number of claimed sightings of the Virgin from Yugoslavia to Colorado, in the past few years... Whether they hold to those views or not, people in the world over are travelling enormous distances to demonstrate in person their veneration of the Madonna. The late twentieth century has become the age of the Marian pilgrimage."

The article ends with this observation: "It seems clear, though, that the world is crying out for many things from Mary, and in some fashion is receiving them... Renewed expression of her vitality and relevance are signs that millions of people are still moved by her mystery and comforted by the notion of her caring. Whatever aspect of Mary they choose to emphasize and embrace, those who seek her out surely find something only a holy mother can provide."

Three years later, this time the front cover of *Time* featured Pope John Paul II. In proclaiming him the "Man of the Year" in its last issue of 1994, it reported: "The Pope must be a moral force. In a year when so many people lamented the decline in moral values or made excuses for bad behavior, Pope John Paul II forcefully set forth his vision of the good life and urged the world to follow it. For such rectitude - or recklessness, as his detractors would have it - he is *TIME*'s Man of the Year.

Bishop Paolo Hnilica has also often said that John Paul is the Pope who has been chosen by Mary, prepared by her to be the apostle of the consecration, and that under the pontificate of her "most beloved son" has to come the fulfillment of the promise of Fatima made on July 13, 1917: "In the end my Immaculate Heart will triumph, the Holy Father will consecrate Russia to me, Russia will be converted and a certain period of peace will be granted to the world."

Indeed, John Paul II is the Pope of Fatima in a special way. It is no coincidence, therefore, that the blood of this Peter called John Paul was shed with an attempt on his life in St. Peter's Square on the anniversary of the first apparition in Fatima, May 13, 1981. Three years later, on March 25, 1984, he fulfilled the consecration requested to Sister Lucia by *Our Lady of Fatima* - the consecration of Russia and the world to the Immaculate Heart of Mary.

With respect to the consecration, let us not forget, however, that in one of her letters to her confessor dated May 18, 1936, Lucia quoted the words of Jesus Himself to her: "I want My whole Church to acknowledge that consecration as a triumph of the Immaculate Heart of Mary, so that it may extend its cult later on, and put the devotion to the Immaculate Heart beside the devotion to My Sacred Heart."

In 1531, she said to the humble Juan Diego in Guadalupe, Mexico: "Am I not here, I who am your Mother... Am I not of your kind?" And so, as a loving Mother she is calling us to the Love of God. As Mother Teresa says so emotionally: "Love until it hurts." It is therefore a call "for lovers only," and for such lovers it has to be the commitment of John Paul II, a "Totus Tuus" commitment - "All Yours."

It is "the first of all the commandments" (Mark 12: 28-31; Luke 10-27; Matthew 22: 36-40). The second is to love our neighbours as ourselves, and the mistake we frequently make is placing this second great commandment before the first. We cannot and must not love the creature more than the Creator of the creature.

But God who is Love is not loved. She is the Mother of Love and she, too, is not loved by so many. Yet, those who have had the personal privilege of seeing her or experiencing her love and protection would readily testify that there is no greater beauty, no greater love, no greater tenderness, no greater faithfulness.

One day the visionaries of Medjugorje asked her what she wanted of them. "Faith and respect for me," she replied. Happy are those of us who have actually seen her, but blessed are those who have not seen her, yet have believed. It is a question of faith — that virtue which bridges the gap between science and religion.

Augustine of Hippo once said: "Faith is to believe what we do not see, and the reward of this faith is to see what we believe." In more recent times, Max Planck (1858-1947) in his 1932 treatise *Where Is Science Going*, acknowledged: "Anybody who has been seriously engaged in scientific work of any kind realizes that over the entrance to the gates of the temple of science are written the words: *Ye must have faith*. It is a quality which the scientist cannot dispense with." However, Luke, a physician queries: "But when the Son of Man comes, will He find any faith on eartth?" (Luke 18:8).

As for respect, just as Yahweh decreed that the ancient Ark was to be respected, her Son likewise demands that we respect her. He observes His own fourth commandment and in His heaven He honours her and still calls her "Mother."

But whereas the Man-God came the first time as a defenseless little babe whom she had to hide from Herod, in His second Advent He will be coming as the God-Man in all His glory as Judge. As Grignon Marie de Montfort (1673-1716) said nearly three centuries ago: 'Being the way in which Jesus came to us the first time, she is the way by which He wil come the second time, though not in the same manner.'"

This is her hour and the time is nigh when, as foretold in Luke 1:48, all generations will call her "blessed." All will love and respect her — for she is **truly** the **Ark of the Covenant**. So says my research.

"*And the sanctuary of God in heaven opened, and the ark of the covenant could be seen inside it*" (Rev. 11:19). "*Now a great sign appeared in heaven: a woman clothed with the sun, standing, on the moon, and with twelve stars on her head for a crown*" (Rev. 12:1).

338.

Statue of the
Queen of Peace in
the church of
St. Mary Major
in Rome
(see p. 334)

The full moon
appears during
an open air
devotion in Trinidad
— "Fair as the moon"
(Song 6:10)
(photo courtesy of
Noel Norton)

# BIBLIOGRAPHY

1. Agreda, Mary of, *The Mystical City of God*, Tan Books and Publishers, Inc., Illinois, 1978.
2. Albright, Judith M., *Our Lady at Garabandal*, Faith Publishing Co., Milford, Ohio, 1992.
3. Aronica, Paul, *A Man Sent by God*, Don Bosco Publications, New Rochelle, NY, 1988.
4. Arratibel, Daniel Lasagabaster, *La Joya de Zaragoza: El Pilar de Santa Maria*, Con La Colaboración de Caja de Ahorros de Zaragoza, Aragon y Rioja.
5. Atya, Aziz, Professor, *The Copts and Christian Civilization*, West Midlands, 1985.
6. Auclair, Raoul, *The Lady Of All Peoples*, Les Presses, Lithographiques Inc., Quebec, 1978.
7. Barbaric, Slavko, *Pray With the Heart*, Franciscan University Press, Ohio, 1988.
8. Bassilli, Mary & Armani, *The Life of the Mother of God, The Virgin Mary*, London, 1988.
9. Bonanno, Raphael, *Jews, Moslems And Christians. Children Of God*, Franciscan Printing Press, Jerusalem, 1988.
10. Bossa, Barry, *Brown Scapular of Our Lady of Mt. Carmel*, AMI Press, Washington, N.J., 1987.
11. Boudreau, Fr. J., *The Happiness of Heaven*, Tan Books and Publishers, Inc., Rockford, Illinois, 1984
12. Breen, Eileen, Mary, *The Second Eve, From the Writing of John Henry Newman*, Tan Books, 1982.
13. Brown, Eugene M, Rev., *Dreams, Visions & Prophecies of Don Bosco*, Don Bosco Publications, New Rochelle, New York, 1986.
14. Brown, Raphael, *The Little Flowers of St. Francis*, Image Books, New York, 1958.
15. Carroll, Warren H., *Our Lady of Guadalupe and the Conquest of Darkness*, Christendom Publications, Virginia, 1983.
16. Carty, Charles M., *The Stigmata and Modern Science*, Tan Books and Publishers, Inc., Illinois, 1974.
17. Carty, Charles M. and Rumble, L., *Eucharist Quizzes To A Street Preacher*, Tan Books, 1976.
18. Chesterton, G. K., *St. Francis of Assisi*, Hodder and Stoughton, 1960.
19. Chettham, Nicolas, *A History of the Popes*, Dorset Press, New York, 1992.

20. Craig, Mary, *Macmillan Kolbe: Priest Hero of a Death Camp*, Catholic Truth Society, London, 1982.
21. Craig, Mary, *Spark From Heaven*, Ave Maria Press, Indiana, 1988.
22. Cruz, Joan Carroll, *Eucharistic Miracles*, Tan Books and Publishers, Inc., Rockford, Illinois, 1987.
23. de Montfort, Louis, *True Devotion To Mary*, Tan Books and Publishers, Inc., Illinois, 1941.
24. de la Sainte Trinité, Michael, *Fatima and "The Last Times,"* Augustine Publishing Co., Devon, 1987.
25. de la Sainte Trinité, Michael, *The Third Secret of Fatima*, Augustine Publishing Co., Devon, 1986.
26. De Marchi, John, *Fatima From the Beginning*, Editors: Miss es Consolata Fátima (Portugal), 1983.
27. Deiss, Lucien, *Mary, Daughter of Sion*, The Liturgical Press, Minnesota, 1972.
28. Delaney, John, *A Woman Clothed With the Sun*, Image Books, New York, 1961.
29. *Dictionary of Mary*, Catholic Book Publishing Co., New York, 1985.
30. *Divine Mercy in My Soul - The Diary of the Servant of God Sister M. Faustina Kowalska*, Marian Press, Massachusetts, 1987.
31. *Dolorous Passion Of Our Lord Jesus Christ: From the Meditations of Anne Catherine Emmerich*, Tan Books and Publishers, Inc., Rockford, IL, U.S.A., 1983.
32. Duff, Frank, *The Woman of Genesis*, Praedicanda Publications, Dublin, 1976.
33. Englebert, Omer, *Catherine Labouré And The Modern Apparitions of Our Lady*, P. J. Kenedy & Sons, New York, 1959.
34. Faricy, Robert and Pecoraio, Luciana, *Mary Among Us. The Apparitions at Oliveto Citra*, Franciscan University Press, Ohio, 1989.
35. Farrell, Gerald J. and Kosicki, George W., *The Spirit and the Bride Say, "Come!,"* AMI Press, Asbury, N.J., 1981.
36. Flanagan, Neal M., *Salvation History—An Introduction to Biblical Theology*, Sheed and Ward Inc., 1964.
37. Fox, Robert J, Rev., *Immaculate Heart of Mary: True Devotion*, Our Sunday Visitor, Indiana, 1986.
38. Giday, Belai, *Ethiopian Civilization*, Addis Ababa, 1992.
39. Gilles, Anthony E., *The People of the Book*, St. Anthony Messenger Press, 1983.
40. Glynn, Paul, *A Song of Nagasaki*, Marist Fathers Books, Australia, 1988

41. Gracia, Juan Antonio, *El Pilar - Historia - Arte - Espiritu*, Talleres Generales de Imprenta de Aragón, S. A., España, Zaragoza, 1989.
42. Greaef, Hilda, *Mary — A History of Doctrine and Devotion*, Christian Classics, Westminister and Sheed & Ward, London, 1985.
43. Green, Julien, *God's Fool. The Life and Times of Francis of Assisi*, Hodder and Stoughton, London, 1986.
44. Haffert, John Mathias, *Sign of Her Heart*, Ave Maria Institute, Washington, N.J., 1971.
45. Haffert, John Mathias, *The Meaning of Akita*, 101 Foundation Inc., Asbury, N.J., U.S.A., 1989.
46. Halley, Shelagh, *Francis of Assisi*, Catholic Truth Society, London, 1982.
47. Hancock, Graham, *The Sign and the Seal*, Simon & Schuster, Inc., 1992.
48. Hanson, Robert W., *Science and Creation*, MacMillan Publishing Co., NY, 1986.
49. Hawking, Stephen, *A Brief History of Time*, Bantam Press, London, 1992.
50. Hebert, Albert, *The Tears of Mary and Fatima*, 1985.
51. Hebert, Albert, *Signs, Wonders and Response*, 1988.
52. Johnston, Francis, *The Wonder of Guadalupe*, Augustine Publishing Company, Devon, 1981.
53. Johnston, Francis, *When Millions Saw Mary*, Augustine Publishing Co., Chulmleigh, Devon, 1980.
54. Johnston, Francis, *Fatima: The Great Sign*, AMI Press, Washington, N.J., 1980.
55. Kaczmarek, Louis, *The Wonders She Performs*, Trinity Communication, Manassas, VA, 1986.
56. Kertzer, Morris N., Rabbi, *What is a Jew?*, Macmillan Publishing Co, New York, 1978.
57. Kowalska, Faustina, M. Sister, *Divine Mercy In My Soul*, Divine Mercy Publications, Dublin, 1987.
58. Kraljevic, Svetozar, *The Apparitions of Our Lady at Medjugorje*, Franciscan Press, Chicago, 1984.
59. Kraljevic, Svetozar, *In the Company of Mary*, St. Francis Press, Nashville, Tennessee, 1988.
60. Larkin, Francis, *Enthronement of the Sacred Heart*, St. Paul Editions, 1978.
61. Laurentin, René, *An Appeal From Mary in Argentina*, Faith Publishing Co., Ohio, 1980.
62. Laurentin, René and Joyeux, Henri, *Scientific and Medical Studies on the Apparition at Medjugorje*, Veritas, Dublin, 1987.

63. Laurentin, René, and Ljudevit, Rupcic, *Is the Virgin Mary Appearing At Medjugorje?*, The Word Among Us Press, Washington, D.C., 1984.
64. Lewis, C. S., *Miracles*, Harper Collins Manufacturing, Glasgow, 1947.
65. Ligouri, Alphonsus, *The Glories Of Mary*, Tan Books and Publishing, Illinois, 1977.
66. Lord, Bob and Penny, *Heavenly Army of Angels*, Journies of Faith, Slidell, LA, 1991.
67. Lord, Bob and Penny, *This is My Body, This is My Blood: Miracles of the Eucharist*, Journeys of Faith, California, 1986.
68. Lubich, Chiara, *The Eucharist*, New City London, 1979.
69. Malaty, Tadros, *St. Mary in the Orthodox Concept*, Palaprint, Australia, 1978.
70. Manuel, David, *Medjugorje Under Siege*, Paraclete Press, Orthodox, Mass, 1992.
71. Marie-Therese, Sr., *Parish Beat*, Imprint Caribbean Ltd., Trinidad, 1976.
72. Meagher, James L., *How Christ Said The First Mass*, Tan Books and Publishers, Inc., Illinois, 1984.
73. *Messages Of Our Lady At San Nicolàs*, Translated by Eleonora O'Farrell De Nagy-Pal and Marie-Helenè Gall, Faith Publishing Co., Milford, Ohio, 1991.
74. Mueller, Michael, Prayer. *The Key to Salvation*, Tan Books and Publishers, Inc., Illinois, 1985.
75. Nassan, Morris, *Meditating on Mary*, Catholic Truth Society.
76. O'Carroll, Michael, *Medjugorje—Facts, Documents, Theology*, Veritas, Dublin, 1986.
77. O'Carroll, Michael, *Theotokos: A Theological Encyclopedia of the Blessed Virgin Mary*, Michael Glazier, Inc., Washington, Delaware, 1982.
78. Odell, Catherine M., *Those Who Saw Her*, Our Sunday Visitor, Indiana, 1986.
79. *Our Lady of Fatima's Peace Plan From Heaven*, Tan Books and Publishers, Inc., Illinois, 1983.
80. *Our Lady Speaks To Her Beloved Priests*, 14th English Edition, U.S.A. National Headquarters of the Marian Movement of Priests, Maine, 1993.
81. Palairet, Michael, *The Life of The Blessed Virgin Mary: From The Visions of Anne Catherine Emmerich*, Tan Books, Rockford, Illinois, 1970.
82. Papali, Cyril, *Mother of God, Mary in Scripture and Tradition*, Augustine Publishing Co., Devon, 1987.

83. Pelletier, Joseph A., *God Speaks at Garabandal*, An Assumption Publication, Worcester, Mass.
84. Pelletier, Joseph A., *The Queen of Peace Visits Medjugorje*, An Assumption Publication, Mass. 1985.
85. Pennington, Basil M., *Mary Today*, Doubleday And Company, Inc., N.Y., 1987.
86. Pius X, Pope, *Encyclical Letter on the Doctrines of the Modernists (1907)*, Daughters of St. Paul, Boston.
87. Ripley, Francis J., *Devotion to the Immaculate Heart of Mary*, Augustine Publishing Co., Devon, 1988.
88. Rolston III, Holmes, *Science and Religion*, Random House, New York, 1987.
89. Roman-Bocabeille, Christiane, *Le Mystere Des Apparitions De Garabandal*.
90. Ryan, Finbar, Archbishop, *Our Lady of Fatima*, The Richview Press, Dublin, 1939.
91. Sammaciccia, Bruno, *The Eucharistic Miracle of Lanciano*, Rev. Francis J. Kubo, Connecticut, 1976.
92. Sarna, Nahum M., *Exploring Exodus*, Schocken Books, New York, 1987.
93. Schökel, Alonso L., *Celebrating the Eucharist*, St. Paul Publications, 1988.
94. Sheen, Fulton, J., *The World's First Love*, Mc Graw-Hill Book Company, Inc., New York, 1952.
95. Sims, Margaret Catherine, Sr., *Apparitions In Betania, Venezuela*, Medjugorje Messengers, Framingham, M.A., U.S.A., 1992.
96. Teresa of Avila, Saint, *The Interior Castle*, Hodder And Stoughton, London, 1988.
97. *The Sermons of St. Francis de Sales on Our Lady*, Translated by the Nuns of the Visitation, Tan Books and Publishers, Inc., Illinois, 1985.
98. Ullathorne, William, *The Immaculate Conception of the Mother of God*, Christian Classics Inc., Maryland, 1988.
99. Verheylezoon, Louis, *Devotion to the Sacred Heart*, Tan Books and Publishers, Inc., Illinois, 1978.
100. Winstone, Harold, *Communion Under Both Kinds. It's Significance*, Catholic Truth Society, London.
101. Wirt, Sherwood, *The Confessions of Augustine*, Lion Publishing, 1971.
102. Yasuda, Teiji, Akita: *The Tears and Message of Mary*,
101 Foundation, Inc., Asbury, NJ, U.S.A., 1989.
103. Zaki, Pearl, *Our Lord's Mother Visits Egypt*, Dar El Alam El Arabi, 1977.
104. Zimdars-Swartz, Sandra L., *Encountering Mary*, Avon Books, New York, 1991.